W9-ATX-486

Senegal

WORLD BIBLIOGRAPHICAL SERIES

General Editors:
Robert G. Neville (Executive Editor)
John J. Horton

Robert A. Myers   Ian Wallace
Hans H. Wellisch   Ralph Lee Woodward, Jr.

John J. Horton is Deputy Librarian of the University of Bradford and currently Chairman of its Academic Board of Studies in Social Sciences. He has maintained a longstanding interest in the discipline of area studies and its associated bibliographical problems, with special reference to European Studies. In particular he has published in the field of Icelandic and of Yugoslav studies, including the two relevant volumes in the World Bibliographical Series.

Robert A. Myers is Associate Professor of Anthropology in the Division of Social Sciences and Director of Study Abroad Programs at Alfred University, Alfred, New York. He has studied post-colonial island nations of the Caribbean and has spent two years in Nigeria on a Fulbright Lectureship. His interests include international public health, historical anthropology and developing societies. In addition to *Amerindians of the Lesser Antilles: a bibliography* (1981), *A Resource Guide to Dominica, 1493-1986* (1987) and numerous articles, he has compiled the World Bibliographical Series volumes on *Dominica* (1987), *Nigeria* (1989) and *Ghana* (1991).

Ian Wallace is Professor of German at the University of Bath. A graduate of Oxford in French and German, he also studied in Tübingen, Heidelberg and Lausanne before taking teaching posts at universities in the USA, Scotland and England. He specializes in contemporary German affairs, especially literature and culture, on which he has published numerous articles and books. In 1979 he founded the journal *GDR Monitor*, which he continues to edit under its new title *German Monitor*.

Hans H. Wellisch is Professor emeritus at the College of Library and Information Services, University of Maryland. He was President of the American Society of Indexers and was a member of the International Federation for Documentation. He is the author of numerous articles and several books on indexing and abstracting, and has published *The Conversion of Scripts, Indexing and Abstracting: an International Bibliography* and *Indexing from A to Z*. He also contributes frequently to *Journal of the American Society for Information Science*, *The Indexer* and other professional journals.

Ralph Lee Woodward, Jr. is Professor of History at Tulane University, New Orleans. He is the author of *Central America, a Nation Divided*, 2nd ed. (1985), as well as several monographs and more than seventy scholarly articles on modern Latin America. He has also compiled volumes in the World Bibliographical Series on *Belize* (1980), *Nicaragua* (1983), *El Salvador* (1988) and *Guatemala (Rev. Ed.)* (1992). Dr. Woodward edited the Central American section of the *Research Guide to Central America and the Caribbean* (1985) and is currently associate editor of Scribner's *Encyclopedia of Latin American History*.

VOLUME 166

Senegal

Roy Dilley and Jerry Eades

Compilers

CLIO PRESS

OXFORD, ENGLAND · SANTA BARBARA, CALIFORNIA
DENVER, COLORADO

British Library Cataloguing in Publication Data

Senegal. – (World bibliographical series; vol. 166)
I. Eades, Jeremy   II. Dilley, R. M.   II. Series
016.9663

DT
549.22
D44
1994

ISBN 1–85109–156–4

Clio Press Ltd.,
Old Clarendon Ironworks,
35A Great Clarendon Street,
Oxford OX4 6AT, England.

ABC-CLIO,
130 Cremona Drive,
Santa Barbara,
CA 93116, USA.

Designed by Bernard Crossland.
Typeset by Columns Design and Production Services Ltd, Reading, England.
Printed and bound in Great Britain by
Bookcraft (Bath) Ltd., Midsomer Norton

THE WORLD BIBLIOGRAPHICAL SERIES

This series, which is principally designed for the English speaker, will eventually cover every country (and many of the world's principal regions), each in a separate volume comprising annotated entries on works dealing with its history, geography, economy and politics; and with its people, their culture, customs, religion and social organization. Attention will also be paid to current living conditions – housing, education, newspapers, clothing, etc.– that are all too often ignored in standard bibliographies; and to those particular aspects relevant to individual countries. Each volume seeks to achieve, by use of careful selectivity and critical assessment of the literature, an expression of the country and an appreciation of its nature and national aspirations, to guide the reader towards an understanding of its importance. The keynote of the series is to provide, in a uniform format, an interpretation of each country that will express its culture, its place in the world, and the qualities and background that make it unique. The views expressed in individual volumes, however, are not necessarily those of the publisher.

VOLUMES IN THE SERIES

Contents

Contents

Contents

Preface

This bibliography is intended to be a representative survey of the main literature in both English and French, rather than a comprehensive listing. The latter would in any case have been impossible. As we have became painfully aware as we have proceeded with the compilation, Senegal, considering its relatively small size, is probably one of the best documented countries in Africa. Porgès' monumental bibliographies contain over 7,000 items up to the mid-1970s, and the flood of material has continued since.

This is due to several factors. The first is the extent of historical literature: the earliest relevant items are from Arab accounts from around the turn of the millennium, with European sources beginning during the 15th century with the arrival of the Portuguese. The second factor is the concentration of the main French educational and research institutions for the whole of French West Africa in Dakar during the colonial period. One result of this was the creation of the magnificent Dakar archives which have provided the basis for literally dozens of excellent monographs in history and the social sciences. Another was the establishment of specialist research institutes and units, the most famous of which is probably the Institut Fondamental (previously Français) d'Afrique Noire (IFAN) which through its journals and monograph series has made much of the research on the country widely available. There are also other examples, such as the psychiatric research group founded by Henri Collomb in the 1950s, the groups of demographers and anthropologists working in the south east of the country, and the Centre for Applied Linguistics in Dakar (CLAD).

Related to this is a third factor. Due to the country's close links with France, Senegalese scholars were among the first Africans to study in France itself, including many of the pioneers of African literature in French. Again, considering the size of the country, it has produced an astonishingly high proportion of Africa's distinguished men and women of letters. The former president, Léopold Senghor, is the best known of these, but there are many others: their work, substantial in itself, has also led to the production of a large secondary critical literature in both French and English.

Finally, there are institutional factors: a very substantial proportion of the literature on Senegal has been produced and disseminated by a few enterprising publishing houses in Europe and West Africa: apart from IFAN itself, they include Nouvelles Editions Africaines in Dakar, Présence Africaine, Karthala and Harmattan in Paris, and the Heinemann African Writers Series in the United Kingdom, among others.

Taking into consideration the size and range of this literature, we have had to be selective. This has meant leaving out 500 or so of the items we had originally annotated, and shortening many of the annotations which we have included in order to reduce the book to a manageable size. The amount of literature in French is perhaps three or four times larger than that in English, although in this volume preference has been given to items in English, where possible, in order to make the work more accessible to the English-speaking reader. Our choice of items is dictated by the scope and coverage of each of the bodies of literature, and in some areas few English works exist. Where several items cover similar ground we have tended to list just one of them in the main bibliography, referring to alternative sources in the notes. In a few cases we have included in the notes references to related work in the same (often rather specialized) series. Furthermore, for reasons of space, our final selection includes relatively few articles from the two major and easily available sources of regular news on Senegal in Europe, *West Africa* and *Jeune Afrique*. The title pages of these are always worth scanning for recent information, as are *Africa Confidential* and the authoritative annuals, *Europa Yearbook* and *Africa Contemporary Record*.

Our depth of coverage of individual topics varies considerably, but generally we have tried to reflect the nature of the actual material and its availability. The sources on literature, recent history and the social sciences are very extensive, readily available and often of excellent quality. Conversely, the sources on subjects such as archaeology or geology are more difficult to find, particularly in English, and are often highly technical and aimed at specialists. This also applies to the very large body of literature on medicine: the items we have annotated are of more general interest, but they do include two substantial bibliographies for those in search of specialist material. In general, even though we have not been able to include everything on Senegal, the works which we have cited will enable the researcher to gain access to almost all of the significant works written on Senegal to the beginning of 1990.

In nearly all sections of the bibliography, items are listed alphabetically by title rather than by author or date of publication. We felt that this would enable the reader to gain easier access to specific topics of interest. The one exception to this ordering is the chapter on literature, especially the Major Authors section. Here we have resorted to ordering by date of publication so that the integrity and development of a particular writer's corpus is maintained. The more general critical literary surveys have been grouped in a section of their own.

Compilation has not been easy, not only because of the size of the task but also because of the lack of any direct contact between the compilers during the period of writing, for most of which Roy Dilley has been based in St Andrews, Scotland and Jerry Eades in Tokyo. In the absence of a reliable computer link we have had to rely on the exchange of discs and on communication by fax machine, but for which the book's completion would have been practically impossible. We would like to thank Bob Neville of Clio Press for his forbearance during the delays which this unusual arrangement has entailed.

Roy Dilley would like to thank the staff of St Andrews University Library for their help and advice; in particular Miss J. M. Young for her assistance with on-line database sources and the inter-library loan staff who have worked untiringly tracing the many requests submitted. The university library staff of both Aberdeen and Edinburgh also provided a good deal of guidance, and Professor Peter Robson and Professor John Hargreaves both provided information on some very useful material. He would like to thank also Barry Reeves for his help with the indexes and a number of last-minute bibliographical queries.

Jerry Eades would like to thank Yusuke Nakamura of the Cultural Anthropology Department at the University of Tokyo for the use of his own collection of Senegambian material, the staff of the National Museum of Ethnology at Osaka and the Institute of Developing Economies (Ajia kei zai kenkysho), Tokyo, for access to what are probably the two best collections of African material in Japan, and the University of Kent for the use of its excellent collection of African literature in French, much of it assembled over the years by Professor Clive Wake.

A note on orthography

The orthography of contemporary Senegalese place names is quite well established, and we have used the conventional spellings to be found in authoritative sources such as the *Atlas National du Sénégal*. Unfortunately, this has not been the case for ethnic groups and pre-colonial states, where a variety of spellings exist in English and

French literature; even the same authors have used different spellings on different occasions. There is no completely satisfactory way of dealing with this problem, and to impose our own standard spellings would be to give an impression of unity where none exists. Our preferred forms, among some of the more common alternatives, either because of simplicity or frequency of usage in the literature, are as follows: Walo (= Waalo, Oualo); Kayor (= Cayor, Kajoor etc.); Jolof (= Djoloff, Diolof etc.); Tukulor (= Toucouleur); Jakhanke (= Diakhanke, Jaxaanke); Diola (= Joola, Dyola, but not the Dyula of Mali and the Ivory Coast); Peul (= Pula, Fula, Fulbe, Fulani); Fuuta Toro (= Fouta Tooro etc.); Bundu (Bundou), etc. A similar variation is found in personal names, of which the most important is probably that of Umar Tal.

Introduction

The country and its peoples

Senegal is a coastal country on the western-most tip of the region of West Africa. It covers an area of around 200,000 square kilometres, and has a population currently estimated to be around 7,000,000. The country takes its name from the river which runs along its northern and eastern borders, forming the frontier with Mauritania and Mali. To the south Senegal shares borders with Guinea-Bissau (the former Portuguese Guinea), and the Republic of Guinea. Also in the south, along the Gambian river, lies the enclave of The Gambia, a former British colony, the effect of which is to isolate the south-western region of Senegal, the Casamance, from the rest of the country. The name 'Senegal' itself is said to be derived from 'Sanhaja' (Sanhadja in French literature), the name of a nomadic Berber group who lived to the north of the present-day country. This group of people were referred to by the early Portuguese travellers as *Azanaga*, a term which might alternatively be derived from the earlier Arabic chroniclers' use of *Zanj* or *Zinj* to designate generally the black inhabitants of West Africa. Certainly the river was referred to as the 'river Senega' rather than 'Senegal' by 15th and 16th European traders. A more poetic etymology from the Wolof people is that the country's name derives from their local term *'sunugal'*, meaning 'our dug-out canoe' (all in the same boat!).

Dakar, the capital since independence from France in 1960, lies on the Cap-Vert peninsula, the most westerly point in Africa. It is by far the largest city in the country, with a population of over a million, and possesses one of the best natural harbours in the region. Prior to independence, Dakar was the capital of the whole of French West Africa (the AOF or l'Afrique Occidentale Française), which included the present countries of Mauritania, Senegal, Guinea, the Ivory Coast, Mali, Burkina Faso, Benin, Togo and Niger. Again, local etymologists, who revel in the art of putative derivations, suggest that 'Dakar' derives from the Wolof term 'daxar', the tamarind tree. It is said that a French colonial officer, pointing to the site of the proposed new capital city, asked after the name of the local Wolof settlement he saw in the distance. The locals, believing him to be inquiring about the scenery, replied 'daxar', a species of tree abundant in the area.

The colonial capital of Senegal itself was at Saint-Louis, at the mouth of the Senegal river to the north, and one of the earliest French settlements in the region. After the transfer of the administration to Dakar, Saint-Louis declined in importance, but with a population of 100,000 it remains the country's fourth largest city after Dakar, Thiès and Kaolack, and is still the administrative headquarters of the Fleuve region, which extends along the Senegal river valley.

Most of the country lies in the Sudan savanna belt of West Africa, in which rainfall and humidity increase as one travels from north to south. The Fuuta Toro region to the north, bordering on Mauritania, and the Ferlo region to the south, receive only about 500mm or less rain annually. Both these areas are part of the West African Sahelian zone, which has been badly affected by drought in recent years. In the Casamance to the south, the annual rainfall rises to as much as 1500mm, making it potentially the most fertile part of the country, and it is here that most of the country's woodland and tropical forest is concentrated. As in the rest of West Africa, rainfall is highly seasonal, most of it being concentrated in the wet season (*l'hivernage*) from around early July to the end of October. The dry season extends from November to June. The coolest temperatures, between eighteen and twenty degrees, are in January, and the hottest, generally around thirty to thirty-five degrees, are in April and May before the onset of the rains. During the dry season the coastal areas benefit from fresh sea-breezes, although inland the scorching easterly wind, *l'harmattan*, can take April temperatures up to forty-five degrees in some areas. The landscape throughout most of the country is predominantly flat, the major exception being the mountainous areas along the border with Guinea in the extreme south east (525 metres at its highest point).

The major geographical features of this region are the great rivers that cut through it: the Senegal itself, the Gambia, and the Casamance, all of which are navigable for long stretches. These rivers were the points of access to the hinterland for sea-borne travellers and traders from Europe, and also important commercial routes and centres for pre-colonial states. They now tend to demarcate post-colonial borders. All three rivers rise in the Fuuta Djallon area of neighbouring Guinea. The Senegal river valley from Saint-Louis to Bakel in the east is where much of the recent developments in irrigated agriculture have taken place, particularly rice cultivation, but the river itself is less important as a transport route than it was previously. The Gambia river, although shorter, could potentially provide a much better access route to the interior of the region were it not for its peculiar political status, an English-speaking finger of a country 'pointing into the belly' of French-speaking Senegal.

Senegal is divided into seven administrative regions (Fleuve, Diourbel, Thiès, Cap-Vert, Sine-Saloum, Sénégal Oriental, and Casamance), and these broadly coincide with the main ecological zones. The most northerly is the Fleuve (river) region, with its capital Saint-Louis, which extends east along the Senegal. To the south of this lie the regions of Diourbel stretching inland from the coast, and of Thiès and Cap-Vert lying mainly along the central coastal belt. Thiès region forms part of the country's groundnut basin, the *bassin arachidier*, on which much of the country's economy still depends. The city of Thiès, with a population of over 125,000, is the country's second largest town, and is a major communications centre as well as a centre of phosphate production. The beaches of the southern coastal area of the Thiès region, on the Petite Côte around M'Bour are an important tourist attraction.

The town of Diourbel lies directly east of Thiès, and is also within the groundnut belt, but the large Diourbel region also extends into the more arid Ferlo area where pastoralism, rather than agriculture, is the main occupation. To the west of Thiès lies the smallest region, Cap-Vert, essentially Greater Dakar, with its satellite towns of Rufisque and Pikine. Rufisque, Dakar, and the small island of Gorée off the coast, together with Saint-Louis, constituted the four historical communes of Senegal during the colonial period, and their inhabitants enjoyed the benefits of French citizenship. Between Diourbel and Thiès and the Gambian border lies the last of the provinces of the groundnut belt, Sine-Saloum region, with its capital at Kaolack, the country's third largest city, which has a population of 120,000. South of The Gambia lies the Casamance with its administrative head-quarters at Ziguinchor. This is a major rice-producing region and is potentially the most fertile part of Senegal, but its development has been hampered by poor communications with the rest of the country, and by the political problems created by the separatist movement which has operated there for the last decade. Finally, the south-eastern quarter of the country consists of the single large and rather remote province of Sénégal Oriental, with its capital at Tambacounda, a centre of cotton production. In the southern part of this, north of the border with Guinea, lies Senegal's largest national park, the Parc National du Niokolo Koba, which is one of the country's major tourist attractions.

The languages spoken in the country fall into two main families: the West Atlantic group, and the Mande group. The West Atlantic languages are divided into a number of subgroups, the most important of which includes Wolof, Serer, and Pulaar, the language of both the Fulbe and the Tukulor. Three of the other subgroups consist of the Cangin languages, such as Palor, which are generally being superseded by Wolof as a dominant language; the Diola dialects; and the languages of minority groups such as the Bassari and Bedik in the extreme south east. The Mande languages are spoken by a smaller proportion of the population of Senegal, but are historically important. They include Manding, the language of the largest ethnic group in The Gambia; Soninke, spoken along the middle reaches of the Senegal river; and Bambara, spoken in neighbouring Mali. Linguistically, therefore, as well as historically and culturally, Senegal is just part of a much larger region which Barry has called 'Greater Senegambia', including all of present-day Senegal, The Gambia, and Guinea-Bissau, together with large parts of Mali, Mauritania and Guinea.

To a large extent, the cultural divisions coincide with linguistic delineations. The Wolof, who make up over one third of the population, are the country's largest ethnic group, concentrated in the northern part of the peanut basin, in the central regions of Thiès and Diourbel. They are predominantly Muslim, and many are members of the powerful Mouride Sufi brotherhood, whose leaders play an important role as peanut barons and as patrons in national politics. The original population of Cap-Vert were the Lebu (Lébou) fishers, similar in both language and culture to the Wolof who are now largely assimilated with them.

The second largest ethnic group is the Serer, forming approximately one-fifth of the total population, although they actually comprise two separate and rather different groups of people. Eighty per cent of the Serer, known as the Serer-Sin, speak a language closely related to Wolof and Pulaar. The remaining twenty per cent consists of smaller subgroups such as the Serer Ndut, who originally spoke Cangin dialects but who increasingly speak Wolof. The Serer were slower to accept Islam than the Wolof, and there is a substantial Serer Catholic minority, from which Léopold Senghor, the country's first president and its leading poet, originated.

To the north, in the Fuuta Toro area along the Senegal river, the main peoples are the Halpulaaren (Pulaar-speakers), consisting of two major branches, the Tukulor and the Fulbe, who together make up a further fifth of the population. They speak a similar language, but their economic roles and their histories are different. The Tukulor, who live mainly in the Fuuta Toro, are mostly sedentary agriculturalists who converted to Islam as early as the 11th century. The Fulbe, known variously as Pula, Fula, Peul and Fulani (originally a Nigerian term for related peoples), are pastoralists who have now spread not only across much of northern and eastern Senegal, but throughout West Africa, from the Atlantic to Cameroon and beyond.

In the south, the largest ethnic groups are the Diola and the Manding, each accounting for about seven per cent of the national population. The Diola are the main ethnic group in the Casamance region. They speak a cluster of related languages, and different Diola groups have been influenced to a greater or lesser extent by Manding culture spreading in from the east. Many of the Diola have converted to Islam, but there is still a substantial Catholic minority, and the indigenous religious beliefs are, by Senegalese standards, still strong. Since the early 1980s, the Casamance has seen the development of a separatist movement, and since 1990 there has been serious violence in the region, involving conflict between local guerrillas and the army.

The Manding, the largest ethnic group in The Gambia, who moved into the region from the east when it was part of the Mali empire (c. 13th-15th century), speak Mandinka, a language closely related to that of the Soninke or Sarakole along the Senegal river. Other groups include the Muslim Jakhanke who are scattered throughout the region, and the Bambara, who live mainly in Mali but who have a few settlements in Senegal. In Sénégal Oriental, in the south east of the country, the Manding and Fulbe live alongside a number of other small minority groups, including the Bassari and Bedik.

Despite this cultural heterogeneity, two factors have tended to transcend ethnic boundaries in Senegal. The first is Islam, and in particular the spread of the major brotherhoods – the Mouridiyya, Tijaniyya and Qadariyya – which have mass followings in many parts of the country. The second is the spread of the Wolof language, which has become a lingua franca in towns and markets, in schools (even though instruction is in French) and in inter-ethnic marriages. Wolof, often heavily laced with loan-words from French, is now spoken by over eighty per cent of the population, and in some areas it is rapidly replacing other local languages, especially among the educated younger generation.

Early history

The peoples of the region, and the kingdoms which they established, first appear in historical records dating back before the first millennium and in the Arabic accounts which began to accumulate as the trans-Saharan trade developed, following the spread of Islam west into north Africa. For the preceding period, we have only archaeological evidence, notably the mysterious megaliths scattered in large numbers, mainly along the Gambia river valley in the south. The trans-Saharan trade stimulated the growth of large states, the most important of which were the Ghana, Mali and Songhay empires along the Niger river in present-day Mali. The Tekrur empire, situated along the Senegal river valley and at the terminus of a trans-Saharan route, was smaller and less influential in the region, although it boasted the conversion of an early West African ruler to Islam in the 11th century. One result of state formation was the development of a system of social stratification which is found, with local variations, throughout much of the Sahelian region. The population came to be divided between the free born, the various occupational castes – including blacksmiths and *griots*, or traditional praise singers – and slaves or domestic bondsmen and women. The occupational castes were endogamous and hereditary, and some have retained their occupations into the 20th century, with groups such as the smiths and *griots* developing new markets for their skills as jewellers and musicians.

The Western Sudan, in the period before the discovery of the New World, supplied Europe with much of its gold, with the major goldfields being situated on the upper Senegal and Niger rivers. The first of the great kingdoms to develop around the trans-Saharan trade was the Soninke kingdom of Ghana, of which we have a detailed account by the Arab writer el-Bakri from 1067, just before its conquest by the Almoravids, Muslim warriors from the north. Ghana lay mainly to the east of the Senegal river, in present-day Mali and Mauritania, but the next major regional power, the Mali Empire, which developed in the early 13th century and flourished until the end of the 14th, controlled virtually the whole of present-day Senegal. From the 14th century, however, the power of Mali declined. It retained control of areas such as the Gambia river valley, in which many Manding had settled, until well after the arrival of the Portuguese. In the north it lost control from the early 15th century onwards, and at the end of the 15th century it was replaced as the major power along the river Niger by the Songhay Empire further east.

Further to the west, the process of state formation at a local level had also begun. Perhaps the earliest state in northern Senegal was the Tekrur state (c. 11th century) which developed among the Tukulor of the Fuuta Toro, but states also developed among the Wolof and Serer from the 14th century onwards. The most important was the Djolof state, which by the 15th century extended into most of the area between the Senegal and Gambia rivers. Later on, its vassal states, Walo, Kayor, Baol, Sine and Saloum asserted their independence. The relations between these states and France provided the framework for many of the events in the region during the 19th century. Djolof itself lay inland, and the ability of its vassals to assert their independence was probably related to the changes in international trade with the arrival along the coast of the Portuguese, followed by the Dutch, British and French.

The Atlantic trade

During the 15th century Portuguese exploration of the African coast was proceeding apace, facilitated by naval developments and navigation techniques which eventually led to contact with Asia and the New World. In West Africa trading posts were established, diplomatic relations created, and in some cases there was intermarriage with the local population; but with the decline of Portuguese fortunes in Europe in the 16th century, it was the French and the British who began to exploit the trade of coastal Senegambia on a larger scale. Increasingly, as the plantations in the New World developed and generated a demand for cheap labour, commerce along the Senegambian coast was dominated by the slave trade, which lasted throughout the 17th and 18th centuries.

There is probably no more emotive an issue in African history than that of the impact of the slave trade on Africa. The seminal work is that of Philip Curtin who tried to determine how many slaves had been shipped to the New World from each region of Africa, even though his figures, his account of the impact of the trade on African society, and way in which he analyses it as simply one of a number of alternative economic activities, have all generated fierce debate. Three things are clear, however. First, the trade must have had a serious demographic effect on the region, even if this is difficult to quantify. In addition to the losses through actual slave exports, there was heavy mortality caused by the warfare and violence which the slave trade engendered. Becker has argued that there were also wider economic and environmental effects, since the disruption of production led to the abandonment of land and more frequent food shortages. Secondly, the slave trade had a major impact on local political development: states became organized around the production and export of slaves; slaves themselves became the major form of local capital accumulation within the region itself. The majority of the slaves exported were male, but females and children tended to be retained and highly valued, and in many areas of Senegambia, a substantial part of the population, if not the majority, was kept in bondage. Finally, the slave trade led to the large-scale involvement of Europeans in the politics and economy of the region, and thus paved the way for the later colonial takeover.

Slavery was also linked to the spread of Islam, although these connections were complex. Firstly, as the conditions of insecurity in the area increased, it was often the large Islamic states which provided most security, and so the population tended to be most heavily concentrated around them. Secondly, although Islam forbade the enslavement of Muslims, it did not forbid slavery itself as an institution – indeed, before the arrival of the Europeans, a vigorous trade in slaves was conducted by Muslim traders operating across the Sahara. Islam saw trade in general as an honourable occupation, and the main trade routes were dominated by networks of Muslims. The availability of slave labour also gave Muslims the opportunity to devote themselves to learning, and therefore the growth of the clerisy itself depended to some extent on the ownership of slaves and forms of bondage. Finally, it was in the wars declared in the name of Islamic reform that many of the slaves were captured from neighbouring 'pagan' peoples, and these wars became increasingly frequent throughout the 18th and 19th centuries.

The role of the Europeans

Control of the coastal trade and the settlements upon which it was based depended largely on the balance of power in Europe. The main staging post for the slave trade in Senegambia, on the island of Gorée off Cap-Vert, was founded by the Dutch in 1588, but was taken over by the French in 1679 and then fought over with the British. British and French companies gradually came to dominate the coastal trade from their respective local bases, the British from the Gambia river, and the French from Saint-Louis and Gorée. During the Seven Years' War the British briefly took control of both Gorée and Saint-Louis. Saint-Louis was returned to France in 1778 but was occupied once more by the British in 1809. French control over both settlements was finally confirmed by the treaties of Paris and Vienna in 1814-15.

The historical sources on the company period in these coastal settlements are excellent, and provide a vivid account of the life and petty intrigues in these little communities. In addition to the Europeans and the Africans, an important element in their populations were the mulattos, people of mixed descent. Inter-racial unions in the region dated back to the arrival of the Portuguese, and the wealthier and more talented African and mulatto women, known as *signares*, became the companions, mistresses and sometimes wives of generations of French officials and traders. They gave their partners access to networks of African traders in the interior, and in return they were able to acquire the capital to become wealthy traders in their own right. Their economic position declined in the early 19th century, along with that of the rest of the mulatto population.

The treaties of 1814-15 required the abolition of the slave trade; however this trade was already in decline as the requirements of the European economy began to change, and as the slave populations in the Americas began to reproduce themselves. The existing slaves in Saint-Louis and Gorée were finally emancipated in 1848. The end of the slave trade raised the question of alternative sources of revenue. An attempt to found agricultural colonies near Saint-Louis failed, and for a while the most important export was gum-arabic, used mainly in the French textile industry. Most of this was exported from Saint-Louis, but Gorée still lacked an obvious economic role. One possibility for stimulating its trade was to reduce the duties charged there: in 1822 the French exempted some goods from taxation, and in 1852 they declared Gorée a free port. In the 1840s, after the discovery that groundnut oil could be used by the Marseilles soap industry, the island also became a centre for groundnut exports and its prosperity, together with that of the colony as a whole, finally revived. This made the French government more willing to listen to the advice of French commercial interests in the region, particularly the merchant firms of Marseilles and Bordeaux, and the result was a more overtly expansionist French policy.

The French conquest

Many groups had an interest in the expansion of French influence in West Africa. The politicians were concerned with competition in Europe, and were willing to annex regions elsewhere simply to keep the rival European powers out. The military and the bureaucracy saw colonial expansion as a means of bettering their own career prospects. The missions needed government protection in order to expand their work, and so did the merchants. France under the Second Empire was more in favour of colonial expansion than under the previous régime, and during the 1850s there were particularly dramatic developments, with the appointment of Louis Faidherbe as Governor in 1854, the foundation of Dakar in 1857, and the beginnings of direct European intervention in the politics of the interior.

Since the late 18th century, wars in the Sudan, from Senegal to northern Nigeria, had become increasingly frequent. Many of them resulted from declarations of *jihad* (holy war) by religious leaders, even though the underlying reason for these wars in the Western Sudan was often economic. One of the most important figures in these movements was al-Hajj Umar Tal. Born of a Tukulor family in what is now eastern Senegal, he spent his early years as an itinerant Muslim scholar, passing long periods in Sokoto and Mecca, where he was initiated into the Tijaniyya Sufi order and was appointed Khalifa for the Sudan. He thus returned to West Africa with a sense of religious and political mission, and in a series of military campaigns during the 1850s he established a substantial empire, mostly in present-day Mali but also including parts of eastern Senegal. He then left his son Ahmadou to administer his conquests in the west, while he turned to the east, where he was killed during a campaign in 1864.

While Umar was establishing his empire in the interior, the French were starting to expand their own influence along the coast. The Bordeaux merchants, having decided that some political involvement in the interior was necessary for the expansion of trade, supported the appointment of Louis Faidherbe, a brilliant military engineer, as Governor of Senegal, who served from 1854 to 1861 and again during 1863-64. By the time he left the region, the French had established control of a considerable area of the mainland, and Senegal had become the largest European colony in West Africa. In the period between 1855 and 1858 Faidherbe was mainly occupied with politics along the Senegal river valley, annexing Walo and restricting Umar's forces to the area east of Bakel. Following this, from 1859 onwards, he launched a series of campaigns in Sine and Salum further south, partly to remove obstacles to trade and missionary work, and partly to pre-empt a British move into the interior. French posts were established at Rufisque, Kaolack, and Thiès. The ruler, or Damel, of Kayor, Lat Dior, who opposed the construction of a telegraph line through his territory, was driven out and his kingdom annexed, linking Cap-Vert to Walo and Saint-Louis for the first time.

Through these campaigns, Faidherbe established the French as the main power-brokers in the region, and laid the basis for the French conquest which continued for the rest of the century. As their power expanded, and as the quality of their military technology improved, the local rulers increasingly realised that French support could be a distinct political asset. However, French policy was once more affected by events in Europe. After the war with Prussia in 1870, fewer resources could be devoted to Africa, and the French even re-instated Lat Dior as ruler of Kayor, where at times he assisted the French in their campaigns against other local rulers. French colonial aspirations only really began to revive from the mid-1870s, with the arrival of a more ambitious governor, Brière de l'Isle, and with elaborate proposals to develop the railway network in the region, by linking Dakar to Saint-Louis, the Niger, and, ultimately, to a trans-Saharan line running down through Algeria. Lat Dior, having agreed to let the Dakar-Saint-Louis line pass through Kayor, changed his mind, and was once more forced into exile. He was finally killed in battle in 1886 and Kayor was annexed permanently.

Sporadic negotiations with the British had been underway for many years regarding the future of their enclave along the Gambia river, but the British price was always too high to make agreement possible (a particularly interesting proposal in 1866 would have given the British the French posts on the Ivory Coast, and in Gabon in exchange, which would have dramatically changed the future shape of West Africa). Eventually in 1889 an agreement was reached, which though regarded by all as unsatisfactory and temporary, established the frontiers which have existed ever since. After a final major push by the French into the interior in 1890 in a war against Ahmadou, the son of Umar Tal, French control over the whole area of present-day Senegal was more or less complete. By 1902, the French had completed the conquest of most of those parts of West Africa not occupied by the British, the Portuguese and the Germans, and Dakar was designated the capital for the whole of the AOF.

Colonial rule: the four communes and the protectorate

The territory which the French had occupied in Senegal was divided administratively into a colony, which consisted of the four historic communes of Dakar, Saint-Louis, Gorée and Rufisque, and a protectorate, which included all the rest. The peoples of the communes and the protectorate had quite different rights. Those born in the four communes, whether they were Europeans, mulattos or Africans, were French citizens and enjoyed full political rights. The policy here was one of 'assimilation' to French culture and citizenship. As the colonial system expanded, however, the idea of the assimilation of all those under French control appeared increasingly implausible, and the peoples of the protectorate were administered under the *indigénat*, a code which granted them few political or civil rights, and which subjected them to the often authoritarian rule of French local administrators. This distinction between the two areas and the rights of their citizens lasted until the abolition of the *indigénat* after the Second World War.

The citizens of the four communes were in fact the only people in Africa to enjoy the benefits of French citizenship, and this was the only part of the French empire where assimilation as a policy was actually put into practice. The result was that the citizens of the four communes had an active political life and regularly elected both their own councils and deputies to serve in Paris. Many of these representatives were mulattos, but in 1914 the citizens of the communes elected Blaise Diagne, an African, to represent them in Paris. He remained deputy until 1934, and in 1918-19 he founded the first African political party in Senegal, the Republican Socialist Party of Senegal. Even though the notion of assimilation has been much criticized for the way in which it was implemented, and also for the fact that it had little meaning for the great mass of the population, it was still remarkably liberal in comparison with other models of colonial rule current in the 19th century, and, through the election of Diagne, it paved the way for the post-war development of nationalist politics.

However, the policy for the administration of the interior was completely different. Much has been made of the administrative differences between British and French territories in West Africa, the former usually seen as relying on forms of 'indirect' rule involving traditional political authorities, and the latter on 'direct' rule, with greater hierarchical centralized control. Even if the philosophies of the two colonizing powers were different, the reality of the situation was not so clear-cut. Although the British and French administrators had to deal with similar problems of large territories and limited resources, which meant usually some accommodation with, or reliance on, the local chiefs, the main difference perhaps was that while the British emphasized the chief's freedom of action, particularly in judicial matters, within the narrow limits defined by the colonial regime, he was seen by the French as just one level in a centralized administrative system, responsible for unpopular tasks such as tax collection and the recruitment of labour. The chiefs under this system gradually evolved into government officials and by the time of independence this transition was complete. Labour relations were governed by the *indigénat* code, which basically gave the employers complete control over employees. Senegalese labour was recruited for a variety of purposes: for the construction of railways and roads; for service in the French army (with wages and working conditions inferior to those of citizens from the communes); or even to provide factory labour when none could be recruited through more conventional means.

The introduction of colonial rule coincided with two other revolutionary changes in Senegalese society. The first was the further spread of groundnut production which made it the mainstay of the economy. The second was the spread of Islam. It appears that with the complete disruption of the social and political order, Islam provided both a social and an intellectual framework within which people could rebuild their lives. This may explain the popularity of the brotherhoods within which the relationship between *marabout* (religious teacher) and *talibé* (disciple) is particularly strong, and it was the marabouts who became the new intermediaries between the peasantry and the political system, a position which they still occupy.

The response of the administration to the rise of Islam was at first negative. Because of their experience in Algeria in the early 19th century, the French saw Islam as a potential threat, a source of resistance to colonial rule. Muslim preachers whom they regarded as dangerous were persecuted or even exiled. This was the fate of Ahmadu Bamba, the founder of the powerful Mouride order, which spread particularly rapidly among the Wolof of the groundnut basin. His sufferings at the hands of the French became the stuff of legend, and only served to enhance his reputation among his followers. When he returned from exile, however, he made his peace with the colonial government, which by this time, thanks to the work of Marty, Delafosse and other scholarly administrators, had begun to regard Islam in more favourable light, as a conservative rather than a radical force. Certainly Bamba helped the French with recruitment campaigns during the First World War (as did Blaise Diagne, who was appointed to a ministerial post in France for that purpose). The administration came to rely on the *marabouts d'arachide* as intermediaries between them and the rural population, just as the peasants became reliant on the marabouts as patrons. Some of the Mouride marabouts, through the labour of their disciples, became wealthy farmers, responsible for an increasing percentage of the country's total output.

The other economic beneficiaries of the colonial system were the French firms. In the precolonial period commerce had been dominated by the mulatto population, but they gradually lost ground to the Lebanese and small French businesses on the one hand, and the large French companies, particularly CFAO and SCOA which dominated the import-export trade, on the other. French colonialism is often criticized, particularly by Marxist scholars, for preventing the development of an indigenous bourgeoisie, for concentrating on the export trade in goods which were useful to France rather than developing a balanced economy locally, and for making the peasant farmers dependent on a world market which they were unable to control, while the main profits from the trade went to the French companies.

Even in the pre-war period, however, the foundations were being laid for the political changes which were to follow it. Galandou Diouf and Lamine Guèye emerged as the leading African politicians in the generation after Blaise Diagne, and the latter founded the Parti

Socialiste Sénégalais in 1927. Senghor had links with both Diagne and Guèye, the former as his legal guardian during his early days in France, and the latter as his sponsor in the early part of his political career.

Senghor was also involved in developments in literature. The concentration of the region's educational institutions in Senegal meant that many of the students travelling to France for further studies, including Senghor and his contemporaries, Birago Diop and Ousmane Socé Diop, were Senegalese. Senghor was starting to write poetry, and together with the Caribbean poets Damas and Césaire, he was beginning to think about problems of African identity and formulate the concept of *négritude*, a theme with which he was preoccupied for the next fifty years.

The Second World War and its aftermath

France's position as an imperial power ultimately depended on its position in Europe, and this was destroyed by the German invasion and occupation in 1940. The West African colonies were at first administered by the Vichy régime, and an expedition to take over Dakar, mounted by the British at the insistence of De Gaulle, ended in farce. Senegal remained under Vichy control until 1943 when the West African colonies, sensing that the tide was turning, began to support the Free French. African troops served in the Second War as they had in the First. Senghor himself was captured by the Germans and imprisoned for two years, which he spent, rather characteristically, improving his German by reading Goethe, and writing some of the poems in his second collection, *Hosties noires*.

The years after the war were years of rapid development, both in politics and literature, and Senghor was again involved in both. On the literary side he published in quick succession his first three collections of poems (*Chants d'ombre, Hosties noires,* and *Chantes pour Naëtt*), and a major anthology of black poetry, for which Jean-Paul Sartre wrote the introduction. Birago Diop published his *Tales of Amadou Koumba*, and Alioune Diop founded Présence Africaine which was responsible for publishing much of the work by Senegalese writers in the years that followed. On the political side, the French government brought in reforms in the colonies: the *indigénat* was abolished, together with the distinction between the peoples of the four communes and the protectorate. Senegal elected two deputies to the French assembly, with Lamine Guèye representing the rural areas, and Senghor, his protégé, the rural. The alliance between the two men did not last long however: Senghor soon founded his own party, the Bloc Démocratique Sénégalaise, and soon proved himself adept at building political alliances, even among the Muslim peasantry. In the 1951 election Guèye's party was heavily defeated, and Senghor emerged as the dominant figure in Senegalese politics, a position which he was to hold for the next thirty years.

Politics, literature and négritude

The link between Senghor's roles as poet and as a politician was, of course, the concept of *négritude*, even if there was a gradual shift in its meaning. In his early work, Senghor was preoccupied with the distinctiveness of black personality and culture, which he regarded as fundamentally different from white identity. In the run-up to independence, negritude became more overtly political, the basis for Senghor's version of African socialism. In his later work, negritude has come to refer to the unique qualities of black culture which will contribute to the 'universal civilization' which Senghor hopes will develop.

This kind of mysticism is, however, far removed from practical politics, and what really kept Senghor in power for so long was not his philosophy, but his ability to do deals, build alliances, and successfully neutralize his political rivals. Negritude and similar ideas were probably of greater importance in the development of Senegalese literature, as in Senghor's own poetry or in the reworking of myth and folk tales by Abdoulaye Sadji and Birago Diop. They also provided an agenda for the highly idiosyncratic historical research of Cheikh Anta Diop. Ultimately, they contributed to a repertoire of themes dealing with the clash between African and European cultures, and the alienation of the black man in the white-dominated world – themes which have been worked and reworked from different philosophical standpoints in Senegalese poetry, novels and films ever since. Senegal has produced a crop of major writers out of all proportion to the country's size. As well as Senghor and his immediate contemporaries, Birago Diop, Ousmane Socé Diop, and Abdoulaye Sadji, these have included the poet David Diop, the novelist and politician Cheikh Hamidou Kane, the novelist and film director Sembène Ousmane, the dramatist Cheikh Aliou Ndao, and the women writers Nafissatou Diallo, Mariama Bâ and Aminata Sow Fall.

The transition to independence

The 1950s were as eventful in France's relations with its colonies as the 1940s had been: a decade marked by major colonial wars in Indochina and Algeria. The crisis in Algeria led directly to the collapse of the Fourth Republic and the return of De Gaulle to power, and this in turn resulted in the acceleration of the decolonization process in West Africa. In 1956, the French extended universal enfranchisement to the colonies as a step towards ultimate independence, and after the advent of De Gaulle the question of the future of the French West African federation was high on the agenda. Senegal had a great deal to lose with its breakup, as did Senghor personally. Dakar was the regional capital, and most of the industry, educational facilities and administrative infrastructure were located there. Senghor would probably have preferred to play a role on a regional rather than a national stage. However, France and the Ivory Coast, whose leader Houphouët-Boigny was the other major political personality in the region, both opposed the idea of a self-governing regional federation, and the result was the dissolution of the AOF into its constituent territories.

A referendum was held in these territories in 1958 on the form of independence to be taken. There was to be either administrative autonomy coupled with a continued association with France, or immediate independence. Senghor argued at a regional congress in Cotonou in 1958 that the colonies were not yet ready for independence, however the delegates voted almost unanimously against him. Fortunately, the French modified the wording of the available options slightly, so that 'continued association with France' also entailed the possibility of independence. This was a compromise which most of the African leaders felt able to recommend to their electorates. Guinea alone voted for immediate independence, and the French left in great haste, plunging the country into chaos.

Senghor had already consolidated his position within Senegal through a merger with opposition parties in 1956, and a further merger in 1958 with Lamine Guèye's party led to the formation of the Union Progressiste Sénégalaise (UPS), which despite changes of name is currently still in power. The question was now whether Senegal could salvage anything from the former federation at all. With Guinea independent, Mauritania wanting separation, and with Guinea-Bissau and The Gambia still colonies, Senegal's only alternative to a totally independent path seemed to be a deal with Modibo Keita, the leader of the Soudan (now Mali). The result was the Mali Federation which was given independence on 20 June 1960, but which rapidly collapsed in acrimony. The fact was that though both leaders seem to have been committed to the idea of federation, neither was prepared to risk their local power base on its behalf. Mali and Senegal declared their mutual independence and Senghor was elected president of Senegal, with Mamadou Dia as his prime minister. The capital was moved from Saint-Louis to Dakar to fill the void left by the departing AOF administration.

Independence

At independence, Senegal inherited from the AOF one of the best infrastructures in West Africa: a good industrial base and communications network, a thriving export trade in groundnuts, and excellent relations with France, in part due to Senghor's own reputation and contacts there. On the other hand, the French connection also meant the perpetuation of Senegal's status as an appendage of the French economy. Most of the foreign capital invested in Senegal was French, and the administration was mainly manned by French advisers. France also retained a military presence in Senegal, which it still maintains.

The new country was soon beset by political and economic problems. The first crisis, which erupted in 1962, was the rift between Senghor and his prime minister Mamadou Dia over political reforms and the nature of future links with France. Dia was in favour of greater self-reliance and the creation of a modern state which would bypass the patron-client networks of the marabouts. He had initiated a far-reaching programme of agricultural reorganization, centred around the cooperative movement (to organize marketing and distribution), *animation rurale* (to motivate the farmers and establish a dialogue between them and the state), and *centres d'expansion rurale* (to act as social and economic growth poles in the rural areas). Senghor himself was more pragmatic: he could see the necessity of maintaining links with both the marabouts and the French. In the ensuing showdown between the two leaders, plans for a coup were allegedly uncovered, and Dia was tried and imprisoned until 1974, leaving Senghor to run the country on his own. A new constitution in 1963 created a strong executive presidency, and in the elections of the same year the UPS gained over ninety-four per cent of the vote. Senegal was now effectively a one-party state, and this was confirmed by a ban on opposition parties.

The political system still remained periodically volatile, and in 1968 and 1969 there were student strikes. A general strike was called by the union movement to which the government responded by declaring a state of emergency, and the creation of a new government-sponsored union confederation. There was also dissent in the countryside, when the farmers, hard hit by drought and a drop in groundnut prices due to the French withdrawal of price supports, refused to repay their loans to the state marketing organizations.

Senghor's response was the introduction of a clause in the constitution which would allow the reappointment of a Prime Minister, and his choice was Abdou Diouf, an able young technocrat. The situation hardly improved, however: peasant and student unrest continued, and the drought situation worsened. But instead of a political crack-down, which would have been the instinctive response of many African leaders, Senghor's response was the liberalization of the political system, perhaps in an attempt to channel the dissent into a more manageable form, on the understanding that his political survival was still underwritten by French troops.

In 1974, therefore, he announced a political amnesty, which included Mamadou Dia, and allowed the legalization of Abdoulaye Wade's Parti Démocratique Sénégalais (PDS). Two years later, he decreed that in future there would be a three party system: a party of the centre-left (his own); a party to the right of it (the PDS); and an official Marxist Leninist party led by Majhmout Diop, who had been allowed to return from exile. The liberalization strategy worked to the extent that Senghor's party won another overwhelming victory in the 1978 elections, but, again, it did little to solve the country's underlying economic problems. Senghor, however, had also paved the way for his retirement by yet another change to the constitution which made the Prime Minister his automatic successor. In 1979 he announced that he would stand down at the end of the year, making him the first African post-independence leader to voluntarily cede power, and leaving Abdou Diouf to make the necessary difficult decisions concerning the economy.

The era of structural adjustment

Despite his long service under Senghor, Diouf quickly proved to be capable of making his own decisions. He brought in his own appointees, and lifted the limits on the number of opposition parties, although parties based on region, ethnic group or religion were still banned. Opposition parties proliferated. Diouf also gained relative success as an international statesman: as a Muslim he was able to take an active part in international Islamic diplomacy, and this proved to be a useful source of new financial aid. His international standing was also helped by his appointment as chairman of the Organization of African Unity in 1985-86.

However, the country's economic crisis continued, and in 1981 Senegal was forced to negotiate an IMF restructuring programme. This has involved deregulating the economy, allowing producer prices to rise, and cutting back on government expenditure. These measures have in turn had the effect of raising the cost of living in the cities, but do not appear to have had much impact on production, which is still stagnant in spite of a rapidly growing population. It seems, therefore, that despite its compliance with these programmes, Senegal's economic recovery will be a slow and protracted process.

At the time of writing, there are four main sectors which contribute to export earnings. The first of these is agriculture, in which there are obvious environmental constraints on production in many parts of the country. The widespread cultivation of groundnuts has led to the acceleration of the processes of deforestation and desertification. However, as some of the largest groundnut farmers are the marabouts, on whose political support the government has traditionally depended, this environmental destruction went unchecked for a long time. Under the 'New Agricultural Policy' introduced in 1984, the government has tried to persuade farmers to move to the production of foodstuffs, in order to reduce these problems and to make the country eighty per cent self-sufficient in food supplies, thus cutting down the cost of imports. The problem which arises from this policy is a potential reduction in foreign exchange earnings from groundnuts, so that the effect on the balance of payments may in fact be small or even negative. There are also difficulties concerning the management of agricultural development. Almost every study of Senegalese agriculture since independence has been critical of the way in which the bureaucracy has tended to impose its ideas and policies on the peasantry, whether or not they are suitable for the local situation, making the peasantry extremely sceptical of the value of government initiatives. Regarding deforestation, firewood and charcoal remain the main sources of energy for the cities. The prices of both remain relatively low thus ensuring a high rate of consumption, and providing little economic incentive for farmers to plant trees. Thus deforestation may well continue until the price of fuel rises to make tree-planting sufficiently attractive, by which time of course the damage to the environment could well be irreversible.

The second sector is fishing, and as far as fish stocks are concerned, Senegal has some of the richest territorial waters in Africa. The fishing industry is divided into two sectors: a small-scale sector relying on traditional techniques and canoes; and a capital-intensive sector. Most of the latter is foreign owned, as attempts to develop a modern Senegalese fishing fleet have been relatively unsuccessful. The small-scale sector has fared much better, largely through the motorization of the traditional canoes. However, it appears that foreign fishing fleets are reaping the greatest benefits, so much so that according to some authorities, the waters are already being over-exploited. The third economic sector concerns the extraction of phosphates. The production of phosphates is limited, however, by technical problems and stagnant prices on the international market as well as other factors.

The fourth sector of the economy which affects the balance of payments is tourism. Senegal is West Africa's largest tourist destination, with 300,000 visitors per year coming in search of sun, the sea and the exotic. Tourist developments are mainly centred around the coastline and the national parks, but an additional attraction are the *campements*, which provide basic accommodation for visitors to rural areas while trying to integrate the tourists into rural life. The most detailed study of the comparative effects of tourist development suggests that this type of integrated rural tourism has a less serious impact on the environment than the intensive enclave seaside developments. The long-term concerns are different: there must be a limit on the number of tourists that Senegal can absorb without serious disruption of its social life, and therefore a ceiling on the contribution which tourism can make to solving the country's economic problems.

International relations

It is not surprising that given these rather limited economic options, the government of Senegal should have looked once more to wider regional groupings as a way of finding solutions to some of its problems. Many organizations have been established in the region over the years, but not all have been successful. The Senegal River Organisation which was set up in the late 1960s collapsed amid bickering between Sekou Touré of Guinea and the other members. Its more modest successor, the OMVS (Organisation for Senegal River Development) may be more fortunate as new irrigation projects come into operation. Senegal is also a member of ECOWAS (Economic Organisation of West African States); but the Organisation's ambitious aims of greater economic and political integration are proving difficult to realize.

This leaves the possibility of an association with The Gambia, which would give Senegal greater control over its trade, as well as allowing it to rationalize its transport system and develop the full potential of the Casamance. However, the whole history of Senegal's relations with The Gambia since independence illustrates how difficult the legacy of the colonial period is to eradicate. When Britain and France carved up the map of the region in 1889, the arrangement was regarded as both temporary and unsatisfactory, but with the colonial powers seemingly uninterested in further rationalization of the map, or even in cooperation during the colonial period, the existing frontiers have survived by default.

Despite the obvious cultural and historical links between the two countries, different sets of administrative, educational, and (above all) economic policies have over the years created a formidable series of obstacles to unity. The British pursued a more liberal trade régime, which meant higher prices for groundnuts, and lower prices for imports, and the predictable result was massive smuggling to and fro over the frontier. As the transit trade is one of The Gambia's major assets it is reluctant to do anything to change the situation. Indeed, one of the main obstacles to unity is the Gambian perception that Senegal would gain much more from a federation than The Gambia itself. A United Nations report in 1964 concluded that unification was impossible, and the best that could be hoped for was a confederation in which both countries would maintain their sovereignty.

In 1981, however, unity between the two nations suddenly seemed likely to become a reality. Senegal's response to a coup attempt in The Gambia was to send in troops to support the régime of President Jawara. With the dramatic improvement in relations between the two countries, a plan to establish a confederation was swiftly agreed, and negotiations initiated the unification process. Defence was one of the first issues to be dealt with, and a joint military force was established. Given that the Jawara government was still not sure of the loyalty of the Gambian army, the continued presence of Senegalese troops was a perhaps a guarantee of survival.

However, as time went on the Gambian régime became less enthusiastic about further moves towards unity, to the evident impatience of Dakar. Strains in the Federation were usually officially denied, and the confederation secretariat continued to issue bullish statements about progress, but the reality was one of stalemate on key issues such as trade. Eventually, in 1989, there was a swift denouement: the Gambians demanded that the presidency, held by Senegal under the 1982 agreement, be transferred. The Senegalese withdrew their troops from the joint force, and the leaders of the two countries declared that the union had been dissolved. Relations have since improved enough for the two countries to sign a treaty of friendship and cooperation, but confederation and unity are no longer being discussed. There are still suspicions in The Gambia that Senegal may one day attempt annexation, but this seems to be unlikely under the present Senegalese régime.

Senegal's relations with its other neighbours are also troubled. To the south there is a long-running border dispute with Guinea-Bissau over rights to territorial waters which may or may not contain oil. This dispute arises because of Guinea-Bissau's rejection of agreements originally negotiated by the Portuguese. Much more serious, however, are the problems with Mauritania in the north. Moors from Mauritania have long occupied an important position in Senegal's trading system as small shopkeepers, and many of the skilled workers in Mauritania have long been Senegalese. The problems developed from an incident in early April 1989, in which two Senegalese were shot and killed on the border, apparently after a dispute about grazing rights. This was followed by disturbances in local towns and the looting of Mauritanian shops.

Efforts by both governments to placate the parties involved were ineffective and by the end of the month serious ethnic rioting had broken out in the towns of both countries. More than 200 Senegalese were believed to have been killed in Mauritania, and perhaps fifty or sixty Mauritanians in Senegal. Many more were injured, and shops and stores were looted. Both groups of migrants began to flee over the border to safety, and an international airlift evacuated a further 45,000 people. There were also allegations by black Mauritanians arriving in Senegal that they were being expelled from their farms along the Senegal river by their northern neighbours who claimed they were of Senegalese descent. It seemed that the various ethnic groups in Mauritania were using the crisis for their own purposes. The Chairman of the Organization of African Unity (OAU) at that time, President Mubarak of Egypt, became involved in mediation attempts, but relations remained tense.

The Casamance situation

Ethnic tensions were also apparent in the conflict in the Casamance, where violence started to escalate in 1990. Because of the frontiers with The Gambia, the Casamance is relatively remote from the rest of Senegal: it is also culturally different, and it is the only part of Senegal with a substantial Christian and animist population. The relations between its peoples and state officials from other regions have not always been ideal and in 1982 the discontent led to demonstrations, followed in 1984 by serious violence. A classic regional separatist movement, the Mouvement des Forces Démocratiques de Casamance (MFDC) developed with both civilian and military wings and, reputedly, with support from Catholic churchmen as well as from the Diola in Guinea-Bissau. So far this movement has been too fragmented to pose a serious military threat, but it has been capable of sporadic attacks on government targets.

In 1990 the government signalled its decision to crush the movement with the appointment of an uncompromising retired general as the region's military governor. Since then there have been numerous allegations of atrocities by both sides and Amnesty International issued a report highly critical of the government. With the movement still active and with the government unwilling or unable to make concessions, contained but serious violence could well continue for some time.

Conclusion: the management of a chronic crisis

Despite these foreign and regional problems, the major issues facing the leadership are still economic, and the constraints which these create do much to explain the course of government policy over the years. It has been a long-term process of crisis management, with the presidency oscillating between different policy options and constitutional arrangements, thereby giving itself some room for manoeuvre, but never overcoming the basic problems. As a result, many of the processes in recent Senegalese history appear to be cyclical – the concentration and devolution of power, the elimination and the re-incorporation of political opponents, and the alternation of techno-cratic and free-market development programmes. It is therefore worth considering both the basic framework of constraints and the available options within them which have produced this pattern.

The basic constraints fall into two categories. First, given the limited resource base of the country and its dependency on international capital and markets, there is unlikely to be any dramatic improvement in the economic situation in the near future. Had Senegal become the commercial and industrial powerhouse of a united West African Federation, its history might have been very different: as soon as the AOF broke up, many of the assets which Senegal possessed during the colonial period lost much of their potential value. Secondly, there are the continuing links with France and the rest of the international community. Given its chronic economic weakness, Senegal is dependent on these links both for continuing flows of credit and aid, and, in the case of France, for an implicit guarantee of the maintenance of the régime. It is not difficult to imagine, for instance, what the French reaction to a coup attempt might be.

But within this framework, Senegal is unlikely to solve any of its basic problems, and the most it can hope to do is to play off, or pay off, the various interest groups in the country so as to minimize the risk of serious political disorder. These interest groups include major players such as the marabouts, the bureaucracy, the party, the military, and perhaps the trade unions, and less powerful but still potentially disruptive groups such as the students and the peasantry. From time to time opposition groupings have emerged which have gained the support of fractions of these interest groups, but in general the government has been extremely skilful at keeping the political opposition fragmented.

The problem is that, with the limited resources available, the state cannot pay off all of these groups at the same time. Programmes based on strong bureaucratic control and management may suit the bureaucracy, but not the marabouts or wealthy members of the ruling party. These groups usually prefer policies which channel resources through the free market, so as to raise the returns on their capital. The problem is that such policies also tend to increase the living costs of state employees or, for that matter, students (in 1987, the government faced major confrontations with both the students and the police). The state also has to keep an eye on the kinds of policies which are currently in favour with the international financial community, and these in the 1980s generally involved deregulation of the market.

The President has limited options as to how to present and operate these policies. He can either concentrate power in his own hands and take a strong lead, which allows him greater personal control but means accepting the blame in the case of failure; or he can devolve power, reducing the pressure on himself, at the risk of reduced efficiency. His subordinate's failure means that he has to centralize power once more, and the cycle begins again.

These constraints and limited policy options help to explain some of the vagaries of Senegalese politics over the years. In many other Third World states similar constraints produce an alternation between civilian and military régimes, with neither retaining political legitimacy for very long. In Senegal, however, with its relatively strong guarantee against military intervention, the process is one of oscillation between strong presidential control over what is in effect a bureaucratic one-party state, and a more devolved system, with other interest groups or parties being allowed greater involvement in decisions. In a review of Senegalese politics in the early and mid-1980s, Coulon and O'Brien suggested that Diouf was relying more on the bureaucracy and his own network of technocrats and advisers, notably the tough, French-born general secretary of the presidency, Jean Collin, and depending less on the marabouts and party bosses. This had led to increasing militancy among some of the marabouts, as well as disarray in the party. Many of the senior party members had been pushed aside as the president assumed greater power after his accession, and in abolishing the office of Prime Minister, he had followed Senghor's lead of two decades earlier.

Since the late 1980s, however, the pendulum may have begun to swing the other way. The death of the leader of the Mourides in 1989 gave Diouf the chance to convey his sympathy to the Brotherhood in person. In 1990 Jean Collin's retirement was announced, ostensibly on the grounds of age (he had just turned sixty-five). In April 1991 Diouf reinstated the post of Prime Minister, and reappointed Habib Thiam, the former incumbent, to fill the post. At the same time, and with true Senghorian panache, he offered Abdoulaye Wade the position of Minister of State in the government, which the opposition leader duly accepted.

Whatever these events tell us about Diouf's need for broad-based support to continue with the structural adjustment programme, they also suggest some continuity with the Senghor era. The basic domestic economic constraints remain the same, though the situation has if anything gradually worsened with continued poor weather and population growth. The basic external situation remains the same, with reliance on France and on external sources of finance leading to the perpetuation of dependency. The alignment of local interest groups also remains largely the same, even if the state bureaucracy has been expanded at the expense of the traditional patron-client networks.

What the future holds for Senegal is therefore also most likely to be more of the same, with the presidential office ringing the changes both in economic policy, to appease the international community and local interest groups, and in constitutional changes in order to allow crisis management to continue. At both of these President Diouf is proving as adept as his predecessor, and thus the remarkable capacity of the Senegalese state to maintain relative stability amidst apparent economic disaster may yet be demonstrated for some time to come.

Postscript

During the period in which this book has been in press, and since the completion of the Introduction in 1992, events in Senegal have been unusually turbulent. In March 1993, Abdou Diouf was declared to have been elected for a further seven-year presidential term, but only after three weeks of dispute over the election results. His share of the vote dropped dramatically whilst Abdoulaye Wade won a significant majority of the vote in Dakar. Legislative elections in May also produced a victory for the ruling *Parti Socialiste*, albeit with a reduced majority. A major crisis erupted during the same month with the assassination of Babacar Seye, the Vice President of the Constitutional Council. Predictably, Abdoulaye Wade, the opposition leader, was detained and eventually charged in connection with the affair; but he denied the charge.

A further crisis resulted in January 1994 with the massive devaluation of the CFA franc (to 1FF=100 CFA). Under pressure from the IMF and from the French conservative government – returned after a victory in France in the 1993 elections – Diouf, who had strenuously opposed devaluation, was left humiliated and his government's relations with France were soured. Serious riots, fuelled by popular discontent over price rises and shortages of goods, then erupted in Dakar on February 16th. Islamic fundamentalists and opposition parties were quickly blamed by the government for the breakdown, and Wade was once more detained.

Thus, with the continuing economic gloom, with relations with France called into question, and with opposition to the government being demonstrated on the streets of Dakar, the art of crisis management in Senegal now, in early 1994, generally looks rather more difficult than it did in the summer of 1992.

March 1994

The Country and Its People

1 **Area handbook for Senegal.**
Compiled by Harold D. Nelson (et al.). Washington, DC: American
University Foreign Area Studies Division; Washington, DC:
Government Printing Office, 1974. 2nd ed. 410p.
This is a major reference source for the country. Its individual chapters provide
overviews of Senegal's history, economy, politics and administration, along with a
wealth of bibliographical material. The first edition, compiled by T. D. Roberts was
published in 1963.

2 **Carte d'identité du Sénégal.** (Identity card of Senegal.)
Dakar: Nouvelles Editions Africaines for the Ministère du Plan et de la
Coopération, [n.d.] 175p.
A concise official guide to the country (the copy consulted referred to 1984) containing
brief sections on climate, demography and history; the political institutions; and human
resource development and the quality of life.

3 **Esquisses sénégalaises.** (Senegalese sketches.)
Abbé David Boilat. Nendeln, Leichtenstein: Kraus Reprint, 1973. 495p.;
Paris: Karthala, 1984. 499p. (Originally published by P. Bertrand, Paris,
1853.)
This book, completed in France in 1852, is a massive survey of Senegalese life and
history with chapters on Gorée and Dakar, together with the major kingdoms and
ethnic groups in the region. The conclusion contains an assessment of African progress
under French occupation and policies for the future.

4 **Etude sur le Sénégal.** (Study of Senegal.)
   M. Courtet.   Paris: Augustin Challamel, 1903. 183p.

A useful overview of the state of the Senegalese economy at the turn of the century, with short sections on all the major products, vegetable, animal and mineral. At the end of the book is a miscellany of sections on ethnography, local industries, public health and public works, and a long and useful chronology of major historical events.

5 **French West Africa.**
   Virginia Thompson, Richard Adloff.   London: Allen & Unwin, 1958. 626p.

This large-scale survey of the region written on the eve of independence is still a standard work in English, and contains chapters on the history, politics and administration of French West Africa, followed by sections on the economy, including finance, transportation, agriculture, industry, trade and labour, education, the media, urban development and religion. It also includes a useful sixteen-page bibliography.

6 **French West Africa, vol. II. The colonies.**
   Oxford: Oxford University Press for HMSO, 1944. 596p.

A wartime naval intelligence handbook, dated, but still useful as an introduction to the physical geography and coastline of Senegal.

7 **The Gambia and Senegal.**
   Edited by Philip Sweeny.   Hong Kong: Insight Guides, APA Publications (HK), 1990. 343p.

Presents a well-produced comprehensive guide to the country, illustrated with particularly fine photographs by Michel Renaudeau. The text is divided into short readable chapters on various aspects of Senegambian history, geography and society by a team of established experts.

8 **Haut-Sénégal-Niger.** (Upper Senegal and Niger.)
   Maurice Delafosse.   Paris: Larose, 1912. 3 vols. (Reissued by Maisonneuve & Larose, 1972.)

Although the main focus of these volumes is on the regions to the east of the national boundaries of present-day Senegal, they deal with the origins, societies and cultures of groups who extend into Senegal such as the Soninke, Tukulor and Fulbe (Peul). Volume one is entitled *Les pays, les peuples, les langues* (The country, the people, the languages), volume two, *L'histoire* (The history) and volume three *Les civilisations* (The civilisations).

9 **Où va le Sénégal? Analyse spectrale d'une nation africaine.** (Whither Senegal? Spectral analysis of an African nation.)
   Pierre Fougeyrollas.   Dakar: IFAN; Paris: Editions Anthropos, 1970. 274p.

This work is an attempt to explain the transformations occurring in Senegalese society during the 1960s, and examines the living conditions of the peasant population, the problems of underdevelopment and ways of escaping from it through regional cooperation.

10   **Les peuplades de la Sénégambie: histoire – ethnographie – moeurs et coutumes – légendes, etc.** (The peoples of Senegambia: history, ethnography, morals and customs, legends etc.)
L.-J.-B. Bérenger-Féraud.   Paris: Ernest Leroux, 1879. 420p. (Reissued by Kraus Reprints. Nendeln, Liechtenstein, 1973)

This survey consists of individual chapters on the Wolof, Moors, Peul, Soninke, Manding, Bambara, and Serer peoples, as well as on the Casamance and the Rio Nunez regions. Each chapter covers similar lists of topics: history, geography, language, manners and customs of each group. The last chapter gives suggestions for the more effective French exploitation of the region.

11   **Le Sénégal.** (Senegal.)
G. Haurigot.   Paris: H. Lecène & H. Oudin, 1887. 235p.

Covers the physical geography, the local people, the arrival of the French, politics, economic exploitation, meteorology, climate and diseases. The text is illustrated with line engravings, and ends with a list of the territory's governors.

12   **Le Sénégal.** (Senegal.)
Gouvernement Général de l'Afrique Occidentale Française.   Paris: Editions Géographiques, Maritimes et Coloniales, 1931. 274p.

Produced for an international exhibition, this volume, dating from 1931, covers the history, geography, cultures, economy and administration of the territory. There are a number of graphs and maps.

13   **Sénégal.**
Christian Saglio.   Paris: Petite Planète, Editions Seuil, 1980.

A useful introduction in French to the history, culture, economy and the regions of Senegal.

14   **Senegal: an African nation between Islam and the West.**
Sheldon Gellar.   Boulder, Colorado: Westview; Aldershot: Gower, 1982. 145p.

One of the most useful general books on the country in English, this is an account of the ways in which the modern political development of Senegal has been shaped by Islam, French colonialism and Western imperialism, with good summary chapters on the historical background, post-independence government and politics, the economy, international relations, and Senegalese culture and society.

15   **Le Sénégal, Dakar.** (Senegal, Dakar.)
Edmond Séré de Rivières.   Paris: Editions Maritimes et Coloniales, 1953. 127p. (Pays Africains, 4).

This is a concise, official introduction to Senegal and Dakar with brief chapters on the country, history, administration, and economy. A brief survey of Dakar, a short section on tourism and hunting, as well as a short bibliography and a list of maps complete the volume.

16   **Le Sénégal et la Gambie.** (Senegal and The Gambia.)
Jacques Lombard.   In: *Histoire générale de l'Afrique noire: Tome I: Des origines à 1800.* Edited by Hubert Deschamps.   Paris: Presses Universitaires de France, 1970, p. 57-80.

This brief chapter by a French anthropologist, taken from one of the standard French histories of Africa, deals with the early history of the country, concentrating on the major ethnic groups: Tukulor, Wolof, Serer, the peoples of the Casamance, and the Europeans.

17   **Le Sénégal et la Gambie.** (Senegal and The Gambia.)
Hubert J. Deschamps.   Paris: Presses Universitaires de France, 1975. 3rd ed. 125p.

Originally published in 1964, this book has chapters on Senegal's geography, peoples, history, and contemporary situation. It ends with a short chapter on The Gambia and a brief select bibliography.

18   **Le Sénégal: étude intime.** (Senegal: in-depth study.)
F. Ricard.   Paris: Chalamel Aîné, 1865. 425p.

The first half of the book is a survey of geography, economy and society. The second half comprises a description of the economic and social transformations brought about by the French, and suggestions for the future administration and economic development of the territory.

19   **Le Sénégal – La Sénégambie.** (Senegal – Senegambia.)
Eric Makédonsky.   Paris: L'Harmattan, 1987. 2 vols.

Essays on Senegambia by a long-serving African correspondant of the Agence France Presse. The first volume gives a broad picture of the country and its history, and the second volume deals with Senghor's foreign policy and visits, the politics of dam construction, and Senegal's relations with France and with The Gambia, and the rest of Africa. There are useful appendices on political parties, constitutional changes, Senegal's currency, cinema and literature.

20   **Sénégal: l'expérience du précurseur.** (Senegal: previous experience.)
Albert Bourgi, Siradiou Diallo, Sennen Andriamirado, Elimane Fall. *Jeune Afrique* (19 Dec. 1990), p. 1564-5.

This special section in the leading French popular journal on Africa contains articles by its regular correspondents on the state of the country's politics, international relations, economic difficulties and the development of the tourist industry.

21   **Le Sénégal: organisation politique, administration, finances, travaux publics.** (Senegal: political organization, administration, finance, public works.)
Paris: Augustin Challamel, 1900. 430p.

A major official reference source compiled at the turn of the century for the Exposition Universelle of 1900, with an enormous mass of information on the political and economic structure of Senegal. The sections deal with fiscal organization, administration, and the economy. There are many tables and graphs, and some fine engravings and maps.

22 **Sénégal-Soudan: agriculture, industrie, commerce.** (Senegal-Sudan: agriculture, industry, commerce.)
Paris: Augustin Challamel, 1900. 124p.

A second, much shorter, volume prepared for the Exposition Universelle of 1900, providing brief official accounts of Senegalese topography, industry, trade (including tables on the origins, destinations and values of imports and exports, 1889-1900), agriculture, communications, and mining. It ends with a general note on administration, imports and customs, and some fascinating estimates on the capital necessary for the prospective European immigrants to establish themselves.

23 **Sénégal: porte de l'Afrique.** (Senegal: gateway of Africa.)
Christine Garnier, Philippe Ermont.   Paris: Hachette, 1962. 201p.

A concise guide to the country with chapters on the history of Dakar, the regions, the colonial period, the collapse of the Mali Federation, the political system of the new Republic, the economy and the 'soul and spirit' of Senegal, dealing with festivals, Islam, education, the press and literature.

24 **Senegambia: proceedings of a colloquium at the University of Aberdeen, April 1974.**
Edited by R. C. Bridges.   Aberdeen, Scotland: Aberdeen University African Studies Group, 1974. 185p.

An edited collection of ten papers, this volume deals with the history and diversity of the region, contemporary issues, and the prospects for cooperation between Senegal and The Gambia.

25 **Special report on Senegal.**
West Africa (13 Nov. 1988), p. 2095.

West Africa, the leading British-based newspaper on the region, carried this special section on the eve of the visit by President Diouf to London. It contains brief articles on the country: the media, government and opposition, Senegal's relations with the UK, and its economic structural adjustment programme.

Connaissance du Sénégal. Géographie humaine. (Knowledge of Senegal. Human geography.)
See item no. 27.

Guide de Dakar et du Sénégal. (Guide to Dakar and to Senegal.)
See item no. 84.

Le Sénégal aujourd'hui. (Senegal today.)
See item no. 86.

Traveller's guide to West Africa.
See item no. 87.

The Country and Its People

West Africa: a travel survival kit.
See item no. 88.

West Africa: the rough guide.
See item no. 89.

Geography

General

26 **Bioclimatologie humaine de Saint-Louis du Sénégal. (Essai de
méthodologie bioclimatologique).** (Human bioclimatology of Saint-Louis,
Senegal: essay on bioclimatological methodology).
Jean-Paul Nicolas. Dakar: IFAN, 1959. 340p. (Mémoires no. 57)
Analyses the complex inter-relationship between human activities and climatic
conditions.

27 **Connaissance du Sénégal. Géographie humaine.** (Knowledge of Senegal.
Human geography).
Jacques Lombard. Saint-Louis, Senegal: CRDS-Sénégal, 1963. 183p.
(Etudes Sénégalaises, 9).
An important study dealing with demography and population, habitat and economic
activity, and life in Senegalese towns.

28 **Haut-Sénégal-Niger (Soudan Français). Géographie économique. Tomes I
& II.** (The Upper Senegal and Niger, French Sudan. Economic
geography.)
Jacques Meniaud. Paris: Larose, 1912. 2 vols.
A companion to the volumes published by Delafosse under the same title (see item 8),
this work focuses primarily on the area to the east of present-day Senegal. However, it
contains useful chapters on the Senegal river, and provides a good overview of
agriculture and production in the region as a whole.

29 **Répertoire des villages.** (Directory of villages.)
Dakar: Ministère du Plan et du Développement, 1964. 196p.
An official directory of the villages of Senegal, listed according to region with details of their population structure. An alphabetical index is provided at the end of the volume.

30 **West Africa.**
R. J. Harrison Church. London: Longman, 1974. 7th ed. 526p.
A standard regional text, frequently revised since its original publication in 1960, which provides systematic coverage of the physical geography of the region, with a detailed a country-by-country survey of climate, geology and relief, the major regions, economic resources, and transport.

French West Africa, vol. II. The colonies.
See item no. 6.

Le Sénégal. (Senegal.)
See item no. 11.

Le Sénégal: étude intime. (Senegal: in-depth study.)
See item no. 18.

Tableau géographique de l'Ouest Africain au moyen âge d'après les sources écrites, la tradition et l'archéologie. (A geographical picture of medieval West Africa, based on written sources, oral tradition and archaeology.)
See item no. 201.

Vie de rélations au Sénégal: la circulation des biens. (Life of relationships in Senegal: the circulation of goods.)
See item no. 375.

Regions and cities

31 **L'agglomération dakaroise: quelques aspects sociologiques et démographiques.** (The Dakar agglomeration: some sociological and demographic aspects.)
P. Mercier, L. Massé, A Hauser. Saint-Louis, Senegal: Centre IFAN, 1954. 83p. (Etudes Sénégalaises, 5).
The three essays in this volume discuss social organization, including the neighbourhood and the family, marriage and fertility, and the development of industry.

32 **La croissance urbaine dans les pays tropicaux: Ziguinchor en Casamance. Une ville moyenne du Sénégal.** (Urban growth in tropical countries: Ziguinchor in the Casamance. A medium-sized town in Senegal.) Jean-Claude Bruneau. Bordeaux, France: Centre d'Etudes de Géographie Tropicale, Domaine Universitaire de Bordeaux, 1979. 163p. (Travaux et Documents de Géographie Tropicale).

A study of the capital of the Casamance, with chapters on the geographical setting, the origins and development of the town, spatial organization, communications, trade, industries, regional administration, demography, and its heterogeneous social and ethnic composition. It is well illustrated with maps, diagrams and photographs, and a useful bibliography of maps, statistical sources and reference works completes the volume.

33 **Dakar en devenir.** (The development of Dakar.) Groupe d'Etudes Dakaroises. Paris: Présence Africaine, 1968. 517p.

An important collection of essays with chapters on many aspects of the city's history, geography, population and social life.

34 **Dakar: métropole ouest-africaine.** (Dakar: a West African metropolis.) Assane Seck. Dakar: IFAN, 1970. 516p. (Mémoire de l'Institut Fondamental d'Afrique Noire, 85).

A massive standard study of the Senegalese capital in the early years of independence, dealing with many aspects of its physical, human and economic geography and history. It contains maps and tables, as well as a section of forty-eight black-and-white plates. There is also a thirteen-page bibliography, with extensive coverage of official sources. A short account of Dakar by the same author was published in *Cahiers d'Outre-Mer*, vol. 14, no. 56 (1961), p. 172-92.

35 **Daoudane-Pikine. Etude démographique et sociologique.** (Daoudane-Pikine. A demographic and sociological study.) Luc Thoré. *Bulletin de l'IFAN*, vol. 24(B), no. 1/2 (1962), p. 155-98.

A study of a satellite town, thirteen kilometres from Dakar, which was established in 1952 to house those affected by redevelopment in Dakar, and whose population totalled 28,000 in 1960. The paper deals with sex ratios, ethnic groups, education, religion and occupations, and with the paradoxical effect of economic growth strengthening rather than weakening family ties.

36 **Espace Dakar-Rufisque en devenir. De l'héritage urbain à la croissance industrielle.** (The spatial development of Dakar-Rufisque. From urban heritage to industrial growth.) Alain Dubrisson. Paris: ORSTOM, 1979. 371p. (Travaux et Documents, 106).

Examines the growth of Rufisque, one of the country's four historical communes, but now effectively an extension of Dakar, discusses its development, economic functions, and the growth of industry. A discussion of the problems of supplying the town with basic resources, and the effects of industry on its social structure complete the volume.

37 **Louga et sa région (Sénégal): essai d'intégration des rapports ville-campagne dans la problématique du développement.** (Louga and its region, Senegal: rural-urban links from the perspective of development.) M. Sar. Dakar: IFAN, 1973. 305p. (Initiations et Etudes Africaines, 30).

Systematically examines the Louga region, dealing with its physical and human geography, the growth of the town, and its economy. It also discusses the agricultural and environmental crises and their effects on the life of the district.

38 **La moyenne vallée du Sénégal: étude socio-économique.** (The middle Senegal valley: a socio-economic study.) J.-L. Boutillier, P. Cantrelle, J Caussé, C. Laurent, Th. N'Doye. Paris: Presses Universitaires de France, 1962. 368p.

This large-scale, detailed study of the middle valley of the Senegal river focuses on northern Senegal and southern Mauritania, and deals with the physical geography, economy and social organization. It is well illustrated with numerous tables, graphs and some excellent black-and-white photographs, and there are eleven appendices on methodology.

39 **Saint-Louis du Sénégal. Evolution d'une ville en milieu africain.** (Saint Louis, Senegal. Evolution of a town in an African setting.) C. Camara. Dakar: IFAN, 1968. 292p. (Initiations et Etudes 24).

Discusses the former capital, dealing with its history, economic role and social composition. Maps, illustrations and plates as well as a useful bibliography are also included.

40 **Sob: étude géographique d'un terroir sérèr (Sénégal).** (Sob: a geographical study of a Serer region in Senegal.) André Lericollais. Paris: ORSTOM/ Ecole Pratique des Hautes Etudes (vie section) & Mouton, 1972. 110p. (Atlas des Structures Agraires au sud du Sahara, 7).

Based on research carried out in the late 1960s, this is a study of the Serer village of Sob, which has a population of 547, located to the south of Diourbel. It deals systematically with population density, land tenure, natural resources, livestock, agricultural work and techniques, and the village economy. A collection of plates with excellent aerial photographs, as well as black-and-white photographs of village life, and a portfolio of three remarkable maps which show respectively the terrain, the land use, and individual landholdings in 1967 are appended.

41 **Tambacounda: capitale du Sénégal oriental.** (Tambacounda: capital of Eastern Senegal.) Jean-François Dupon. *Cahiers d'Outre-Mer*, vol. 17, no. 66 (1964), p. 175-214.

Examines the capital of Sénégal Oriental, and describes the town's layout, building styles, the ethnic groups which make up its population, and its economic and administrative roles.

42 **Un village de la vallée du Sénégal: Amadi Ounaré.** (A village in the
   Senegal valley: Amadi Ounaré.)
   C. Le Blanc. *Cahiers d'Outre-Mer*, vol. 66 (1964), p. 117-48.
This is a short study of a village situated on the Senegal river in the north-east of the
country, and of its economy, incuding weaving, for which it is widely known.

43 **Les villages-centres du Sénégal.** (Village centres of Senegal.)
   Alain Galaup. *Cahiers d'Outre-Mer*, vol. 43, no. 174 (1991),
   p. 187-206.
Since the early 1970s, the Senegalese government has made an effort to correct the
imbalance between urban and rural development by encouraging the creation of
villages as local economic growth poles. This is a study of four such villages in the
groundnut basin, and it describes their demographic development, their infrastuctures,
and their roles in trade, craft production and administration.

44 **La ville de Thiès: étude de géographie urbaine.** (The town of Thiès: a
   study in urban geography.)
   G. Savonnet. Saint-Louis: Centre IFAN, Sénégal, 1955. 178p.
This study of Senegal's second largest city, 50km east of Dakar, deals with its economic
functions as a centre of mining and communications, its history, ethnic composition,
and economy.

Geology and Natural Resources

45 **Africa's shared water resources: legal and institutional aspects of the Nile, Niger and Senegal river systems.**
Bonaya Adhi Godana.   London: Frances Pinter, 1985. 370p.
An important study which describes the major rivers of northern and western Africa, their geography and the legal issues surrounding their use. The sections of the book deal with water law as it developed in Europe, the physical, hydrological and economic characteristics of the African rivers systems, and legal and administrative issues which developed during the colonial period and after independence.

46 **Afrique de l'ouest: introduction géologique et terms stratigraphiques.**
(West Africa: an introduction to geology and stratigraphical terms.)
Edited by J. Fabre.   Oxford: Pergamon Press, 1983. 396p. (Léxique Stratigraphique International, Nouvelle Série, 1).
Contains two accessible introductions, one in French and a second in English, to the geology of West Africa. It includes twenty-nine pages of bibliographical references and a paper specifically covering the geology of Senegal by R. A. Rayment.

47 **Les bassins des fleuves Sénégal et Gambie: étude géomorphologique.**
Tomes I-III. (The Senegal and Gambia river basins: a study of the geomorphology, vols. 1-3.)
P. Michel.   Paris: ORSTOM, 1973. 752p. (Mémoires ORSTOM, 63).
Presents a monumental, comprehensive and definitive account of all the major aspects of riverine geology in the region, profusely illustrated with tables, graphs and maps. The third volume contains a portfolio of geological maps of the river basin areas of Senegal, The Gambia and Mauritania, and there is also a valuable series of ninety-one black-and-white plates.

48 **Contribution à l'étude écologique des côtes rocheuses du Sénégal.**
(Contribution to the ecological study of the rocky coasts of Senegal.)
A. R. Sourie. Dakar: IFAN, 1954. 342p. (IFAN Mémoires, 38).
The two parts of this work deal with the physical geography of the coast line, and its biology. It contains a lengthy bibliography and forty-five black-and-white plates.

49 **Energie et espace au Sénégal. Tome 1.** (Energy and space in Senegal. Vol. 1.)
G. Di Meo, R. Guerrero J. P. Jambes, P. Grenier. Talance: Editions CEGET-CNRS, 1987. 171p. (Travaux et Documents de Géographie Tropicale, 60).
The major study in its field, based on research in the Ferlo, the groundnut basin, the Casamance, Dakar and Ziguinchor, this two-volume work contrasts regional energy requirements and the problems of provision. Senegal's continued reliance on wood as the main fuel creates obvious environmental problems, to which there is no easy solution. Volume 2 is the work of A. Cheneau-Loquay, P. Grenier, B. Shauvet, P. Entz and J. Pilleboue (Talance, Senegal: Editions CEGET-CNRS, 1988. 277p.).

50 **Le problème de l'eau au Sénégal.** (The problem of water in Senegal.)
Gerard Brasseur. Saint-Louis, Senegal: Centre IFAN, 1952. 99p.
(Etudes Sénégalaises, 1).
This study of water resources and usage covers the traditional methods of extraction, colonial measures to improve the supply, agriculture and irrigation along the Senegal river, and the urban water supply.

51 **Les problèmes forestiers dans le contexte économique du Sénégal.**
(Forestry problems in the economic context of Senegal.)
Arthur Tibesar. *Canadian Journal of African Studies*, vol. 25, no. 3 (1991), p. 432-47.
A study of deforestation in Senegal and its relationship to the low level of fuel prices, which mean that it is not profitable to conserve or replant trees. Similar ground is covered in a paper co-authored with Rodney White, 'Pricing policy and household energy use in Dakar, Senegal', *Journal of Developing Areas*, vol. 25, no. 1, (1990), p. 33-47.

52 **Sources et consommation d'énergie à Dakar.** (Energy sources and consumption in Dakar.)
Evelyne Berlureau, Patrick Berlureau. *Cahiers d'Outre-Mer*, vol. 34, no. 134 (1981), p. 257-71.
A survey of the energy problems facing Dakar, a city which is home to twenty per cent of the population of Senegal. It covers the use and sources of supply of traditional energy sources, firewood and charcoal, the alternatives (namely petrol, electricity and gas), and the possibilities of new energy sources in the future, which are likely to be slow in appearing.

Flora and Fauna

Flora

53 **Contribution à l'étude de végétation du Sénégal.** (Contribution to the study of the vegetation of Senegal.)
J. Trochain.   Paris: Librairie Larose, 1940. 433p. (Mémoires de l'IFAN, 2).

A comprehensive specialist study of vegetation in Senegal covering climatic and environment conditions, methods and techniques of study, as well as a description of species presented according to their botanical classification and their geographical and ecological habitat. The work contains numerous plates and figures, together with a large bibliography.

54 **Flore du Sénégal: 2e édition plus complète, avec les forêts humides de la Casamance.** (Flora of Senegal: second enlarged edition including the humid forests of the Casamance.)
Jean Berhaut.   Dakar: Editions Clairafrique, 1967. 485p.

A manual for plant identification according to their major morphological characteristics, by which they can be grouped and then matched against a series of line drawings of individual species. The book also contains coloured plates, a vocabulary of botanical terms, a list of plant families, an alphabetical index of species by their scientific names, and additional indexes by name in French, Bambara, Diola, Serer and Wolof.

55 **A handbook of West African flowers.**
Harold N. Saunders.   London: Oxford University Press, 1958. 124p.

A useful pocket reference source for identifying plants, which lists 364 species, about a third of which are illustrated with black-and-white line drawings. At the end is a glossary and an index of botanical names.

14

56 **Noms vernaculaires de plantes du Sénégal.** (Vernacular names of the plants of Senegal.)
J.-G. Adam.   Paris: Laboratoire d'Ethnobotanique, Muséum National d'Histoire Naturelle, 1970. 112p.
Lists of botanical names with their local equivalents in Diola, Mande, Peul (including Tukulor), Serer, Tada and Wolof.

57 **West African trees.**
D. Gledhill.   London: Longman, 1972. 72p. (West African Nature Handbooks).
A well-illustrated survey of the most important species in the full range of West African environments, from swamp forest to savannah.

Fauna

58 **Birds of the West African town and garden.**
J. H. Elgood.   London: Longman, 1960. 66p. (West African Nature Handbooks).
A well-illustrated guide to a hundred species of bird, with information on their distributions, habits and calls. Longman also published in the same series *Small mammals of West Africa* by A. H. Booth (London: Longman, 1960. 68p.); and *West African snakes* by G. S. Cansdale.   London: Longman, 1961. 74p.).

59 **Diet of wild chimpanzees *(Pan troglodytes verus)* at Mt. Assirik, Senegal: I. Composition.**
W. C. McGrew, P. J. Baldwin, C. E. G. Tutin.   *American Journal of Primatology*, vol. 16, no. 3 (1988), p. 213-26.
A study of chimpanzee diet in what is an unsually dry environment for the species. The bibliography lists a number of other specialist papers on this group of chimps by the same authors.

60 **A field guide to the birds of West Africa.**
William Serle, Gérard J. Morel.   London: Collins, 1977. 351p.
The major English-language reference source on the subject, with information on nearly 1100 species, 726 of which are discussed in detail.

61 **The forest dwellers.**
Stella Brewer.   London: Collins, 1978. 254p.
This book tells the compelling and intimate story of the rehabilitation and subsequent resettling of chimpanzees taken from The Gambia to Mount Assirik in the Niokolo-Koba National Park, Senegal, where large populations of these apes live in the wild. This book has also been published in the United States under the title *The apes of Mt Assirik* (New York: Knopf, 1978).

62 **Les oiseaux de l'Ouest africain. Fascicules I, II & III.** (Birds of West Africa, volumes 1-3.)
P. L. Dekeyser, J. H. Derivot. Dakar: IFAN, 1966-68. 507p. (Initiations et Etudes, no. 19).

This is a magnificent work which presents a detailed zoological survey of 1160 species. The first volume includes entries for each species, illustrated and indexed by their Latin, French and English names. The second volume contains a set of 140 colour plates, and the third volume is a 112-page guide to the written sources on the subject, including a bibliography of over 550 items as well as further notes on the species documented in volume 1.

63 **Poissons de mer du Sénégal.** (Saltwater fish of Senegal.)
J. Cadenat. Dakar: IFAN, 1950. 345p. (Initiations et Etudes Africaines, 3).

A standard reference work, the bulk of which consists of an annotated catalogue of species, many of them illustrated with line drawings. There are lengthy appendices, mainly relating to the collection of the Laboratoire de Biologie Marine de l'IFAN at Gorée. In general, the *Etudes et initiations* series published by IFAN remain the major specialist works on the fauna of West Africa. Other titles included *Les animaux protégés de l'Afrique noire* (The protected animals of Black Africa), P. L. Dekeyser and A. Villiers. (Dakar: IFAN, 1951, 128p.); *Hémiptères de l'Afrique noire (puaises et cigales)* (Hemiptera of Black Africa: bugs and cicadas), A. Villiers. (Dakar, IFAN, 1952. 256p.); *Les mammifères de l'Afrique noire française* (The mammals of French Black Africa), P. L. Dekeyser. (Dakar: IFAN, 1955. 426p. bibliog); *Tortues et crocodiles de l'Afrique noire française* (Turtles and crocodiles of French Black Africa), A. Villiers. (Dakar: IFAN, 1958. 354p.); *Les lépidoptères de l'Afrique noire occidentale* (Lepidoptera of Western Black Africa), P. C. Rougeot. (Dakar: IFAN, 1962. 214p.); *Les serpents de l'Ouest africain* (Snakes of West Africa), A. Villiers. (Dakar, IFAN, 1963. 190p.).

Recherches scientifiques dans les parcs nationaux du Sénégal. (Scientific research in the national parks of Senegal.)
See item no. 808.

Sénégal: ses parcs, ses animaux. (Senegal, its parks and animals.)
See item no. 809.

The Environment

64 **Les crises de subsistance dans les villages soninké du cercle de Bakel, de 1858 à 1945: problèmes méthodologiques et perspectives de recherches.**
(The crisis of subsistence in Soninke villages in the circle of Bakel, from 1858 to 1945: Methodological problems and research perspectives.)
Monique Chastanet. *Cahiers d'Etudes Africaines*, vol. 23, no. 1/2, (1983), p. 5-36.
This paper reconstructs the chronology of periods of scarcity, famine and extreme famine in eastern Senegal, using a combination of documentary and oral sources in the absence of detailed statistical data.

65 **Draft environmental report on Senegal.**
University of Arizona Office of Arid Lands Studies, Arid Lands Information Center. Tucson, Arizona; Washington, DC: US Agency for International Development, 1980. 105p.
A useful technical report, discussing Senegal's natural resources, including soils, vegetation and fish, and the problems arising from the slow rate of technical change. Over half of the report consists of appendices, including lists of citations, environmental organizations, counter-desertification activities in progress, proposals to combat desertification, and bibliographies of the major topics discussed.

66 **Environmental management and national sovereignty: some issues from Senegal.**
Rodney White. *International Journal* (Canada), vol. 45, no. 1 (1989-90), p. 106-37.
A useful discussion of general issues of the food crisis in sub-Saharan Africa, and policies which governments might adopt, using Senegal as an example. The paper deals with the relationship between chronic drought and agricultural practices, urban growth and the water supply, the lack of alternative (for example, mineral) resources for exploitation, and the shortage of economic capital.

67 **The great West African drought, 1972-1974.**
J. Derrick. *African Affairs*, vol. 76, no. 305 (1977), p. 537-86.

A useful general survey of the causes and consequences of the drought in both the region and the main countries affected. Pages 555-7 deal with the situation in Senegal.

68 **Human action and the desertification of the Sahel.**
Henri Lo, Abdoulaye Sene. *International Social Science Journal*, vol. 41, no. 3 (1989), p. 449-56.

Presents a brief analysis of human factors in the spread of the desert in Sahelian Senegal, focusing on deforestation.

69 **The Sahel facing the future – increasing dependence or structural transformation. Futures study of the Sahel countries, 1985-2010.**
Jacques Giri (et al.). Paris: OECD, 1988. 267p.

A report consisting of an historical overview of the development of poverty and dependency, a discussion of present trends, and a discussion of possible future scenarios.

70 **Sécheresses et famines du Sahel. Tomes I & II.** (Droughts and famines of the Sahel. Volumes 1 and 2.)
Edited by Jean Copans. Paris: François Maspero, 1975. 2 vols. (Dossiers Africains).

The first volume deals with the general issues of ecology, malnutrition and development aid in the whole Sahel region of Africa. Volume two includes detailed case studies of specific regions. Chapter five, by Copans himself, investigates the problems of drought in the Mouride areas in central Senegal, and the attitudes of farmers towards the problems.

71 **Seeds of famine: ecological destruction and the development dilemma in the West African Sahel.**
Richard W. Franke, Barbara H. Chasin. Montclaire, New Jersey: Allanheld; New York: Universe, 1980. 266p.

A valuable regional survey and a forceful critique of the disastrous effects of short-sightedness by policy makers and administrators in the region, based on an analysis of the 1968-74 drought. The cases cited include several from Senegal: Mouride agriculture, the USAID Bakel livestock project and its nutritional and ecological implications, and the development of the Senegal river basin. The volume includes an important seventeen-page bibliography.

72 **Stratégies de lutte contre la disette au Sénégal oriental.** (Strategies in the struggle against food shortage in eastern Senegal.) Marie-Thérèse de Lestrange, Monique Gessain, Danielle Fouchier, Ghislaine Crépy-Montal. *Journal des Africanistes*, vol. 56, no. 1 (1986), p. 35-50.

A discussion of the stategies used by the local farmers to cope with a shortfall in food caused by the severe drought of 1983, including fishing, sales of cattle and labour migration.

73 **The West African Sahel: human agency and environmental change.** J. Gritzer. Chicago: University of Chicago Press, 1988. 170p. (Geography Research Paper no. 226).

A general study of the Sahelian environment, its history, dynamics and the possibilities of rehabilitation. The three parts of the book discuss the basic features of the region's environment, the impact of human economic activity, and the flow of energy. The analysis is generally technical and there is little discussion of the wider political and economic issues. The appendices contain useful lists of tree and shrub species and birds, and a table showing the climatic distribution of browse species.

A provisional historical schema for Western Africa based on seven climate periods (ca. 9000 BC to the 19th century).
See item no. 199.

Conditions écologiques, crises de subsistance et histoire de la population à l'époque de la traite des esclaves en Sénégambie. (Ecological conditions, subsistence crises and population history during the slave trade era in Senegambia.)
See item no. 215.

Notes sur les conditions écologiques en Sénégambie aux 17e et 18e siècles. (Notes on the ecological conditions in Senegambia in the 17th and 18th centuries.)
See item no. 238.

The ecology of malnutrition in the French-speaking countries of West Africa and Madagascar.
See item no. 613.

Maps and Atlases

74 **Africa north and west. 1:4,000,000.**
Paris: Pneu Michelin, 1965. One sheet.
This map, sheet 153 of the Michelin map series, is the most readily available road map of West Africa as a whole, and packs an enormous amount of information into a very limited space, including the location of scenic routes and national parks. It is also good on the location of frontier crossing points and road conditions in the more isolated Sahel and desert areas.

75 **Atlas des colonies françaises, protectorats et territoires sous mandat de la France.** (Atlas of French colonies, protectorates and mandated territories.)
Directed by G. Grandidier. Paris: Société d'Editions Géographiques, Maritimes et Coloniales, 1934. 236p.
A large-sized and beautifully produced atlas from the inter-war period including a twenty-eight-page section on West Africa. Essays on the physical and human geography of the area, and twelve pages of coloured maps are also included.

76 **Atlas national du Sénégal.** (National atlas of Senegal.)
Production co-ordinated by Régine Van Chi-Bonnardel (et al.). Paris: Institut Géographique National, 1977. 147p.
Produced by a team of over forty Senegalese and French scholars, this very large and beautifully produced book is one of the major reference sources on the country. The sixty-five plates cover many aspects of Senegalese geography, history, social organization and economy, and there are plans of many of the major towns as well as maps of each of the main regions. Each map is preceded by a short essay and a select bibliography, and there are also a large number of ancillary maps and diagrams.

77   Cartes ethnodémographiques de l'Afrique occidentale. 1.
(Ethnodemographic maps of West Africa. 1.)
Prepared by J. Richard-Molard.   Dakar: IFAN Dakar, 1952. 4 sheets.

This is one of a series of clear and well-drawn maps issued in the 1950s showing the distribution of population and ethnic groups in French West Africa. In this portfolio, two of the four maps cover Senegal, dealing with population and ethnic groups respectively. They are both drawn to the scale 1:1,000,000, and are accompanied by a four-page note prepared by Paul Pélissier.

78   Cartes pour servir à l'aménagement du territoire. (Maps for use in territorial development.)
Produced under the direction of P. Metge.   Dakar: Ministère du Plan, 1965. 42p.

Containing thirty-nine thematic maps on a scale of 1:2,000,000, this atlas covers topics which include demography, climate, physical geography, the economy and administration.

79   République du Sénégal. Carte administrative. (Republic of Senegal. Administrative map.)
Paris: Institut Géographique National, 1969. 1p.

This small sheet map (scale 1:2,000,000) shows the adminstrative divisions and centres within the country. The boundaries of the country's regions, départements and arrondissements are given, along with their respective administrative centres.

80   République du Sénégal. Carte de l'Afrique de l'ouest à 1:200,000.
(Republic of Senegal: Map of West Africa, scale 1:200,000.)
Paris: Institut Géographique National, 1971. Separate sheets.

This series of well-produced small-scale maps covers the whole of Senegal in great detail, suitable for researchers requiring detailed information on a specific locality of the country, such as the situation of small hamlets, nomadic camps or water-courses. Each sheet in the series covers an area of approximately 108 by 110 kilometres.

81   Sénégal.
Paul Pélissier (et al.).   Paris: Jeune Afrique, 1983. 2nd ed. 72p.
(Les Atlas Jeune Afrique).

This excellent atlas, aimed at the general reader as well as the specialist, includes both clear thematic maps in colour and an informative text by some of the leading authorities on the region. The topics covered include physical geography, peoples and ethnic groups, population and migration, agriculture, livestock production and fishing, mining, and urban development. There are also brief essays on each of the main regions of the country, a short glossary, and an index.

82   Sénégal. Carte au 1: 1 000 000. (Map of Senegal, scale 1:1,000,000.)
Paris: Institut Géographique National, [n.d.]. 1p.

Intended for general use, this informative, larger scale map from the National Institute of Geography shows clearly the major geographical features, the road and transport

21

network, as well as 'towns' with more than 1,000 inhabitants. Detailed inserts of the Cap-Vert peninsula and of the urban centres of Saint-Louis and Dakar are also given.

83 **Sénégal et Niger: La France dans l'Afrique occidentale 1879-83.** (Senegal and Niger: France in West Africa 1879-83.)
Paris: Challamel Aîné for the Ministère de la Marine et des Colonies, 1884. [n.p.].

A series of maps from the start of the colonial period, with six maps covering West Africa, and sixteen plans of the main towns and forts.

Travel Guides

84 **Guide de Dakar et du Sénégal.** (Guide to Dakar and to Senegal.)
Christian Saglio. Paris: Société Africaine d'Edition, 1979. 148p.
Complementing Saglio's other book on Senegal (item 13), this French-language
volume covers aspects of the country's geography, history, economy and socio-cultural
life, and includes informative maps and tourist itineraries for the various towns and
regions.

85 **Sénégal.**
Paris: Groupe JA (Jeune Afrique), [1978] 161p. (World Markets:
A country-by-country guide).
One of a series of guides published in both French and English aimed at the
prospective business person. It contains brief sections, illustrated with tables and
graphs on the socio-political base, the economy, imports and exports, investing in
Senegal, transport and commuications, 'life at an African pace' (useful information on
life and sightseeing in Dakar and Gorée) and business addresses. At the end is a thirty-
page supplement of advertisements by firms with Senegalese connections.

86 **Le Sénégal aujourd'hui.** (Senegal today.)
Mylène Rémy. Paris: Editions j.a. (Jeune Afrique), 1974. 238p.
Well illustrated, if now dated, this guide consists of three sections. The first deals with
the country and people, literature and the arts, the economy and history in seventy-
eight pages. This is followed by a guide to thirty-five main towns and tourist sites in
alphabetical order, and a sixty-three page section giving more general travel
information.

Travel Guides

87 **Traveller's guide to West Africa.**
Edited by Alan Rake.   London: IC Publications; Edison, New Jersey:
Hunter Publishing 1988. rev. ed. 274p.

A regional travel-guide including introductory sections on currency, climate, planning
a trip, a guide to package tours, food, and a country-by country guide. The fifteen
pages on Senegal contain concise information on geography, history, parks, travel
notes, hotels, and the regions, and a sketch-map of Dakar.

88 **West Africa: a travel survival kit.**
Alex Newton.   South Yarra, Australia: Lonely Planet Publications,
1988. 459pp.

The Senegal section consists of thirty-four pages with information on history, peoples,
climate, money, and getting around. There is a thirteen-page section on Dakar, and
shorter sections on the Petite Côte, Sine Saloum, the Casamance and northern
Senegal. At the end of the book is a brief stop-press section of latest information.

89 **West Africa: the rough guide.**
Jim Hudgens, Richard Trillo.   London: Harrap-Columbus, 1990.
1232p.

One of the best and most comprehensive guides to travel in West Africa currently
available. Pages 345-431 deal with Senegal, comprising: maps, information on
transport, hotels and restaurants; a brief history, information and a directory on
Dakar; information on the regions; and an index. At the end of the book there are
valuable sections, also organized by country, on music, cinema (including Sembène
Ousmane), and literature.

The Gambia and Senegal.
See item no. 7.

Explorers' and Travellers' Accounts

General

90 **Les explorations au Sénégal et dans les contrées voisines, depuis l'antiquité jusqu'à nos jours.** (Explorations in Senegal and the neighbouring regions, from antiquity until the present day.)
J. Ancelle. Paris: Maisonneuve Frères et Ch. Leclerc, 1887. 445p.

This is the major work of the late 19th century on the history of exploration in the Senegambia and neighbouring regions of West Africa, from the earliest times to the colonial period. It includes chapters on the ancient world, Arab travellers and geographers (10th-16th centuries), the Portuguese (15th century), the English in the Gambia (16th and 18th centuries), and the French explorations (17th and 18th centuries). All of the major explorers are covered, including Adanson, Golberry, Park, Mollien, Caillié, Raffenal, Mage and Colin. At the end of the text is a map of the routes they followed.

91 **Les grandes missions françaises en Afrique occidentale.** (The great French missions to West Africa.)
Le Ct. Chailley.   Dakar: IFAN, 1953. 132p. (Initiations Africaines, 10).

A brief account of French exploration and colonial pentration of the region, including sections on the origins of Saint-Louis, and on Faidherbe, Charles Monteil and Jules Ferry. There are some interesting, if poorly printed illustrations. The book ends with a chronological table of events in different parts of the region and a set of illustrative maps.

92   **Power and knowledge: the representation of the Mande world in the works of Park, Caillié, Monteil and Delafosse.**
      M. Grosz-Ngaté.   *Cahiers d'Etudes Africaines*, vol. 28, no. 3/4 (1988), p. 485-511.

A fascinating study of the descriptions of the Mande world by four major writers on French West Africa: the 18th/19th-century explorers Park and Caillié; and the early 20th-century administrators Charles Monteil and Maurice Delafosse. It considers the ways in which the Mande world is constructed in their texts, and the power relationships which these texts reflect.

Arab sources (until the 16th century)

93   **Corpus of early Arabic sources for West African history.**
      Translated by J. F. P. Hopkins, edited and annotated by N. Levtzion, J. F. P. Hopkins.   Cambridge, England: Cambridge University Press, 1981. 492p.

This work overlaps both in aim and in content with the Cuoq collection (see next item), but is more accessible for the English-speaking reader. Particularly important are the observations on the ancient empire of Takrur, which was established in the middle Senegal river valley around the turn of the millennium in an area known today as the Tukulor territory of Fuuta Toro.

94   **Recueil des sources arabes concernant l'Afrique occidentale du VIII au XVI siècle (Bilad Al-Sudan).** (Collection of Arab sources concerning West Africa from the eighth to the sixteenth centuries: Black Sudan.) Translated with notes by Joseph M. Cuoq.   Paris: Editions du Centre National de la Recherche Scientifique, 1985. 515p. (First published by CNRS in 1975.)

A large compendium of Arab sources by over eighty authors, dealing mainly with the ancient Ghana, Mali and Songhay empires. Some of these empires extended their influence into parts of present-day Senegal. After introductory chapters on the growth of knowledge of the area, the main Arab authors and their historical value, the bulk of the book consists of translations of the relevant passages of their work. At the end is a glossary of Arabic and Sudanese terms, an index of authors cited and an index of place, ethnic and personal names. This is a ground-breaking work, even though it has been criticized by Levtzion and Hopkins for extracting quotations from non-existent sources (see previous item).

Early European (pre-1800)

95 **Civilisation wolofo-sérère au XVe siècle d'après les sources portugaises.**
(Wolof-Serer civilization up to the 15th century according to Portuguese sources.)
Sékéné M. Cissoko. *Présence Africaine*, vol. 62, (1967), p. 121-47.

A useful overview of the rich body of material available on the study of early Wolof and Serer social and political organization is based on information from Portuguese travellers in the seventy-year period between 1440 and 1510. The paper covers the chronology of the rulers during this period, centralized and uncentralized political systems, the main economic activities, and the economic bases of political power in the control of slaves, horses and villages.

96 **Description de la Côte d'Afrique de Ceuta au Sénégal par Valentim Fernandes (1506-1507).** (Description of the coast of Africa from Ceuta to Senegal by Valentim Fernandes [1506-1507].)
Edited by P. De Cenival, Th. Monod. Paris: Librairie Larose, 1938.
214p. (Publications du Comité Historique et Scientifique de l'Afrique Occidentale française, Série A, no. 6).

This is an edition of the original Portuguese text with a parallel French translation of an account of the West African coast compiled from previous reports and first-hand information from travellers. It is our longest and most complete Portuguese source on the Western Sahara. The second part, translated and edited by Monod, deals with coastal areas of the present-day Mauritania and northern Senegal, and there is a useful introduction by the editors which discusses the author's identity and his sources. There are also extensive notes and a twenty-four-page historical bibliography.

97 **Europeans in West Africa, 1450-1560. 2 vols.**
Edited and translated by John William Blake. London: Hakluyt Society, 1942. 461p.

Volume I deals with documents referring to the voyages to the West African coast – from Senegal to the Equator – and the occupation of coastal sites by the Portuguese. Volume II includes accounts of early English voyages to West Africa. Trade, fortification and navigation of the Senegal river are variously referred to, as well as the conversion of Bemoym, Prince of the Jalofo (the Wolof kingdom of Jolof), and the attempt to build a fort at the river's mouth in 1488.

98 **The golden trade or a discovery of the River Gambra, and the golden trade of the Aethiopians.**
Richard Jobson. London: Dawsons, 1968. 210p.

One of the most detailed early accounts of the region, Jobson's voyage in 1620 resulted from the efforts of London merchants to find a more direct route to the gold-producing areas of West Africa: he failed, but did collect valuable information on the region, its peoples, including the Mandinka and the Peul, its cultures, climate, wildlife, and trade. This work was originally published by N. Bourne of London in 1623.

99 **Journal d'un voiage fait en Bambouc en 1744.** (Journal of a voyage to
    Bambouk made in 1744.)
    Pierre-Félix-Barthélemy David, edited by André Delcourt.   Paris:
    Société Française d'Histoire d'Outre-Mer, 1974, 303p.

David (1710-95) was Governor of the French concession in Senegal of the trading
enterprise *La Compagnie des Indes* and, in 1744, he sailed up the Senegal river as far
as Galam and Bambouk. This edition of his journal includes a valuable ninety-two-
page introduction by André Delcourt, which relates it to the archival sources and oral
traditions. There are also a number of appendices, notes and plates, the latter
including contemporary maps, as well as a three-page English summary and a lengthy
index.

100 **Mungo Park's travels in Africa.**
     Edited by Roland Miller.   London: Dent, 1969. 386p.

Park made two visits to West Africa, in 1795-57 and 1805-06, the main aim of which
was to determine the course of the River Niger. His route took him up the River
Gambia and through eastern Senegal, into Mali. On his second trip he successfully
followed the Niger for most of its course, but was killed at Bussa, in north-western
Nigeria in 1806. Park wrote an account of his first expedition in *The life and travels of
Mungo Park in Africa* (Edinburgh: William P. Nimmo, 1871. 336p.). This is a major
source of observations on the region and its peoples, particularly the various Manding-
speaking groups of Senegal and Mali.

101 **Travels in Africa performed during the years 1785, 1786 and 1787 in the
     western countries of that continent, comprised between Cape Blanco in
     Barbary and Cape Palmas.**
     Silva Meinhard Xavier Golberry, translated from the French by Francis
     Blagdon.   London: James Ridgway, 1802. 2 vols.

An account of voyages up the Senegal river to Galam, and along the coast from Saint-
Louis to the Gambia river. Golberry includes some acute observations on the peoples
of the region and its trade, commerce and agricultural practices. Several chapters are
also devoted to observations on flora and fauna. This edition contains a useful index
and some beautifully engraved copper-plate illustrations.

102 **Travels into the inland parts of Africa, containing a description for the
     space of six hundred miles up the River Gambia. . . .**
     Francis Moore.   London: The author, 1738. 234p.

Moore worked as a clerk for the Royal African Company on James Island, near the
mouth of the River Gambia between 1730 and 1735. His book therefore deals mainly
with areas now in The Gambia. However, it also contains valuable historical
information on the slave trade, as well as on the major peoples of the Senegambian
region, including the Peul, Mandinka, Wolof and Diola.

103 **Premier voyage du Sieur de la Courbe fait à la coste d'Afrique en 1685.**
(The first voyage of Sieur de la Courbe made to the coast of Africa in 1685.)
Edited by Pierre Cultru. Paris: Champion et Larose, 1913. 319p.
(Reprinted, Nendeln, Liechtenstein: Kraus, 1973.)

La Courbe was the director of the Senegal Company on two occasions in the late 17th and early 18th centuries, but he also made a visit there in 1685 at a time when the company employees at Saint-Louis had revolted against their commandant and expelled him. As well as an account of the dispute, the book describes the region around Saint-Louis and the desert trade with the Moors.

104 **Voyage au Sénégal, pendant les années 1784 et 1785, d'après les mémoires de Lajaille, ancien officier de la Marine française.** (Voyage to Senegal, during the years 1784 and 1785, according to the accounts of Lajaille, former officer in the French Navy.)
P. Labarthe. Paris: Dentu, 1802. 262p.

This account of a voyage to West Africa consists of twenty-five letters and detailed notes made by Lajaille, which together give a fascinating picture of the state of trade and travel in the region in the late 18th century. The text of a memorandum to the French government on the subject of free trade is appended.

105 **A voyage to Senegal.**
Jean-Baptiste-Léonard Durand. London: Richard Phillips, 1806. 181p.

An English translation of a book first published in Paris in 1803, Durand was a director of the Senegal Company, and his book combines his observations on the country and its peoples along with the history of European trade in the region. Durand had already published an atlas to illustrate his voyage, *Atlas pour servir au voyage du Sénégal* (Atlas for use in the voyage to Senegal) (Paris: Henri Agasse, 1802), some of the illustrations for which are reprinted in this volume.

106 **A voyage to Senegal, the Isle of Gorée and the River Gambia.**
M. Adanson. London: J. Nourse in the Strand, 1759. 337p.

This is an early English translation of one of the most important 18th-century European accounts by a French natural historian who visited the region between 1749 and 1754. Much of the narrative consists of detailed observations of the local flora and fauna around Sor, Podor, Gorée, Cap-Vert and the Gambia River.

107 **The voyages of Cadamosto, and other documents on Western Africa in the second half of the fifteenth century.**
Translated and edited by Gerald Roe Crone. London: Hakluyt Society, 1937. 154p.; reprinted Nendeln: Kraus Reprint, 1967. 159p.

Alvise da Ca' da Mosto or Cadamosto was Venetian by birth and set sail under the sponsorship of Prince Henry of Portugal for the African coast in 1455, where he explored the mouth of the Senegal, Kayor, and, the following year, the river Gambia. His work is an important early first-hand account of the area by an open-minded observer, and this edition contains an informative editorial introduction.

19th and 20th-century accounts

108 **Courrier d'Afrique: Sénégal-Soudan-Guinée.** (African courier: Senegal – Sudan – Guinea.)
Maurice Martin du Gard.   Paris: Flammarion, 1942. 2nd ed. 210p.
An evocative account from the late 1920s of travels in French West Africa during the height of French colonialism. The sections on Senegal include descriptions of schools and missions in Dakar, and an encounter with the African politician Blaise Diagne in Saint-Louis.

109 **Description nautique des Côtes de l'Afrique occidentale comprises entre le Sénégal et l'équateur.** (A nautical description of the West African coast between Senegal and the Equator.)
Cte. Bout-Willaumez.   Paris: Robiquet, Librairie-Hydrographe, 1959. 304p.
Pages 1-52 of this work describe the coastline from Saint-Louis to the Casamance, and include observations on the seasons, the winds, the marshes and the currents along the coast, as well as more detailed information on navigation up the Casamance river and the sand bar across the river Senegal.

110 **Une explorateur sénégalaise: Léopold Panet, 1819?-1859.** (A Senegalese explorer: Léopold Panet, 1819?-1859.)
Roger Pasquier.   *African Historical Studies*, vol. 2, no. 2 (1969), p. 307-17.
Panet was a Franco-Senegalese mulatto who worked both for the French administration and the trading companies, and was a pioneering explorer of the Sahara in Mauritania, as well as one of the earliest African writers in French. The report he wrote on his expedition to the north in 1849-50 is an important source of information not only on the area, but on the relations between the French, the mulattos and the Africans. His writing is discussed at length by Dorothy Blair (see item no. 749).

111 **Une française au Soudan.** (A French woman in the Sudan.)
Raymonde Bonnetain.   Paris: Librairie-imprimeries Réunis, 1894. 377p.
Raymonde Bonnetain left Bordeaux on 5 November 1892 on a trip that took her through Senegal into present-day Mali. She arrived in Dakar, visited Gorée, and travelled by train east to Thiès and north to Saint-Louis. From there she travelled up river, and stayed in Matam, before venturing further east to Kayes and Mali. She returned to France in 1893 after becoming seriously ill. This diary is of interest as the first account of travel in the region by a European woman.

112 **Mes aventures au Sénégal: souvenirs de voyage.** (My adventures in Senegal: travel reminiscences.)
V. Verneuil.   Paris: Librairie Nouvelle, 1858. 279p.
A popular mid-19th-century account of life in the colony which provides a mixture of adventure, racism and the exotic, combined with insights into the local sexual and social mores, and ends with a description of a memorable encounter with a *griot* or praise-singer.

113 **Narrative of a voyage to Senegal in 1816 undertaken by order of the French government comprising an account of the shipwreck of the *Medusa*, the sufferings of the crew, and the various occurrences on board the raft, in the desert of Zaara, at St. Louis and at the camp of Daccard.**
J. B. Henry Savigny, Alexander Corréard. London: Henry Colburn, 1818. 360p.

Savigny and Corréard were travelling together as part of an expedition to Senegal when one of the vessels in the convoy sent from France, the frigate *Medusa*, was grounded on the bank of Arguin, some way north of the Senegal river, an incident which later inspired the great painting by Géricault. The greater part of this narrative recounts the trials and tribulations of the survivors who marched to Saint-Louis, enduring thirteen days of hardship in the desert. Only fifteen of the 150 people who took to the raft launched from the stranded frigate survived. The narrative was republished by Dawsons of Pall Mall in 1968.

114 **Nouveau voyage dans le pays de nègres suivi d'études sur la colonie du Sénégal et de documents historiques, géographiques et scientifiques, tomes I & II.** (New voyage to the country of the negroes followed by studies on the colony of Senegal and historical, geographical and scientific documents. Volumes 1 and 2.)
Anne Raffenel. Paris: Imprimerie et Librairie Centrales des Chemins de Fer, 1856. 2 vols.

Raffenel, an officer in the French Navy, made two expeditions into the interior. His first voyage is described in *Voyages dans l'Afrique Occidentale* (Paris: Arthus Bertrand, 1846), in which he recounts his trip up the Senegal river from Saint-Louis to the Falème in 1843-44 with observations and notes on the peoples of the area. These two volumes describe his second trip, from Saint-Louis up river to Bakel and Galam, and from there into present-day Mali, where he was imprisoned for eight months by the Bambara. The second volume describes the history and operation of the Senegal colony, and also includes material on local peoples, cultures and languages.

115 **Travels in the interior of Africa to the sources of the Senegal and Gambia, performed by command of the French Government in the year 1818.**
G. Mollien, edited by T. E. Bowditch. London: Frank Cass & Co., 1967. 379p.

Mollien had originally planned to follow the same route as Mungo Park but instead went from Saint-Louis through the kingdoms of Kayor, Jolof and Fuuta Toro, before travelling further south and eastwards in search of the source of the Senegal river. He appears to have been observant and open-minded, and gives a lively account of the region and its peoples, despite his experiences in the Fuuta Toro where he was robbed and later held prisoner. This account was first published by Henry Colburn in 1820.

116 **Trois voyages dans l'Afrique occidentale: Sénégal, Gambie, Casamance, Gabon, Ogooue.** (Three voyages in West Africa: Senegal, Gambia, Casamance, Gabon, Ogooue.)
A. Marche.   Paris: Librairie Hachette, 1882. 376p.

The first of Marche's journeys took him from Saint-Louis, where he arrived in 1872, south to Gorée, Dakar, Bathurst (Banjul) and the Gambia river, and finally to the Casamance. His second and third trips were to other parts of West Africa. The book is an account of these travels and includes descriptions of the local inhabitants he met and his own activities, including hunting expeditions.

117 **Voyage au Soudan français.** (Voyage to French Soudan.)
Le Commandant Gallieni.   Paris: Librairie Hachette, 1885. 623p.

This is an account of a military mission through Senegal to the Niger. The party passed up the Senegal river, staying at Saint-Louis and Bakel before passing on through present-day Mali. The first two chapters of the book describe Gallieni's observations on the river valley.

118 **Voyage au Soudan Occidentale (1863-1866).** (Voyage to Western Sudan, 1863-1866.)
Eugène Mage.   Paris: Karthala, 1980.

Mage was sent by Faidherbe in 1863 from Saint-Louis to investigate the possibility of a direct link from Senegal to the Niger, and thence to the city states of Northern Nigeria. This meant travelling through the empire of Umar Tal, who was already embroiled in a war in the east and who was to die in an explosion the following year. By this time Mage had made contact with Tal's son, Amadou, at Segou, with whom he was eventually able to negotiate a treaty, and he was thus the first European to learn of the fate of Umar himself. This work was first published by Hachette in 1872.

Population

General demography

119 Dynamique d'une population traditionnelle: Démographie, apparentement et mariage dans une population d'effectif limité: Les Peul Bandé (Sénégal oriental). (Dynamics of a traditional population: demography, relationships and marriage in a population of limited size: the Bande Peul, Eastern Senegal.)
Gilles Pison. Paris: Presses Universitaires de France, 1982. 278p. (Institut National d'Etudes Démographiques, Travaux et Documents, Cahier 99).

One of the most detailed demographic studies available of any Senegalese people, this monograph deals with a group of Peul (Fulbe) in the Kédougou region of Sénégal Oriental. It contains sections on the social organization and history of the Bande, on methods, the age profile, migration, mortality and fertility, polygamy, kinship and choice of spouse. A brief conclusion lists the main problems which the study encountered. The book is profusely illustrated throughout with maps, tables and graphs and it ends with extensive technical appendices and a bibliography. Material on marriage choice has also been published as 'Méthode statistique d'étude de l'endogamie: application à l'étude du choix du conjoint chez les Peul Bandé' (A statistical method for the study of endogamy: application to the study of the choice of partner among the Bande Peul) by Mark Lathrop and Gilles Pison, *Population*, vol. 37, no. 3 (1982), p. 513-41.

120 **Essai de présentation méthodologique pour une étude sur la différentiation rurale dans l'arrondissement de Paos-Koto (Département de Nioro du Rip-Sénégal).** (Description of the methodology for a study of rural differentiation in the region of Paos-Koto, Department of Nioro, Rip-Senegal.)

B. Lamy, J. C. Roux.   *Cahiers ORSTOM* (Sciences humaines), vol. 6, no. 4 (1969), p. 75-91.

An example of the kind of intensive study of a region in Senegal, based on repeated visits, in which demographers of Senegal have specialized. This paper deals with research in a region of Sine-Saloum. The data collected includes a breakdown of the entire population according to age and sex, ethnic origin, religion and marital status of household heads, migration, village size and size of family land holdings.

121 **Etude démographique et sociale d'un groupe poly-ethnique de villages du Sénégal oriental (Département de Kédougou): Sibikiling, Seguekho, Niéméniki.** (A demographic and social study of a multi-ethnic group of villages in Eastern Senegal, Department of Kédougou: Sibikiling, Seguekho, Niéméniki.)

Bruno de Lestrange.   *Bulletin et Mémoires de la Société d'Anthropologie* (Paris), Series 12, vol. 5, no. 1-4 (1969), p. 17-99.

One of an important series of studies to be carried out in an area to the north-west of Kédougou in Eastern Senegal which has a population of 1,200 divided between Peul, Malinke, Bassari and Diakhanke. The paper describes variations in age pyramids, marriage patterns and patterns of migration between these different groups.

122 **Orientations de la recherche démographique au Sénégal.** (Approaches to demographic research in Senegal.)

Pierre Cantrelle.   *Cahiers ORSTOM* (Sciences humaines), vol. 6, no. 4 (1969), p. 3-10.

Cantrelle and his ORSTOM colleagues have been responsible for much of the demographic work in Senegal over the years, and this is a brief survey both of the methods used by the group to adapt to research conditions in Africa, and of the areas which they have studied intensively.

123 **Fakao (Sénégal): Dépouillement de registres paroissaux et enquête démographique rétrospective. Méthodologie et résultats.** (Fakao, Senegal: Examination of parish registers and retrospective demographic survey. Methods and results.)

Bernard Lacombe.   Paris: ORSTOM, 1970. 156p.

This study is based on data collected from parish registers and other official records relating to Fakao, a village in Sine-Saloum. Lacombe plots the population movements over a twenty-five-year period from 1940 to 1965, and the levels of fertility from 1930 to 1965. He also analyses data on marriage, birth rates and mortality rates and gives a description of the methodology employed.

124 **Sources démographiques de l'histoire de la Sénégambie.** (Demographic sources for the history of Senegambia.)
Charles Becker, Mamadou Diouf, Mohamed Mbodj. *Annales de Démographie Historique* (1987), p. 15-31.
Using the Senegambian example, this paper argues the importance of considering population factors and processes in historical research, despite the lack of attention given to these elements in the past. By combining all the existing sources, including unconventional ones, it is often possible to give a detailed history of a region's demography, even in the absence of conventional censuses.

L'Agglomération dakaroise: quelques aspects sociologiques et démographiques. (The Dakar agglomeration: some sociological and demographic aspects.)
See item no. 31.
Daoudane-Pikine, étude démographique et sociologique. (Daoudane-Pikine, a demographic and sociological study.)
See item no. 35.

Migration

125 **Bassari migrations: the quiet revolution.**
Riall W. Nolan. Boulder, Colorado: Westview, 1986. 199p.
An important addition to the literature in English on southern Senegal, this study deals with the effects of migration on the Bassari village of Etyolo. Paradoxically, migration has not undermined the village social structure: returning migrants are reintegrated into village life, and use their cash to reinforce existing patterns of social organization. The book ends with a lengthy Bassari glossary and a ten-page bibliography, but unfortunately there is no index. A shorter account of Bassari migration by the same author was published as 'L'histoire des migrations bassari, influences et perspectives' (The history of Bassari migration: influences and perspectives), *Journal des Africanistes*, vol. 47, no. 2 (1977), p. 81-102.

126 **De la captivité à l'exil. La vallée du Sénégal. Histoire et démographie des migrations paysanes dans la moyenne vallée du fleuve Sénégal.** (From captivity to exile. The Senegal valley. History and demography of peasant migrations in the middle of the valley Senegal river.)
Daniel Delaunay. Paris: ORSTOM, 1984. 217p. (Travaux et Documents, no. 174).
A large-scale account of migration in the central section of the Senegal river valley. The first part of the study contains a historical account of migration and the penetration of the market economy, with chapters on the slave trade and the subsequent trade in agricultural products, controlled by the Bordeaux merchants. The second part deals with the outflow of migrants which this type of integration into the world economy produced. The author is highly critical of government development

administration, and concludes that the current returns from agriculture are unlikely to halt the exodus in search of other employment.

127 **Kanel: l'exode rural dans un village de la vallée du Sénégal.** (Kanel: rural exodus in a village in the Senegal valley.)
François Revault. *Cahiers d'Outre-Mer*, vol. 17, no. 65 (1964), p. 58-80.

A study of migration from a village of nearly 3,000 people in the middle Senegal valley, with an economy based on the cultivation of sorghum and millet. The author links the high rates of migration to the local caste-based social structure and high land rentals. The low return to agricultural labour is the cause of seasonal emigration and the abandonment of cultivation in the dry season.

128 **Migration artisanale et solidarité villageoise: le cas de Kanèn Njob, au Sénégal.** (Migration of craftsmen and village solidarity: the case of Kanèn Njob, Senegal.)
M. B. Diouf. *Cahiers d'Etudes Africaines*, vol. 21, no. 4 (1981), p. 577-82.

An account of the commercialization of production and distribution, by a group of migrant blacksmiths from a Kayor village, living in Dakar. It describes the group of producers, the distribution network and the ways in which the traditional divide between blacksmiths and other castes is being broken down.

129 **Migration et production domestique des Soninké du Sénégal.** (Migration and domestic production among the Soninke of Senegal.)
J. Y. Weigel. Paris: ORSTOM, 1982. 133p.

An important study of the rural areas around Bakel in north-east Senegal on the Senegal river, for a long time an area of high out-migration following the collapse of the precolonial trading system and the imposition of taxation. The sections of the book deal with the extent and composition of the migrant flows, the traditional system of production, with its ecological constraints, land tenure, modes of consumption and accumulation, and the development of irrigated agriculture in the area which began to transform the local economy after about 1975, about the time that the French attempted to slow down the flow of migrants into France.

130 **Les migrations en Basse Casamance (Sénégal): rapport final.** (The migrations in the Lower Casamance, Senegal: final report.)
Klaas de Jonge, Jos van der Klei, Henk Keilink, Roeland Storm. Leiden, The Netherlands: Afrika-Studiecentrum, 1978. 180p.

A lengthy, mimeographed report by a Dutch team, based on research carried out in 1974-75. The chapters of the study provide summaries of migration theory, the Senegalese development plans from 1973-81, the geography of the region itself, and the results of agricultural and migration surveys carried out there. The study highlights a number of demographic and economic variables which contribute to male migration and examines its consequences for the region and the wider economy.

131 **Paysans migrants du Fouta Toro (Valleé du Sénégal).** (Migrant farmers of the Fuuta Toro, Senegal River valley.)
Jean-Paul Minvielle. Paris: ORSTOM, 1984. 282p. (Travaux et Documents no. 191).

A detailed study of production and migration carried out in and around Matam, on the Senegal river in the extreme north east of the country, with a mixed population of Tukulor, Wolof and Soninke. The conclusion contains a comparison of the different adaptations of the main ethnic groups to migration. The study is well documented with maps, tables and graphs and there is an eight-page glossary of local vernacular terms used in the text.

132 **Société toucouleur et migration: enquête sur l'immigraton toucouleur à Dakar.** (Tukulor society and migration: an investigation of Tukulor immigration to Dakar.)
Abdoulaye Bara Diop. Dakar: IFAN, 1965. 232p. (Initiations et Etudes Africaines, 18).

A sociological account, from the early years of independence, of migration from the Senegal valley to Dakar – due to economic stagnation in the migrants' home area – together with an account of their problems on arrival in the capital. It contains sections on Tukulor society, the social characteristics of the migrants, and their adaptation to urban life. The study also contains a useful bibliography on the Tukulor and a map of the Senegal river valley.

133 **The uprooted of the Western Sahel: migrants' quest for cash in the Senegambia.**
Lucie Gallistel Colvin, Cheikh Ba, Boubacar Barry, Jaques Faye, Alice Hamer, Moussa Souma, Fatou Sow. New York: Praeger, 1981. 385p.

This book contains an important collection of essays on the history and contemporary organization of labour migration in Senegambia, Mauritania and Mali. It was partly funded by USAID and was published in both French and English versions. Chapters include a historical survey of the economic anthropology of the region (by Boubacar Barry), regional surveys, historical studies of labour migration during the colonial period (by Colvin), a study of migration to Dakar (by Sow), and a study of migration among Diola women (by Alice Hamer). It ends with a discussion of the relationship between migration and public policy (by Colvin). It is well illustrated with extensive statistical tables and maps.

134 **Urban migration, cash cropping, and calamity: the spread of Islam among the Diola of Boulouf (Senegal), 1900-1940.**
Peter Mark. *African Studies Review*, vol. 21, no. 2 (1978), p. 1-14.

An important study of conversion to Islam, which in this area is related to historical patterns of migration and changes in agriculture. Migration to the towns, involvement in trade, and the cultivation of groundnuts as a cash crop, all brought increasing financial autonomy to many younger men, who converted to Islam in order to enhance their status and reduce the power of the elders. The rate of conversion accelerated during a series of natural calamities in the 1930s, and by 1939 a majority of the Diola of Boulouf had become Muslim.

Slavery, emancipation and labour migration in West Africa: the case of the Soninke.
See item no. 299.

International migration

135 **De la brousse sénégalaise au Boul'Mich: le système commercial mouride en France.** (From the Senegal bush to the Boul'Mich: the Mouride commercial system in France.)
Gérard Salem. *Cahiers d'Etudes Africaines*, vol. 21, no. 1/3 (1981), p. 267-88.

An important study of trading networks among Senegalese migrants in France, where West African traders have become a common sight in the main towns. With some fascinating maps, case histories and genealogies, Salem shows how these networks, based on kinship and membership of the Mouride brotherhood, have been formed.

136 **De la calabasse à la production en série: les réseaux commerciaux Laobé au Sénégal et en France.** (From the calabash to mass production: Laobe commercial networks in Senegal and France.)
Gérard Salem. In: *Struggle for the city: migrant labor, capital and the state in urban Africa.* Edited by Frederick Cooper. Beverly Hills, California; London: Sage Publications, 1982, p. 195-247. (Sage Series on African Modernization and Development, vol. 8).

A study of the production of Laobe wood-carvings in Senegal and their distribution in Senegal and in Europe, carried out by a network of producers and traders using 'traditional' forms of apprenticeship and kinship organization. It argues that this particular sector of the 'informal' economy is in fact extremely complex and efficient.

137 **Le long voyage des gens du Fleuve.** (The long voyage of the people of the River region.)
Adrian Adams. Paris: Maspero, 1977. 222p.

The first of two important books on the Fleuve region by an American anthropologist who has lived in that area for many years. The three sections provide a history of the Fleuve area from before the 17th century to the present, an account of the migration to France, and of the attempts by agricultural development and agricultural crisis within the region itself. It contains interesting case material from the village of 'Jamané', as well as a lengthy interview with Sally N'Dongo, leader of a union of Senegalese workers in France.

138 **The 'patriarchal ideal' of Soninke labor migrants: from slave owners to employers of free labor.**
Edouard François Manchuelle.   *Canadian Journal of African Studies,* vol. 23, no. 1 (1989), p. 106-25.
A useful historical discussion of migration and agricultural labour among the Soninke of Mali, Senegal and Mauritania, which describes the transition from slavery to wage labour following colonial occupation. Previously, free men migrated and invested their gains in slave labour. In later years, the Soninke migrated to France and used their remittances to employ wage labour from other areas to cultivate their land.

139 **Le prolétariat africain noir en France.** (The black African proletariat in France.)
Michel Samuel.   Paris: Maspero, 1978. 262p.
A study of the Soninke labourers from Mali, Senegal and Mauritania who made up between seventy and eighty per cent of the black immigrants to France, based largely on interviews carried out in 1974 in Dakar and Paris. The three parts of the book deal with the history of emigrant labour, social relations between the migrants and their areas of origin, and the process of proletarianization within the migrants' home areas, which is both a cause and a consequence of the migration.

140 **La répartition géographique des travailleurs immigrés d'Afrique Noire à Paris et à Lyon.** (The geographical distribution of immigrant workers from black Africa in Paris and Lyon.)
Jacques Barou.   *Cahiers d'Outre-Mer,* vol. 28, no. 112 (1975), p. 362-75.
This comparison of the African communities in Paris and Lyon deals with the numbers of African workers at that period, the problems of receiving them, and their distribution in the two cities. The conclusion is that the Muslim migrants from Mali and Senegal living in Paris are largely isolated from the rest of the population, whereas the mainly Christian migrants from Guinea, the Ivory Coast and Cameroon living in Lyon who are more able to speak French are more dispersed and better integrated.

141 **A socio-economic survey of Malian, Mauritanian and Senegalese immigrants resident in France.**
Julien Condé.   *International Migration* (Netherlands) vol. 22, no. 2 (1984), p. 144-51.
This paper attempts to construct a demographic profile for three groups of African migrant workers in France, and shows well the difficulties involved. The absence of accurate official figures is due to low rates of literacy among the immigrants, as well as to the fact that many of them are illegal residents.

Censuses

142 **La Chrétienté africaine de Dakar. Partie descriptive et statistique. 1er, 2ième, 3ième cahiers.** (African Christianity in Dakar. Descriptive and statisticial section. 3 books.)
V. Martin. Dakar: Fraternité Saint-Dominique, 1964. 293p.
The body of Martin's study of Dakar Christianity contains over 100 tables. Topics covered include population size and structure, ethnic groups, church attendance, baptisms, household and domestic arrangements, marital status, parish structure, age structure, socio-professional status and lifestyles.

143 **Notes d'instructions à une étude socio-religieuse des populations de Dakar et du Sénégal.** (Instruction notes for a socio-religious study of the populations of Dakar and Senegal.)
V. Martin. Dakar: Fraternité Saint-Dominique, 1964. 82p.
Martin, who was responsible for the second volume of the 1955 Dakar Census, was also a Catholic priest, and he went on to produce a demographic study of Christianity in Dakar (see previous item). This introduction includes general comments and notes on the Christian population in the city, including physical surroundings and ethnic composition; a history of Catholicism in Dakar; and a survey of the contemporary state of Christianity.

144 **Les premiers recensements au Sénégal – le Sénégal centre-ouest et son évolution démographique (Siin, Saalum, Bawol, pays de l'ouest) Partie I: Présentation des documents.** (The first censuses in Senegal: West-Central Senegal and its demographic evolution in Siin, Saalum, Bawol, and western regions. Part 1: Presentation of documents).
Charles Becker, V. Martin. *Annales de Démographie Historique* (1981), p. 367-86.
A chronological list of attempts to estimate the population of the regions of western Senegal since the 17th century.

145 **Recensement démographique de Dakar (1955) Résultats statistiques du recensement générale de la population de la commune de Dakar, effectué en avril et mai 1955. Fascicule 1.** (Demographic census of Dakar. Statistical results of the general census of the population of the commune of Dakar, conducted in April and May 1955. Volume 1.)
Paris: Haut Commissariat de la République en Afrique occidentale française. Etude et Coordination statistiques et de la Mécanographique, 1958. 126p.
The first of two volumes which resulted from this census, the most comprehensive to have been held in Dakar, this work contains general notes on the commune and the techniques used, followed by tables on the African and non-African populations according to sex, age, ethnic group, religion, marital status, place of birth, nationality, educational qualifications, and economic activity.

146 **Recensement démographique de Dakar (1955). Résultats définitifs (2e fascicule). Etude socio-demographique de la ville de Dakar.** (Demographic census of Dakar (1955). Definitive results, 2nd volume. Socio-economic study of the town of Dakar.)
V. Martin.   Dakar: Ministère du Plan, Service de la Statistique, 1962. 212p.

This second volume from the 1955 census is an important social survey of Dakar. It contains information on the main districts of the capital, the ethnic composition of the population, education, religion, migration and occupations. It ends with chapters on family and household composition and on housing. There is an appendix on Dagoudane-Pikine, a satellite town which, perhaps as a result of the availability of this information has been much studied by social scientists, and a sixty-nine-page section of statistical tables. The copy consulted included a separate large and very attractive coloured map of the distribution of ethnic groups within Dakar.

147 **Recensement général de la population d'avril 1976. Résultats définitifs, données corrigées.** (General census of the population, April 1976: definitive results, corrected data.)
Dakar: Bureau National du Recensement, 1976/1982. 36p., 67p.

The 1976 census was comprehensive in its coverage, and subsequent publications based on these data comprise provisional results, a national analysis as well as regional data. It was conducted by the national census office, with financial support from the United Nations, after three years of preparation and planning. The country was divided into eight main regional units, Cap-Vert, Casamance, Diourbel, Fleuve, Louga, Senegal-Oriental, Sine Saloum and Thiès, further subdivided into departments and districts. The provisional results appeared c.1978, and the final corrected results were supposed to have been published in 1982, although extensive searches have failed to locate this version of the census. The most recent census was carried out in 1988, with the publication of the final results scheduled for 1992.

148 **Senegal.**
In: *The handbook of national population censuses: Africa and Asia.* Edited by Eliane Domschke, Doreen S. Goyer.   New York: Greenwood Press, 1986. p. 377-83.

An invaluable annotated check-list of the ten main attempts to estimate the Senegalese population, starting with estimates from the Ministère de la Marine et des Colonies in 1876, and ending with the first comprehensive national population census, held in 1976. For this, there is a summary covering methods, definitions used, special features, quality control, and publications.

Cultural and Linguistic Divisions

General

149 **Esquisses sénégalaises (Walo, Kayor, Dyolof, Mourides, un visionnaire.)**
(Senegalese sketches: Walo, Kayor, Jolof, Mourides, a religious
visionary.)
Vincent Monteil. Dakar: IFAN, 1966, 243p. (Initiations et Etudes
Africains 21: Textes revus et mis à jour).
This collection of essays brings together five of Monteil's previously published articles
dealing with the oral history of the Wolof, the career of Lat Dior who is seen now as a
hero of the resistance against the French; a study of the Jolof kingdom, and its last
king, Al-Bouri Ndiaye (d. 1902); the Mouride Muslim brotherhood and its founder,
Amadou Bamba; and a Muslim visionary whose dreams are transcribed and analysed
in terms of their contents, their revelations and their meanings within a contemporary
Islamic culture.

150 **Muslim peoples: a world ethnographic survey.**
Edited by Richard V. Weekes. Westport, Connecticut; London:
Greenwood Press, 1978. 546p.
A useful source of information on ethnic groups throughout the world which are either
predominantly or substantially Muslim. The book consists of short, general summary
articles and lists of references, some of which are quite substantial, by leading
authorities. Of relevance to Senegal are the sections on the Diola (Mark), Fulani
(Hopen), Manding (Gingiss), Serer (Klein), Soninke (Gerteiny), Tukulor (Gerteiny),
and Wolof (Gamble). The book also contains a general introduction, statistical
appendices on Muslim populations and an index.

Esquisses sénégalaises. (Senegalese sketches.)
See item no. 3.

Haut-Sénégal-Niger. (Upper Senegal and Niger.)
See item no. 8.

Les peuplades de la Sénégambie. (The peoples of Senegambia.)
See item no. 10.

Le Sénégal et la Gambie. (Senegal and The Gambia.)
See item no. 16.

Cartes ethnodémographiques de l'Afrique occidentale. 1. (Ethnodemographic maps of West Africa. 1.)
See item no. 77.

Les paysans du Sénégal: les civilisations agraires du Cayor à la Casamance. (The peasants of Senegal: the agrarian civilizations from Kayor to the Casamance.)
See item no. 346.

Diola (Jola, Joola)

151 **Les Diola: essai d'analyse fonctionelle sur une population de Basse-Casamance.** (The Diola: a functional analysis of a population of the Lower Casamance.)
Louis-Vincent Thomas.   Dakar: IFAN, 1959. 2 vols. (Mémoire, 55).
One of the most comprehensive monographs ever written on a West African people, by the author of a long series of other papers on aspects of Diola life. Volume one covers: technical activities such as craftwork, agricultural production, house construction and transport; attitudes and beliefs with respect to infant behaviour; human personality; and social life in terms of political, economic and legal organization. Volume two deals with Diola art, music, dance, folklore, science; systems of knowledge and classification relating to time, space, history, medicine etc; morality in theory and practice, traditional religious beliefs and practice, and the impact of Christianity and Islam. This work also contains thirty-two illustrations and plates, as well as a comprehensive bibliography of materials relating to the Diola.

152 **Genèse du pouvoir charismatique en Basse Casamance (Sénégal).** (Genesis of charismatic power in the Lower Casamance region of Senegal)
Jean Girard.   Dakar: IFAN, 1969. 372p.
This is a study of the traditional society and religion of the Diola of the Lower Casamance region of southern Senegal. The work covers various aspects of their traditional religious beliefs, in particular the symbolic centrality of the king and the charismatic powers which he and his descendants are thought to have possessed. It also compares parts of the area which were converted to Islam after the arrival of groups of Manding, and where the French were able to administer the area through local Muslim officials, and the largely traditional southern areas which resisted Islam. The volume

contains numerous illustrations and plates, a collection of funeral chants in French translation, and an extensive bibliography.

153 **Power, prayer and production: the Jola of Casamance, Senegal.**
Olga F. Linares. Cambridge, England: Cambridge University Press, 1992. 258p.

In this book, one of the most important recent ethnographic monographs on Senegal to be written in English, Linares brings together many of the themes on which she has written during nearly thirty years of research in the area: differences between Diola villages in ecology and agriculture, gender relations, social stratification, Islamization, and the impact of Manding culture, and how all of these factors are related. The analysis is based on a comparison of three villages: Sambujat, where the economy is still based on rice, and where Diola culture is still strong; Jipalom, where Islam and groundnut production have had a greater impact; and Fatiya, where Manding culture and Islam have had the greatest impact and where economic and gender relations have also been transformed. In the epilogue the author reflects on the changes which have taken place in the three villages over the years and their position within the modern Senegalese state. The author's other papers relating to themes in this book include 'Households among the Diola of Senegal: should norms enter by the front or the back door?' in *Houshold Changes in Space and Time*, edited by R. McC. Netting (Berkeley, California: University of California Press, 1984, p. 407-44); 'Cash crops and gender constructs: the Jola of Senegal', *Ethnology*, vol. 24 (1985), p. 83-93; 'Kuseek and Kuriimen: wives and kinswomen in Jola society' *Canadian Journal of African Studies*, vol. 22, no. 3 (1988), p. 472-490; and 'From tidal swamp to inland valley: on the social organization of wet rice cultivation among the Diola of Senegal', *Africa* (London), vol. 51, no. 2 (1981), p. 557-95.

A cultural, economic, and religious history of the Basse Casamance since 1500.
See item no. 217.

Deferring to trade in slaves: the Jola of Casamance, Senegal, in historical perspective.
See item no. 219.

Anciens et nouveaux droits fonciers chez les Diola au Sénégal et leurs conséquences pour la répartition des terres. (Old and new property rights among the Diola of Senegal and their consequencs for land distribution.)
See item no. 472.

Capitalism and legal change: an African transformation.
See item no. 473.

Customary land tenure and land reform: the rise of new inequalities among the Diola of Senegal.
See item no. 475.

Essai sur quelques problèmes relatifs au régime foncier des Diola de Basse-Casamance (Sénégal). (Essay on some problems related to the land tenure system of the Diola of the Lower Casamance, Senegal.)
See item no. 477.

Legal innovation and social change in a peasant community: a Senegalese village police.
See item no. 479.

Responsabilité, sanction et organisation judiciaire chez les Diola traditionels de Basse-Casamance (Sénégal). (Responsibility, sanction and judicial organization among the traditional Diola of the Lower Casamance, Senegal.)
See item no. 485.

Animisme, religion caduque: étude qualitative et quantitative sur les opinions et la pratique religieuse en Basse-Casamance (pays diola). (Animism, an obsolete religion. A qualitative and quantitative study of religious opinions and practice in the Lower Casamance among the Diola.)
See item no. 537.

Bukut chez les Diola-Nioumon. (Bukut initiation among the Diola-Nioumon.)
See item no. 538.

Diffusion en milieu diola de l'association du Koump bainouk. (The spread of the Bainouk Koump association among the Diola.)
See item no. 540.

Le Diola et le temps. (The Diola and time.)
See item no. 542.

Kujaama: symbolic separation among the Diola-Fogny.
See item no. 546.

Leper, hyena, and blacksmith in Kujamaat Diola thought.
See item no. 548.

La quête de l'enfant: représentation de la maternité et rituels de stérilité dans la société Diola de Basse-Casamance. (The quest for children: the representation of maternity and rituals to deal with sterility in Diola society of the Lower Casamance.)
See item no. 552.

Un système philosophique sénégalais: la cosmologie des Diola. (A Senegalese system of philosophy: the cosmology of the Diola.)
See item no. 557.

The emergence of a Diola Christianity.
See item no. 588.

Dictionnaire français-dyola et dyola-français précédé d'un essai de grammaire. (French-Diola and Diola-French dictionary, preceded by an essay on grammar.)
See item no. 660.

Cultural and Linguistic Divisions.

Halpulaaren – Tukulor and Fulbe (Peul, Fulani)

Un exemple d'oralité négro-africaine: les fables djugut (Basse Casamance). (An example of black African oral literature: Djugut fables from the Lower Casamance.)
See item no. 673.

Nouvel exemple d'oralité négro-africaine: récits Narang-Djiragon, Diola-Karaban et Dyiwat (Basse Casamance). (A new example of black African oral literature: recitations from Narang-Djiragon, Diola-Karaban and Dyiwat, Lower Casamance.)
See item no. 674.

Les Diola et les objets d'art. (The Diola and art objects.)
See item no. 755.

Diola-Fogny funeral songs and the native critic.
See item no. 771.

Musical style and social change among the Kujamaat Diola.
See item no. 774.

The iconography of the Diola *ebanken* shield.
See item no. 786.

The Wild Bull and the Sacred Forest: form, meaning and change in Senegambian initiation masks.
See item no. 800

Halpulaaren – Tukulor and Fulbe (Peul, Fulani)

154 **Le célibat en pays toucouleur.** (The Tukulor bachelor.)
Yaya Wane. *Bulletin de l'IFAN*, vol. 31(B), no. 3 (1969), p. 717-32.
A summary by a Tukulor writer of attitudes to batchelors in his own society. It appears that their lot is not a happy one, as they are despised, mistrusted and treated as irresponsible minors.

155 **Etat actuel de la documentation au sujet des Toucouleurs.** (The present state of documentation on the Tukulor.)
Y. Wane. *Bulletin de l'IFAN*, vol. 25(B), no. 3/4 (1963), p. 457-77.
A bibliography of the main historical, anthropological, economic and archival sources for this important northern Senegalese people.

156 **Le Fouta Toro au carrefour des cultures. Les Peuls de la Mauritanie et du Sénégal.** (The Fuuta Toro at the crossroads of cultures. The Peul of Mauritania and Senegal.)
Oumar Ba. Paris: L'Harmattan, [1976]. 424p.

A large miscellany of information on the Tukulor and Peul of northern Senegal and Mauritania, with sections on history, language and social structure assembled in a loose order, but, unfortunately, with no index to guide the reader.

157 **L'honneur dans les sociétés Ouolof et Toucouleur du Sénégal.** (Honour in the Wolof and Tukulor societies of Senegal.)
Boubackar Ly. *Présence Africaine*, vol. 61 (1967), p. 32-67.

An extended study of the concept of honour in two of Senegal's main cultural groups, this paper covers the meaning of the concept, with reference to Wolof and Tukulor social structure, and the main components of morality and good behaviour.

158 **Organisation sociale des Peul: étude d'ethnographie comparée.** (Peul social organization: a comparative ethnographic study.)
Marguerite Dupire. Paris: Librairie Plon, 1970. 624p.

A monumental comparative survey dealing with the Peul scattered across West Africa, their social organization, formation of local groups, social stratification based on age, and marriage strategies and their relation to the distribution of power. Dupire has also dealt with Peul marriage in 'Matériaux pour l'étude de l'endogamie des Peul du cercle de Kédougou (Sénégal Oriental)', (Materials for the study of endogamy among the Peul of the Kédougou area of Eastern Senegal), *Bulletin et Mémoires de la Société de l'Anthropologie* (Paris), vol. 5, no. 3/4 (1963), p. 223-98.

159 **Les Peuls du Diolof au XIXe siècle.** (The Peul of Jolof in the 19th century.)
Oumar Ba. *Bulletin de l'IFAN*, vol. 37(B), no. 1 (1975), p. 117-36.

An account of the organization of the Peul in the Jolof area during the last century, their political organization and leadership, and their relations (generally friendly) with the Wolof among whom they moved and lived.

160 **Peul du Ferlo.** (The Peul of the Ferlo.)
Ph. Grenier. *Cahiers d'Outre-Mer*, vol. 13, no. 49 (1960), p. 28-58.

An account of transhumance and social organization among the Peul, at that time numbering between 70,000 and 90,000, in a particularly arid area of Senegal. Settlements were small, the nuclear family was the most important social unit, and the population was seasonally scattered and concentrated depending on the availability of fodder.

161 **La polygamie en pays toucouleur.** (Polygamy in Tukulor country.)
Oumar Ba. *Afrique Documents*, no. 64 (1962), p. 165-79.

An account of the social and economic functions of polygamy in the Fuuta Toro, and consideration of its causes, together with an outline of the rules relating to the seniority of wives.

Cultural and Linguistic Divisions.

Halpulaaren – Tukulor and Fulbe (Peul, Fulani)

162 **Les Toucouleur du Fouta Tooro (Sénégal). Stratification sociale et structure familiale.** (The Tukulor of the Senegalese Fuuta Toro. Social stratification and family structure.)
Yaya Wane. Dakar: IFAN, 1969. 250p. (Initiations et Etudes Africaines, 25).

Written by a native Tukulor and prominent social scientist at IFAN in Dakar who has documented numerous aspects of this society, this book covers social stratification (age, caste), social organization based on kinship, marriage and descent, and the impact of social change on Tukulor society. It also includes forty plates and an extensive bibliography.

163 **Les Toucouleur du Sénégal et la modernisation.** (The Tukulor of Senegal and modernization.)
Yaya Wane. *Bulletin de l'IFAN*, vol. 32(B), no. 3 (1970), p. 888-900.

A discussion of the continuing attachment of the Tukulor to their home region, the traditional social structure based on hierarchy and the family, and Islam, despite high levels of migration.

Dynamique d'une population traditionnelle: Démographie, apparentement et mariage dans une population d'effectif limité: Les Peul Bandé (Sénégal oriental). (Dynamics of a traditional population: demography, relationships and marriage in a population of limited size – the Bande Peul, Eastern Senegal.)
See item no. 119.

Cattle and inequality: herd size differences and pastoral production among the Fulani of Northeastern Senegal.
See item no. 366.

The pastoral environment of northern Senegal.
See item no. 367.

Les rapports du système foncier Toucouleur de l'organisation sociale et économique traditionnelle. Leur évolution actuelle. (The links between Tukulor land tenure and traditional social and economic organization, and their present development.)
See item no. 481.

Du régime des terres de la vallée du Sénégal au Fouta antérieurement à l'occupation française. (On the land use of the Senegal valley in Fuuta before the French occupation.)
See item no. 483.

Raison pastorale et politique de développement: les Peul sénégalais face aux aménagements. (Pastoral reasoning and development policy: the Peul of Senegal facing change.)
See item no. 639.

Grammaire moderne du Pulaar. (A modern grammar of Pulaar.)
See item no. 664.

La langue des Peuls ou Foulbé. (The language of the Peul or Fulbe.)
See item no. 665.

Le poular, dialecte peul du Fouta sénégalais Tome II: Lexique poular-français.
(Pulaar, the Peul dialect of the Senegalese Fouta volume 2: Pulaar-French
lexicon.)
See item no. 666.

La parole à travers quelques proverbes peuls du Fouladou (Sénégal).
(The Fulani concept of speech, based on proverbs from Fouladou, Senegal.)
See item no. 675.

Proverbes et maximes peuls et toucouleurs, traduits, expliqués et annotés.
(Peul and Tukulor proverbs and maxims, translated, explained and
annotated.)
See item no. 676.

Performance and ambiguity: a study of Tukulor weavers' songs.
See item no. 775.

Dreams, inspiration and craftwork among Tukulor weavers.
See item no. 783.

Secrets and skills: apprenticeship among Tukulor weavers.
See item no. 794.

Tukulor weavers and the organisation of their craft in village and town.
See item no. 798.

Tukulor weaving origin myths: Islam and reinterpretation.
See item no. 799.

Serer

164 **Dynamisme interne de la famille sérère.** (Internal dynamism of the Serer
family.)
Henri Gravrand. *Afrique Documents,* vol. 85/86, no. 2/3 (1966),
p. 95-122.
A study of changing kinship organization among the Serer which discusses: the
declining importance of lineage ties; the increasing importance of the conjugal family;
changes in descent; and the escalating cost of marriage payments despite the attempts
of the Church, the Mourides and the administration to keep them down.

165 **Dynamisme sérèr dans le Sénégal moderne.** (The dynamism of the Serer in modern Senegal.)
Henri Gavrand. *Afrique Documents*, vol. 105/06 (1969), p. 291-318.

A study of social change among the Serer which suggests that, despite the decline of many of the old political, kinship, economic and ritual institutions because of the development of the state, the market economy and the spread of education, Serer culture remains dynamic, and can still make a positive contribution to modern Senegal.

166 **L'égalitarianisme économique des Sérèr du Sénégal.** (The economic egalitarianism of the Serer of Senegal.)
Jean-Marc Gastellu. Paris: ORSTOM, 1981. 808p. (Travaux et documents, 128).

The first part of this study traces the roots of Serer egalitarianism in the traditional social structure and land tenure systems, and the second considers the ways in which this ideology of equality was preserved despite the political upheavals of the 19th century. There are useful discussions of the spread of the Mouride order and the Catholic church, and the final section discusses the organization of labour and descent.

167 **Des goûts et des odeurs: classifications et universaux.** (Tastes and smells: classifications and universals.)
Marguerite Dupire. *L'Homme*, vol. 27, no. 104 (1987), p. 5-25.

An examination of Ndut Serer categories of taste and smell. These differ from those of European culture, which are inappropriate for the local environment.

168 **Résidence, tenure foncière, alliance dans une société bilinéaire (Sérèr du Sine et du Baol, Sénégal).** (Residence, land tenure and alliance in a bilinear society: the Serer of Sine and Baol, Senegal.)
Marguerite Dupire, André Lericollais, Bernard Delpech, Jean-Marc Gastellu. *Cahiers d'Etudes Africaines*, vol. 14, no. 3 (1974), p. 417-52.

An important, but highly technical, account by four major writers of the Sine Serer, who make up four-fifths of the total Serer population. The article deals with the complexities of residential organization, land tenure and marriage patterns.

169 **Une société rurale au Sénégal. Les structures foncières, familiales et villageoises des Sérèr.** (A rural society in Senegal: the structures of land tenure, family and the village among the Serer.)
Jean-Claude Reverdy. Aix-en-Provence, France: Centre Africain des Sciences Humaines Appliquées, [1968], 115p.

A study of social structure and social change among the Serer based on research carried out in the mid-1960s. It deals with land tenure, kinship and social relations, residential structure, and the creation and operation of agricultural cooperatives.

Ordres, castes et états en pays sérèr (Sénégal): essai d'interprétation d'un système politique en transition. (Orders, castes and estates in Serer country, Senegal: an interpretative essay on a political system in transition.) *See* item no. 239.

Chasse rituelle, divination et reconduction de l'ordre socio-politique chez les Sérèr du Sine (Sénégal). (Ritual hunting, divination and renewal of the sociopolitical order among the Serer of Sine, Senegal.) *See* item no. 539.

Nomination, réincarnation et/ou ancêtre tutélaire? Un mode de survie: l'exemple des Sérèr Ndout (Sénégal). (Name giving, reincarnation and/or guardian ancestor? A mode of survival: the example of the Serer Ndut of Senegal.) *See* item no. 550.

Rites d'initiation et vie en société chez les Sérèrs du Sénégal. (Initiation rites and social life among the Serer of Senegal.) *See* item no. 554.

Les 'tombes de chiens': mythologies de la mort en pays sérèr (Sénégal). (Dogs' tombs: mythologies of death among the Serer of Senegal.) *See* item no. 558.

Totems sereer et contrôle rituel de l'environnement. (Serer totems and ritual control of the environment.) *See* item no. 559.

Quelques proverbes sérères recueillis à Fadiout (Sénégal). (Some Serer proverbs collected at Fadiout, Senegal.) *See* item no. 678.

Wolof

170 **L'alimentation et la stratégie de l'apprentissage de l'échange avec les frères chez l'enfant wolof.** (Food and strategies of training the Wolof child to exchange with brothers.)
J. Zempleni-Rabain. *Psychopathologie Africaine*, vol 4. no. 2 (1968), p. 279-311.
Another of the series of detailed accounts of child socialization by Zempleni-Rabain, this paper deals with the development of relationships between brothers and age-mates through exchanges of gifts and hospitality.

171 **Modes fondamentaux de relations chez l'enfant wolof, du sevrage à l'intégration dans la classe d'âge.** (Fundamental types of relationships among Wolof children: from weaning to the integration into age classes.)
J. Zempleni-Rabain. *Psychopathologie Africaine*, vol. 2, no. 2 (1966), p. 143-77.

An investigation of child development based on the study over 6-18 months of twenty-three children between three and five years old in the mid-1960s, which focuses on different types of physical contact.

172 **La société wolof: tradition et changement. Les systèmes d'inégalité et de domination.** (Wolof society: tradition and change. Systems of inequality and domination.)
Abdoulaye-Bara Diop. Paris: Karthala, 1981. 355p.

This book originated from the author's large-scale doctoral thesis completed in 1978. It deals with social stratification, and the intersecting systems of inequality, traditional inequalities based on caste, political order, and new systems based on Islam which have largely replaced them. The section of Diop's thesis dealing with kinship and marriage in historical perspective has been published separately as *La famille wolof: tradition et changement* (Paris: Karthala, 1985. 262p.), and he has covered similar ground in two papers: 'Parenté et famille wolof en milieu rural' (Kinship and family among the rural Wolof), *Bulletin d'IFAN*, vol. 32 (B), no. 1 (1970), p. 216-29; and 'La famille rurale wolof: mode de résidence et organisations socioéconomique' (The rural Wolof family: pattern of residence and socio-economic organization), *Bulletin de l'IFAN*, vol. 36 (B), no. 1 (1974), p. 147-63.

173 **When is genealogy history? Wolof genealogies in comparative perspective.**
Judith T. Irvine. *American Ethnologist*, vol, 5, no. 4 (1978), p. 651-74.

A study of genealogies among the Wolof and the ways in which they are maintained and transmitted by the griots, the caste of praise-singers. Irvine argues that the existence of this caste is one reason why genealogies among the Wolof are historically more accurate than in many other parts of Africa. On the other hand, the griots may manipulate the details of the genealogies during actual performance to suit the particular needs of their clients.

174 **The Wolof of Saloum: social structure and rural development in Senegal.**
L. B. Venema. Wageningen, The Netherlands: Centre for Agricultural Publishing and Documentation, 1978. 228p.

A large-scale study by a rural sociologist of agricultural and social change among the Wolof of the Saloum area of Senegal. After an account of the changing political context, there are chapters on agricultural policy and implementation, the Wolof farming system, age organization, the fragmentation of the compound and household, social hierarchy, traditional and modern forms of cooperation, and local men of influence. The book ends with a summary in French, and twenty-seven historical, statistical and methodological appendices.

175 **The Wolof of Senegambia, together with notes on the Lebu and the Serer.**
David Gamble. London: International African Institute, 1957. 110p. (Ethnographic Survey of West Africa 14).

The standard ethnographic survey in English, still useful as a synthesis of the earlier literature, with brief sections on demography, history, language, the economy, social organization, the political system, the life cycle, religion and social change. It also contains brief notes on the neighbouring Serer and Lebu. Some of the material in this book has been updated in *Peoples of The Gambia: I The Wolof*, co-authored by Gamble, Linda K. Salmon and Alhanji Hassan Njie, and published as number seventeen in his Gambian Studies Series (San Francisco, 1985. 78p: obtainable through Blackwell North America Inc, 6024 SW Jean Rd. Bldg. G, Lake Oswego, Oregon USA 97034).

Civilisation wolofo-sérère au XVe siècle d'après les sources portugaises. (Wolof-Serer civilization in the 15th century according to Portuguese sources.)
See item no. 95.

L'honneur dans les sociétés ouolof et toucouleur du Sénégal. (Honour in the Wolof and Tukulor societies of Senegal.)
See item no. 157.

Aristocrats, slaves, and peasants: power and dependency in the Wolof states, 1700-1850.
See item no. 211.

Chronique du Wâlo sénégalais (1186?-1855). (Chronicle of Walo, Senegal: 1186?-1855.)
See item no. 214.

Le Grand Jolof (xiiie-xvie siècle). (The Grand Jolof kingdom, 13th-16th centuries.)
See item no. 224.

The pre-nineteenth century political tradition of the Wolof.
See item no. 242.

Le royaume du Waalo: le Sénégal avant la conquête. (The kingdom of Waalo: Senegal before the conquest.)
See item no. 245.

The Wolof kingdom of Kayor.
See item no. 255.

La dimension thérapeutique du culte des rab. Ndoup, tuuru et samp. Rites de possession chez les Lébou et les Wolof. (The therapeutic dimensions of the rab cult. Ndop, tuuro and samp. Possession rites among the Lebu and Wolof.)
See item no. 541.

Cultural and Linguistic Divisions. Other ethnic groups. Bassari

L'enfant *nit-ku-bon:* un tableau psychopathologique traditionnel chez les Wolof et les Lébou du Sénégal. (The *nit-ku-bon* child: a traditional psychiatric image among the Wolof and the Lebu of Senegal.)
See item no. 543.

La confrérie sénégalaise des Mourides. (The Mouride brotherhood in Senegal.)
See item no. 562.

The political significance of the Wolof adherence to Muslim brotherhoods in the nineteenth century.
See item no. 576.

The Shaykh's men: religion and power in Senegambian Islam.
See item no. 578.

Dakar Wolof: a basic course.
See item no. 667.

Grammaire de wolof moderne. (Grammar of modern Wolof.)
See item no. 668.

Initiation à la grammaire wolof. (An introduction to Wolof grammar.)
See item no. 669.

Lexique wolof-français. (French-Wolof dictionary.)
See item no. 670.

Other ethnic groups

Bassari

176 Les Bassari du Sénégal – fils du caméléon: dynamique d'une culture troglodytique. (The Bassari of Sengal – sons of the chameleon. The dynamics of a cave-dwelling culture.)
Jean Girard. Paris: L'Harmattan, 1984. 967p.
An ambitious survey and historical reconstruction of Bassari/Beliyan culture in southeastern Senegal, a culture which was perhaps once much more widespread. The sections discuss the economy, migrations, social structure, rituals and belief systems. It is lavishly illustrated with texts, photographs and line drawings. The appendices provide lists of villages and their caves, including those situated near 'campements' in the Niokolo Koba National Park.

177 **Les Coniagui et les Bassari (Guinée française).** (The Coniagui and the Bassari: French Guinea.)
Monique de Lestrange. Paris: Presses Universitaires de France, 1955. 84p.
A brief systematic survey of two small ethnic groups living on the border between Senegal and Guinea, an area studied intensively by French anthropologists over the years.

Bassari migrations: the quiet revolution.
See item no. 125.

Aspects techniques et sociaux de l'agriculture en pays bassari. (Technical and social aspects of agriculture among the Bassari.)
See item no. 335.

Bedik

178 **Notes sur l'ethnographie des Bedik (Sénégal oriental).** (Notes on the ethnography of the Bedik: Eastern Senegal.)
Jacques Gomila, Marie-Paule Ferry. *Journal des Africanistes*, vol. 36, no. 2 (1966), p. 209-49.
A summary of work on the Bedik, one of the smallest ethnic groups in south eastern Senegal, consisting of 1,400 people in the early 1960s when the research was carried out. The paper deals with a summary of patterns of residence, kinship and authority in the six Bedik villages, the naming system, and with male initiation and the life cycle. Gomila also published a study of the physical anthropology of the group, *Les Bedik (Sénégal oriental): barrières culturelles et hétérogénéité biologique* (Montreal: Presses de l'Université de Montréal, 1971. 273p.), the early chapters of which also contain useful information on this group.

179 **Pour une histoire des Bedik (Sénégal oriental).** (Towards a history of the Bedik.)
Marie-Paule Ferry. *Bulletin et Mémoires de la Société d'Anthropologie* (Paris), Series 12, vol. 2, no. 1/2 (1967), p. 125-48.
An account of the dispersal of this small ethnic group from its original home by the Peul during the wars of the 19th century, their regrouping in four of their original settlements and two Malinke villages, and their integration with the local Malinke population.

180 **Tiges de mil, tiges d'igname: essai sur la parenté chez les Bedik et les Beliyan (Sénégal oriental).** (Millet stalks, yam stems: kinship among the Bedik and Beliyan, Eastern Senegal.) Marie-Paule Ferry, Erik Guignard. *L'Homme*, vol. 24, no. 3/4 (1984), p. 35-60.

Millet stalks are straight, yam stems are flexible and twine around other plants: the two plants are thus used to symbolize the differences between the patrilineages of the Bedik and the matrilineages of the Beliyan and Bassari. The paper provides a description of the Bedik and Beliyan together with a technical analysis of their kinship and marriage systems, and the patterns of the movement of women between kin groups.

Mariage des femmes et initiation des hommes: Beliyan et Bedik du Sénégal oriental. (Female marriage and male initiation: Beliyan and Bedik in Eastern Senegal.) *See* item no. 549.

Ethno-gynécologie et pathologie bedik. (Bedik ethno-gynaecology and pathology.) *See* item no. 614.

Xylophones-sur-jambes chez les Bédik et les Bassari de Kédougou. ('Leg xylophones' among the Bedik and Bassari of Kedougou.) *See* item no. 779.

Badyaranke

181 **Social organization among the Badyaranke of Toughia, Sénégal.** W. Simmons. *Bulletin et Mémoires de la Société d'Anthropologie* (Paris), vol. 2, no. 2 (1967), p. 59-95.

A summary of the economic and social organization of a small ethnic group of 5,000 people divided between Senegal, Guinea and Guinea-Bissau. The paper discusses the matrilineal kinship system, the residence patterns, with men's individual and women's communal houses, the inheritance of names, the role of the headman in these politically uncentralized societies, and patterns of cooperation in work. These differ from village to village, and have been influenced by local Manding culture and Islam.

Eyes of the night: witchcraft among a Senegalese people. *See* item no. 544.

Powerlessness, exploitation and the soul-eating witch: an analysis of Badyaranke witchcraft. *See* item no. 551.

The supernatural world of the Badyaranké of Tonghia (Senegal). *See* item no. 556.

Islamic conversion and social change in a Senegalese village.
See item no. 570.

Ehing

182 **The hatchet's blood: separation, power and gender in Ehing social life.**
Marc R. Schloss. Tucson, Arizona: University of Arizona Press, 1988.
178p.
An anthropological account of a set of ritual prohibitions on social behaviour among
the Ehing, a small group of rice-farming people of the Casamance region in southern
Senegal. The book describes Ehing ritual, myth and notions of power, and links them
to ideas about agricultural production and procreation. It contains material on the
Ehing house, initiation, and useful chapters on women, and their cultivation of rice as
well as their rights in land.

Mande (Manding, Mandinka)

183 **Beyond migration and conquest: oral traditions and Mandinka ethnicity
in Senegambia.**
Donald R. Wright. *History in Africa*, vol. 12 (1985), p. 335-48.
Using oral traditions and written accounts from the 15th and 16th centuries, Wright
questions the generally accepted view that Mandinka culture spread through conquest
and migration, as the followers of the founder of the Mali empire, Sundiata Keita,
moved in from the east. Instead, he argues that Senegambians adopted Mandinka
culture and identities through a slower process of absorption and adaptation.

184 **Mandinko: the ethnography of a West African holy land.**
Matt Schaffer, Christine Cooper. New York: Holt, Rinehart &
Winston, 1980. 116p.
One of the Holt Rinehart series of case studies in cultural anthropology, this is a
concise, clearly written and comprehensive study of the social organization of a
Mandinka community in Southern Senegal between the Gambia and Casamance rivers.

**Power and knowledge: the representation of the Mande World in the works of
Park, Caillié, Monteil and Delafosse.**
See item no. 92.

Histoire des Mandingues de l'Ouest. Le royaume du Gabou. (History of the
Western Manding. The kingdom of Gabou.)
See item no. 227.

La royauté (mansaya) chez les Mandingues occidentaux d'après leurs traditions orales. (Kingship, *mansaya*, among the Western Mandinka as reflected in their oral traditions.)
See item no. 246.

La langue mandingue et ses dialectes (Malinké, Bambara, Diola). Tome II: Dictionnaire mandingue-français. (The Manding language and its dialects (Malinké, Bambara, Diola. vol. 2; Manding-French dictionary.)
See item no. 662.

Proverbes malinké: à l'ombre des grands fromagers. (Malinke proverbs: in the shade of the great kapok trees.)
See item no. 677.

Recueil des traditions orales des Mandingues de Gambie et de Casamance. (A collection of Manding oral traditions from Gambia and the Casamance.)
See item no. 679.

Mandinka drumming.
See item no. 772.

Music in Africa: the Manding contexts.
See item no. 773.

Soninke

185 **La terre et les gens du Fleuve. Jalons, balises.** (The land and the people of the River region. Milestones, beacons).
Adrian Adams.   Paris: L'Harmattan, 1985. 243p.
This is Adams' second volume concerning the life and people of the area around Bakel in northern Senegal. It presents a lively account of the history of the Soninke, and their current struggles to make a living through the annual cycles of fishing and agriculture.

Le long voyage des gens du Fleuve. (The long voyage of the people of the River region.)
See item no. 137.

The 'patriarchal ideal' of Soninke labor migrants: from slave owners to employers of free labour.
See item no. 138.

Le prolétariat africain noir en France. (The black African proletariat in France.)
See item no. 139.

Slavery, emancipation and labour migration in West Africa: the case of the Soninke.
See item no. 299.

Contes et légendes soninké (Mali, Sénégal, Mauritanie). (Soninke tales and legends from Mali, Senegal and Mauritania.)
See item no. 671.

Jakhanke (Diakhanke, Jaaxankhe)

186   **Les Diakhanké: histoire d'une dispersion.** (The Diakhanke: history of a diaspora.)
Pierre Smith.   *Bulletin et Mémoires de la Société d'Anthropologie* (Paris), Series 11, vol. 8, no. 3/4 (1965), p. 263-302.
A study based in part on oral traditions of the origins of this group of marabouts and traders, beginning with the migration of the marabout Bemba Laye Soare from Macina to Bambouk, possibly in the 13th or 14th century. From there the Diakhanke diffused throughout the region, obtaining the support of powerful patrons and concentrating on trade and Islam. In Kédougou, they live alongside Malinke, Peul and Sarakole.

187   **The Jakhanke: the history of an Islamic clerical people of the Senegambia.**
Lamin O. Sanneh.   London: International African Institute, 1979. 276p.
An unusual feature of Jakhanke (Diakhanke) doctrines is the emphasis on pacifism and political neutrality. Based on manuscripts and clan histories in addition to fieldwork, the book describes the history of their diaspora and settlements, Islamic education, prayer, dreams and religious healing. There is also an interesting discussion of the slaves, on whose labour the clerics' ability to devote so much time to religious affairs depended. At the end there is a substantial bibliography containing over 400 entries.

188   **Notes sur l'organisation social des Diakhanké: aspects particuliers de la région de Kédougou.** (Notes on the social organization of the Diakhanke: particular aspects of the Kédougou region.)
Pierre Smith.   *Bulletin et Mémoires de la Société d'Anthropologie* (Paris), Series 11, vol. 8, no. 3/4 (1965), p. 167-230.
This paper describes the relationship of the Diakhanke with the Malinke, whose language they speak, the organization of the main clans, and the division into castes.

189   **Un village Diakhanké du Sénégal oriental: Missirah.** (A Diakhanke village in Eastern Senegal: Missirah.)
Marie-France Fleury.   *Cahiers d'Outre-Mer*, vol. 37, no. 145 (1984), p. 63-85.
A well-illustrated general study of a village in the upper Gambian river basin in southeastern Senegal, with information on demographic structure, layout, and economic activities. The village appears to be extremely conservative with little development of cash cropping, despite the relatively favourable environment. The author concludes that this is due to a shortage of capital rather than of land.

History as identity: the Jaaxanke and the founding of Tuuba (Senegal).
See item no. 229.

Pre-colonial trading networks and traders: the Diakhanke.
See item no. 241.

Slavery, Islam and the Jakhanke people of West Africa.
See item no. 248.

Europeans and Lebanese

190 **Adjustment to West African realities: the Lebanese in Senegal.**
Said Boumedouha. *Africa*, vol. 60, no. 4 (1990), p. 538-49.
A description of the position of the Lebanese thirty years after independence. They
have been able to maintain their position by moving into new areas of investment, by
concentrating their activities in urban centres, and by employing large numbers of local
Senegalese, as well as by obtaining the protection of the Senegalese élite and the
brotherhoods.

191 **Europeans: white society in Black Africa: the French of Senegal.**
Rita Cruise O'Brien. London: Faber; Evanston, Illinois:
Northwestern University Press, 1972. 320p.
The first five chapters of this study deal with the history of the French presence in
Senegal, the emergence of colonial society, the arrival of the lower class whites or *petit
blancs*, and race relations during the period of decolonization. The rest of the book
deals with the life of the expatriate community after independence: their changing role
in commerce and industry, employment and Africanization, technical assistance, their
influence in politics, and their social structure and social life, including the network of
(almost) exclusively European clubs. The final chapter deals with race relations, the
attitudes of the French towards both Africans and Lebanese, and the problems of
mixed marriages. There are appendices on the French population of Dakar, the
samples which formed the basis of the research, and a tabulation of responses to the
questionnaire.

192 **Lebanese entrepreneurs in Senegal: economic integration and the politics
of protection.**
Rita Cruise O'Brien. *Cahiers d'Etudes Africaines*, vol. 15, no. 1,
(1975), p. 95-115.
During the colonial period, the Lebanese in West Africa occupied an important
intermediate position in commerce between the Europeans and the Africans. This
well-researched paper discusses changes in their position in Senegal and their relations
with its rulers before and after independence.

History

General

193 **Contributions à l'histoire du Sénégal.** (Contributions to the history of
Senegal.)
Published under the direction of Jean Boulègue. Paris: Centre de
Recherches Africaines, 1987. 234p (Cahiers du C.R.A., 5).
As its title suggests, this book is a miscellany of fourteen essays on various aspects of
Senegalese history. Though many of the papers focus on the important themes of
relations with the colonial powers and political and religious change, there are also
chapters on more unusual topics such as the uses of linguistic and even blood group
data in historical research.

194 **France and West Africa: an anthology of historical documents.**
Edited by John D. Hargreaves. London: Macmillan, 1969. 278p.
An anthology of sources and documents in English translation which the author found
useful in the preparation of his earlier books on the region. The book is organized
under six headings: African societies and the advent of Europe; the Senegalese colony;
the Muslim counterforce; origins of the French conquest; the purposes of French rule;
and the African presence.

195 **Francophone sub-Saharan Africa 1880-1985.**
Patrick Manning. Cambridge, England: Cambridge University Press,
1988. 215p.
One of the best concise histories of the Francophone countries of West and Central
Africa available in English. After a general introductory section there are chapters on
economy and society, government and politics, and culture and religion for the periods
1880-1940 and 1940-85. It concludes with a short bibliographical essay and an index.

196 **Histoire du Sénégal.** (History of Senegal.)
André Villard. Dakar: Ars Africae; Maurice Viale, 1943. 264p.

A wartime history of Senegal, most of which concentrates on the 19th century, with lengthy chapters on the trading companies, early attempts at colonization, the career of Faidherbe, and the unification of the territory under the governor general. At the end there are useful pull-out ethnographic and historical maps and what was, for the period, an impressive twenty-one-page annotated bibliography, as well as an index which, due to the wartime conditions, was compiled by Th. Monod.

197 **Histoire traditionelle du Sénégal.** (Traditional history of Senegal.)
Félix Brigaud. Saint-Louis, Senegal: CRDS-Senegal, 1962. 335p.
(Etudes Sénégalaises, 9, Connaissance du Sénégal, 9).

A useful volume with a lengthy bibliography. Brigaud was director of the Centre de Recherches et de Documentation Scientifique du Sénégal (formerly the Centre-IFAN) at the time, and was responsible for many of the volumes of the sub-series *Connaissance du Sénégal*, ranging from physical geography to finance. He also published the companion volume *Histoire moderne et contemporaine du Sénégal* (Modern and contemporary history of Senegal) (Saint-Louis, Senegal: CRDS-Senegal, 1966. 149p.), and a more concise history under the title *Histoire du Sénégal: des origines aux traités de protectorat.* (History of Senegal: from its origins to the protectorate treaties.) (Dakar: Editions Clairafrique, 1964. 85p.).

198 **Historical dictionary of Senegal.**
Lucie Gallistel Colvin. Metuchen, New Jersey; London: Scarecrow Press, 1981. 339p.

A useful reference source, of wider interest than its title would suggest. The bulk of the text, p. 121-292, contains an alphabetical series of entries on important places, terms, events and people in Senegalese history up to the date of compilation. This is preceded by a sixteen-page historical survey of the country, a twenty-five-page chronology of important events, and a useful collection of tables including lists of traditional rulers, French governors, the Senegalese cabinet in 1978, economic and demographic statistics, and election results. The final section is an important forty-four-page bibliography divided into sections: general, cultural, economic, historical, political, scientific and social.

199 **A provisional historical schema for Western Africa based on seven climate periods (ca. 9000 BC to the 19th century).**
George E. Brooks. *Cahiers d'Etudes Africaines*, vol. 26, no. 1/2 (1986), p. 43-62.

A bold attempt to provide an environmental framework for the study of West African history. Using a wide variety of evidence, the author argues that the environment has developed through seven major phases, each change having an important impact on the local peoples and their history.

200 **Réflexions sur les sources de l'histoire de la Sénégambie.** (Reflections on the sources of Senegambian history.)
Charles Becker. *Paideuma*, vol. 33 (1987), p. 147-65.
A useful summary of the types of material available to the historian of this region and the kinds of problems associated with them. Becker discusses both locally available material and European documentary sources and concludes that the former are indispensable but have not yet been fully utilized.

201 **Tableau géographique de l'Ouest Africain au moyen âge d'après les sources écrites, la tradition et l'archéologie.** (A geographical picture of medieval West Africa, based on written sources, oral tradition and archaeology.)
Raymond Mauny. Dakar: IFAN 1961. 587p. (Mémoires no. 61).
(Reprinted by Swets and Seitlinger BV, Amsterdam, 1975).
A major account of Africa in the middle ages, based on early European and Arabic records, on archaeology and oral tradition. The sections of the book present a detailed survey of the region's geography, the organization of production and trade, and of its peoples and cultures. There are extensive maps, diagrams and photographs.

202 **West Africa: the former French states.**
John D. Hargreaves. Englewood Cliffs, New Jersey: Prentice Hall, 1967. 183p.
A concise introduction to the history of French West Africa written during the early years of independence. It contains brief sections on the French advance into Senegal, the development of political rights in the Senegalese communes, and an account of the postwar transition to independence. There is a useful list of selected reading at the end.

Sources démographiques de l'histoire de la Sénégambie. (Demographic sources for the history of Senegambia.)
See item no. 124.

Esquisses sénégalaises (Walo, Kayor, Dyolof, Mourides, un visionnaire). (Senegalese sketches: Walo, Kayor, Jolof, Mourides, a religious visionary.)
See item no. 149.

Histoire des classes sociales dans l'Afrique de l'Ouest. Tome II. Le Sénégal. (History of the social classes in West Africa. Volume 2: Senegal.)
See item no. 521.

Archaeology and prehistory

203 **An archeological appraisal of the early European settlements in the Senegambia.**
W. Raymond Wood. *Journal of African History*, vol. 8, no. 1 (1967), p. 39-64.

An useful survey of the main commercial settlements in the region between the late 15th and early 19th centuries, together with details of construction and occupation, as possible sites for archaeological research.

204 **Le laboratoire de radiocarbone de l'IFAN.** (The radiocarbon laboratory of IFAN.)
Cheikh Anta Diop. Dakar: IFAN, 1968. 110p. (Catalogues et Documents, 21).

A description by the historian of *négritude* of the laboratory's activities and faciltities in the late 1960s and some of the results of its research.

205 **Protohistoire du Sénégal: recherches archéologiques. Tome I. Les sites mégalithiques.** (Protohistory of Senegal: archaeological research, vol 1. The megalithic sites.)
G. Thilmans, C. Descamps, B. Khayat. Dakar: IFAN, 1980. 158p. (Mémoire, 91).

The archaeological sites of Senegal are usually divided into river sites, megalithic sites, coastal shell deposits and tumulus sites. This first volume of a projected series deals with stone circles, megaliths and burial sites, found mainly in the Gambia river valley, on the northern side of the river west of Tambacounda. It is based on the detailed excavation of thirteen sites, eight of which been dated with some precision, and four of which originate from the period 594-790 AD, before the development of the trans-Saharan slave trade. These are described together with the human remains found in them, including a detailed study of the teeth. The volume contains a detailed bibliography.

206 **Protohistoire du Sénégal: recherches archéologiques. Tome II. Sintiou-Bara et le sites du Fleuve.** (Protohistory of Senegal: archaeological research. vol. 2: Sintiou-Bara and the Senegal river sites.)
G. Thilmans, A. Ravise. Dakar: IFAN, 1980. 213p.

Reviews both early and more recent work undertaken in sites along the Senegal river valley. The finds, dated between the 5th and 11th centuries, were taken from the Sintiou-Bara cultural complex, named after a particularly rich site near Matam. The authors describe the sites, the techniques of excavation and the objects recovered, including bracelets, pendants, bells, stone beads and pottery. A lengthy bibliography is appended.

207 **Stone circles in the Gambia Valley.**
Sir Herbert Richmond Palmer. *Journal of the Royal Anthropological Institute*, vol. 69 (1939), p. 273-83.
The many hundreds of circles of large stones, found in sites scattered along the Gambia river valley in both The Gambia and Senegal, are the major features of the local archaeology. In this paper, Palmer argues that the circles were funerary in origin and speculates about the identity of the people who had them erected, and the people who carved them.

208 **West Africa before the seventh century.**
B. Wai Andah. In: *UNESCO General History of Africa II: Ancient civilizations of Africa*. Edited by G. Mokhtar. London: Heinneman; Berkeley, California: University of California Press, 1981. p. 593-619.
A general survey of the prehistory of the region during the pre-Islamic period. Pages 615-18 cover archaeological findings in Senegambia.

Nations nègres et culture: de antiquité nègre égyptienne aux problèmes culturels de l'Afrique Noire d'aujourd'hui. (Black nations and culture: from black Egyptian antiquity to cultural problems of Black Africa today.) *See* item no. 691.

Precolonial history

209 **Albouri Ndiaye et la résistance à la conquête française du Sénégal.**
(Albouri Ndiaye and the resistance to the French conquest of Senegal.) Eunice A. Charles. *Bulletin de l'IFAN*, vol. 44 (B), no. 1/2 (1982), p. 33-49.
A discussion of the career of the last independent ruler of the Jolof, including his alliance with Lat Dior, the former ruler of Kayor deposed by the French. Reprisals against Jolof and the threat of a French attack eventually drove Albouri from his kingdom in 1890, and he spent the last ten years of his life in exile.

210 **Ancient Ghana and Mali.**
Nehemia Levtzion. London: Methuen, 1973. 283p.
A standard work by one of the leading experts on the history of the Western Sudan. The ancient kingdom of Ghana was located to the east of the Senegal river, for the most part in present-day Mali, but the Mali empire for a long period included most of southern Senegal, including the basins of the Senegal and Casamance rivers. The book is mainly based on Arabic and Portuguese sources. The first part deals mainly with the history, and the second is a series of chapters on political institutions, trade and Islam. The main treatment of the southern Senegal area is in the chapter on Malinke expansion and political fragmentation (p. 94-102). There is an extensive bibliography of both primary and secondary sources, and a useful index.

211 **Aristocrats, slaves, and peasants: power and dependency in the Wolof states, 1700-1850.**
James F. Searing. *International Journal of African Historical Studies*, vol. 21, no. 3 (1988), p. 475-503.

An important account of slavery in precolonial Wolof society, this paper examines the status of slaves, the role of the slave warriors or *ceddo* in the political economy, and the position of free citizens. The author argues that slavery cannot be discussed in isolation from the rest of society, and that alongside the slaves there existed a thriving peasant sector, so that the lines between the slaves and the free were blurred.

212 **Bundu in the eighteenth century.**
Michael Gomez. *International Journal of African Historical Studies*, vol. 20, no. 1 (1987), p. 61-73.

A brief history of the state, the foundation of which has led to a debate between Gomez and Curtin, and the politics of its ruling Peul/Fulbe lineage based on 18th-century French and Arabic sources.

213 **Chroniques du Fouta sénégalais.** (Chronicles of the Senegalese Fuuta.)
Siré Abbâs Soh, translated from two Arab manuscripts by M. Delafosse and H. Gaden. Paris: Leroux, 1913. 328p.

One of the earliest collections of oral texts dealing with the dynasties that ruled in Fuuta Toro from the time of the Tekrur Empire onward. The work also includes myths and legends on craft groups and their origins. Delafosse and Gaden provide a useful, though at times somewhat prejudiced, introduction.

214 **Chronique du Wâlo sénégalais (1186?-1855).** (Chronicle of Walo, Senegal: 1186?-1855.)
Amadou Wade, translated by Bassirou Cissé with a comment by Vincent Monteil. *Bulletin de l'IFAN*, vol. 26(B), no. 3/4, (1964) p. 440-98. maps.

An important source of information on the history of Walo in northern Senegal. Translated from the original Wolof, it records details of the succession of fifty-two rulers (*Brak*). The paper also includes an outline of Walo politics and society and a list of rulers.

215 **Conditions écologiques, crises de subsistance et histoire de la population à l'époque de la traite des esclaves en Sénégambie (17e-18e siècles).**
(Ecological conditions, subsistence crises and population history during the slave trade era in Senegambia, 17th-18th centuries.)
Charles Becker. *Canadian Journal of African Studies*, vol. 20 (1986), p. 357-76.

A further exploration by Becker of the links between the slave trade, apparent deterioration of the environment, disruption of production, and mass migrations which took place in the 17th and 18th centuries.

216 **Contribution à l'histoire de l'Empire du Mali (xiii-xvie siècles).**
(Contribution to the history of the Mali Empire, 13th-16th centuries.)
Madina Ly Tall.   Dakar: Nouvelles Editions Africaines, 1977. 220p.

This book contains an introduction describing the sources used, followed by a survey of
the main provinces of the empire and a description of the main political institutions.
The survey of regions includes sections on Tekrur, the Fuuta Toro, and the Gambia
river. The latter is based on Arab sources and Mande and Wolof oral traditions.

217 **A cultural, economic, and religious history of the Basse Casamance since
1500.**
Peter Mark.   Stuttgart; Wiesbaden, Germany: Frans Steiner Verlag,
1985. 136p.

This book deals with the early history of the area, using masking traditions as one
source of evidence, and with precolonial religion, the establishment of colonial rule,
and the spread of Islam under French administration between 1890 and 1940. Despite
religious change, some traditional beliefs and rituals do retain their vitality and provide
their participants with a sense of Diola identity. At the end of the book is a ten-page
bibliography and ten black-and-white plates, but no index.

218 **Darbo Jula: the role of a Mandinka Jula clan in the long-distance trade
of the Gambia river and its hinterland.**
Donald R. Wright.   *African Economic History*, vol. 3 (1977), p. 33-45.

An account of trading networks in the Western Sudan, in the area between the
Gambia and Niger rivers. The members of the clan involved depended heavily for their
success on their social and economic networks within the societies in and through
which they traded.

219 **Deferring to trade in slaves: the Jola of Casamance, Senegal, in
historical perspective.**
Olga F. Linares.   *History in Africa*, vol. 14 (1987), p. 113-39.

This paper discusses changes in the precolonial political economy of the Jola between
the 17th and 19th centuries. Originally the Jola (Diola) were pastoralists, but as their
political power expanded, they became involved in rice-farming using slaves as
labourers, and eventually in the slave trade itself.

220 **La dévolution du pouvoir au Fuuta-Toora.** (The devolution of power in
the Fuuta Toro.)
Oumar Kane.   *Bulletin de l'IFAN*, vol. 43(B), no. 3/4 (1981),
p. 278-88.

Discusses succession practices in the region between the 15th and 18th centuries.

221 **The early states of the Western Sudan to 1500.**
Nehemia Levtzion. In: *History of West Africa*, vol 1. Edited by
J. F. A. Ajayi, Michael Crowder. London: Longmans, 1971,
p. 240-69.

A chapter of the standard history of the region (revised twice since its original
publication) which deals with the history of the Ghana, Mali and Songhay empires, and
with trade and Islam in the region, based mainly on Arab sources.

222 **Economic change in precolonial Africa: vol 1. Senegambia in the era of
the slave trade; vol 2. Supplementary evidence.**
Philip D. Curtin. Madison, Wisconsin: University of Wisconsin Press,
1975. 2 vols.

This major history of the Senegambian region is divided into two volumes, the second
of which contains appendices and a bibliography. The first volume opens with a general
description of the region, its agriculture, social organization, government and changing
patterns of religion. The second chapter deals with the local Juula (Dyula) trade
diasporas, while the third examines trade diasporas from overseas: the Afro-
Portuguese, the Europeans, the Afro-French, and the English. The remaining chapters
study the slave trade, production for the market, currency and exchange, the
organization of internal trade, and with external trade. The second volume contains
fifteen appendices on subjects as varied as climate and disease, trade regulations,
chronological outlines of major states, population, slave prices, money, weights and
measures, exports, the river trade, customs payments, wages and salaries, and the
calculation of imports, exports and terms of trade.

223 **Essai sur l'histoire du Saloum et du Rip.** (Essay on the history of
Saloum and Rip.)
Abdou Bouri Ba. *Bulletin de l'IFAN*, vol. 38(B), no. 4 (1976),
p. 812-60.

A lengthy compilation of material gathered from oral traditions from Saloum and Rip.
The subjects include Islam, family histories and social and political organization,
including information on the forty-nine rulers of Saloum, between 1493 and 1969.

224 **Le Grand Jolof (xiiie-xvie siècle).** (The Grand Jolof kingdom,
13th-16th centuries.)
Jean Boulègue. Blois, France: Façades, 1987. 207p. (Les anciens
royaumes wolof (Sénégal) vol. 1).

A reconstruction of the history of the Jolof kingdom using oral tradition and written
sources, which describes the caste and status systems, as well as the decline of the
kingdom which began with the extension of trade along the coast.

225 **Histoire de Boundou.** (History of Bundu.)
Moussa Kamara, edited and translated by Moustapha Ndiaye.
Bulletin de l'IFAN, vol. 37(B), no. 4 (1975), p. 784-816.

This paper presents an annotated translation of a history of an Islamic state in eastern
Senegal, written originally in Arabic in 1924. It contains information on the

genealogical origins of local ethnic groups and on rulers from the 17th to the 20th centuries.

226 **Histoire de la Sénégambie du XVe au XVIIIe siècle: un bilan.**
(Senegambian history from the 15th to the 18th centuries: an overview.)
Charles Becker. *Cahiers d'Etudes Africaines*, vol. 25, no. 2 (1985), p. 213-42.

A useful summary of the current state of knowledge of the precolonial history of the region, which describes the sources available (written, oral and archaeological), periodization and the important issues for future research.

227 **Histoire des Mandingues de l'Ouest. Le royaume du Gabou.** (History of the Western Manding. The kingdom of Gabou.)
Djibril Tamsir Niane. Paris: Editions Karthala [1988]. 221p.

An important study of a Western Mande kingdom in an area comparatively little studied, perhaps because it was divided between the British, the French and the Portuguese during the colonial period and since. The kingdom, which lay along the southern borders of Senegal with Guinea-Biseau and Guinea and which was long involved in the trade with Europe, originated in the 13th century and lasted until its conquest by the Peul in 1867. The chapters deal with Senegambia and the Mande world, the arrival of the Europeans, the origins of Gabou, relations with the Peul, the organization of the state around the capital Kansala, founded during the 17th century, the maintenance of Mande rule, despite the collapse of Mali to the East, Gabou society in the 18th century, animist religion, the end of the slave trade, and the political turmoil from 1800 onwards which resulted in the fall of the kingdom. At the end is a list of constituent states, and a bibliography.

228 **Un historien et anthropologue sénégalais: Shaikh Musa Kamara.**
(A Senegalese historian and anthropologist: Shaikh Musa Kamara.)
David Robinson. *Cahiers d'Etudes Africaines*, vol 28, no. 1 (1988), p. 89-116.

The paper surveys the main periods in the career of the distinguished Senegalese historian, Shaikh Musa Kamara, who wrote prolifically in Arabic on the region, and includes a complete list of his writings and the table of contents of his masterpiece, a lengthy study of the Fuuta Toro.

229 **History as identity: the Jaaxanke and the founding of Tuuba (Senegal).**
Lucy G. Quimby. *Bulletin de l'IFAN*, vol. 37, no. 3 (1975), p. 604-18.

This paper contains English translations of two 20th-century Arabic manuscripts, describing the foundation of the city in what is now Guinea, and the career of its founder, Karamoko Baa.

230 **A history of the Upper Guinea Coast 1545 to 1800.**
Walter Rodney. Oxford: Oxford University Press, 1970; New York: Monthly Review Press, [1980]. 283p.

The standard history of the coastal trade in the area to the south of the Gambia river by a leading Guyanese historian and political activist. It deals with the arrival of the Portuguese, the growth of slavery and the struggle between the European powers to control the slave trade, the rise of a class of mulatto traders and the impact on trade of the Islamic upheavals in the interior.

231 **The Holy War of Umar Tal.**
David Robinson. Oxford: Clarendon Press, 1985. 434p.

A standard history in English of Islamic politics in the Western Sudan in the mid-19th century, based on a wide range of materials both in French and African languages. Umar Tal was an Islamic reformer who managed both to create an empire in what is now Mali, and formulate a *modus vivendi* with the French in Senegal to the west. After introductory chapters which deal with the evidence and the history of the Muslim Peul, the central part of the book deals with Umar's career and the process of reform empire building. Two of the chapters, four and six, deal directly with Senegambia. The final section provides an interpretation of Umar's career and a comparison of his movement with that of the jihad [holy war] in Northern Nigeria. The book also contains an important forty-page list of sources.

232 **The impact of the Atlantic slave trade on the societies of the Western Sudan.**
Martin A. Klein. In: *The Atlantic slave trade: effects on economies, societies, and peoples in Africa, the Americas, and Europe.* Edited by Joseph E. Inikori, Stanley L. Engerman. Durham, North Carolina; London: Duke University Press, 1992, p. 25-47.

An invaluable summary of the debate between Curtin and his critics, notably Barry and Becker, over the place of slavery in the precolonial economy and its impact on African societies. Klein surveys the question of the price of slaves, the use of slaves within Africa, and the relationship between the slave trade and Islam. He concludes that the most important effect of the trade was on the precolonial state which itself depended on the trade and slave labour.

233 **Islam and the state of Kajoor: a case of successful resistance to jihad.**
Lucy Gallistel Colvin. *Journal of African History*, vol. 15, no. 4 (1974), p. 587-606.

The paper traces the course of three unsuccessful attempts at jihad in the coastal Wolof state of Kajoor (Kayor) in the late 18th century. The author argues that the reason for the jihad was not a struggle between Muslims and pagans but a bid for power by politically marginal clerical groups, and that they failed because their political networks were not sufficiently strong.

234 **The Islamic regime of Fuuta Tooro: an anthology of oral traditions transcribed in Pulaar and translated into English.**
Moustapha Kane, David Robinson (et al.). East Lansing, Michigan: African Studies Center, Michigan State University, 1979. 177p.
This collection consists of eighteen texts in Pulaar with a parallel English translation. They cover a range of issues at different historical periods, including the establishment and decline of the Islamic régime, French influence and conquest, and notable historical figures such as Umar Tal and Abdul Bukar. There is a short introduction to the region and the Pulaar language, and the bibliography provides useful information on sources.

235 **Jihad in West Africa: early phases and inter-relations in Mauritania and Senegal.**
Philip D. Curtin. *Journal of African History*, vol. 12, no. 1 (1971), p. 11-24.
This paper gives a concise account of the traditional division between the clerical and political leaders within Islam in the Western Sudan, and the series of holy wars from the 17th century onwards, which the author suggests may have been directly linked. One of the links in the chain was Malik Sy who founded the kingdom of Bundu in south-eastern Senegambia, probably around the end of the 17th century. For an alternative view, see item 243.

236 **Mandingo kingdoms of the Senegambia: traditionalism, Islam and European expansion.**
Charlotte A. Quinn. Evanston, Illinois: Northwestern University Press, 1972. 211p.
This standard history of Islam, state formation and European penetration along the Gambia river, based on research carried out during the 1960s, complements the studies of Klein and others by dealing with similar events and processes in an area further to the south. There are chapters on the organization of the Mandingo kingdoms, the rise of Islam in the Gambia, European settlements, the career of Maba (see also item 285), and the eventual partition of the region between the British and the French as the colonial powers imposed order amid the political chaos which their earlier trade in the area had helped to create.

237 **Les Maures et le Futa-Toro au XVIIIe siècle.** (The Moors and the Fuuta-Toro in the 18th century.)
Oumar Kane. *Cahiers d'Etudes Africaines*, vol. 14, no. 2 (1974), p. 237-52.
An account of the Fuuta-Toro, on the south side of the Senegal river to the east of Podor, in which the role of the Moors from the area to the north and their alliances with one or other of the factions were a constantly destabilizing factor in local politics.

238 **Notes sur les conditions écologiques en Sénégambie aux 17e et 18e siècles.** (Notes on the ecological conditions in Senegambia in the 17th and 18th centuries.)
Charles Becker. *African Economic History*, vol. 14 (1985), p. 167-216.
An important compilation of evidence on the environmental conditions in Senegambia during the early period of the slave trade. While admitting that the evidence is fragmentary, Becker concludes that it points to increasingly frequent droughts and famines, which in turn were related to migration and political instability. As a result of these factors, by the mid-18th century, the population was probably in serious decline.

239 **Ordres, castes et états en pays sérèr (Sénégal): essai d'interprétation d'un système politique en transition.** (Orders, castes and estates in Serer country, Senegal: an interpretative essay on a political system in transition.)
Gabriel Gosselin. *Canadian Journal of African Studies*, vol. 8, no. 1 (1974), p. 135-43.
A study of the changing power and social stratification systems among the Serer, in which the traditional system of orders and castes was weakened by colonialism.

240 **Les portes de l'or. Le royaume de Galam (Sénégal) de l'ère musulmane au temps de négriers (VIII-XVIIIe siècle).** (The golden gates. The kingdom of Galam, Senegal, from the Muslim era to the period of the slave traders, 8th-18th centuries.)
Abdoulaye Bathily. Paris: L'Harmattan, 1989. 379p.
Despite its small size, Galam played a major role in the region's history because of its location in an area rich in gold and iron, and therefore at the centre of the region's commercial networks. The system of production and exchange provided the foundation for the development of a state and class hierarchy which went into decline only during the 18th century when, as a result of the activities of slave traders, the kingdom's role in coastal and hinterland commerce was undermined.

241 **Pre-colonial trading networks and traders: the Diakhanke.**
Philip D. Curtin. In: *The development of indigenous trade and markets in West Africa.* Edited by Claude Meillassoux. London: Oxford University Press for the International African Institute, 1971, p. 228-39.
A discussion of the development of the Diakhanke (Jakhanke) Islamic trading network which flourished in the Senegambian region from the early 17th to the middle of the 19th centuries. Their influence eventually declined because of competition from other trading groups, the collapse of the slave trade and the threat to their Islamic prestige from the rise of the Tijaniyya brotherhood.

242 **The pre-nineteenth century political tradition of the Wolof.**
Victoria Bomba. *Bulletin de l'IFAN*, vol. 36(B), no. 1 (1974), p. 1-13.
A brief account based on oral traditions of the organization of the Wolof states of Jolof and Walo.

243 **The problem with Malik Sy and the foundation of Bundu.**
Michael Gomez. *Cahiers d'Etudes Africaines*, vol. 25, no. 4 (1985), p. 537-53.
Bundu was a small trading state in Eastern Senegal which flourished during the period of the slave trade, and on which both Curtin and Gomez have carried out historical research, and Malik Sy was its 17th-century founder. On the basis of the surviving accounts of his life, Gomez takes issue with Philip Curtin who argued that the foundation of the kingdom was the result of one of a series of related Islamic reform movements. Gomez argues that Sy's war was not a regular jihad, and that his assumption of the Muslim title *eliman* had little real meaning.

244 **La représentation des Sereer du nord-ouest dans les sources européennes (XVe-XIXe siècle).** (The representations of the north-western Serer in European sources, 15th-19th centuries.)
Charles Becker. *Journal des Africanistes*, vol. 55, no. 1-2 (1985), p. 165-85.
This paper is a re-evaluation of the early information available on the Serer, who were often portrayed as savagely independent from the 15th century onwards. Becker claims that this was misleading because most of the information available to Europeans came from Wolof guides and informants.

245 **Le royaume du Waalo: le Sénégal avant la conquête.** (The kingdom of Waalo: Senegal before the conquest.)
Boubacar Barry. Paris: Maspero, 1972. 393p.
After an introduction discussing the sources used, the first part of the book gives an economic, political and social picture of Walo in the 17th century. The second part deals with the arrival of the French and the period of slave trade, Islamic reform and political struggles within Walo, and with extension of French power in the 18th century. The final section deals with the period of colonial conquest from 1819 to 1859. Barry has also written a number of papers on Walo history including 'Le royaume du Walo du traité de Ngio en 1819 à la conquête de 1855' (The kingdom of Walo from the treaty of Ngio, 1819, to the conquest of 1855), *Bulletin de l' IFAN*, vol. 31(B), no. 2 (1969), p. 339-444; 'The subordination of power and the mercantile economy: the kingdom of Waalo, 1600-1831', in *The political economy of underdevelopment: dependence in Senegal*. Edited by Rita Cruise O'Brien (Beverly Hills, California; London: Sage Publications, 1979, p. 39-64. [Sage Series on African Modernization and Development, 3]).

246 **La royauté (*mansaya*) chez les Mandingues occidentaux, d'après leurs traditions orales.** (Kingship, *mansaya*, among the western Mandinka as reflected in their oral traditions.) Sékény-Mody Cissoko. *Bulletin de l'IFAN*, vol. 31(B), no. 2 (1969), p. 325-38.

An account of the small 'kingdoms' of the Mandinka of The Gambia and the Casamance, made up of small groups of villages and confederations of clans, which includes information on succession procedures in different villages, and the limitations of the power of the king.

247 **La Sénégambie du xv au xixe siècle: traite négrier, Islam et conquête coloniale.** (Senegambia from the 15th to the 19th century: slave trade, Islam and colonial conquest.) Boubacar Barry. Paris: Editions l'Harmattan, 1988. 432p.

Barry divides the history of the region into four periods: the period from the 15th to the 17th centuries when external trade was dominated by the Portuguese; the period of the slave trade in the 18th century; the period of 'legitimate' trade in the early 19th century; and the period of conquest and resistance in the late 19th century. This work includes a useful twenty-nine-page bibliography. Barry has also published a number of other general papers on the region, including 'Economic anthropology of precolonial Senegambia from the 15th through the 19th centuries' in *The uprooted of the Western Sahel*, by L. G. Colvin (et al.). (New York: Praeger, 1981. p. 25-57); 'Emiettement politique et dépendance économique dans l'espace géopolitique sénégambien du xv au xvii siècle' (Political decline and economic dependence in the Senegambia geopolitical region from the 15th to the 17th century), *Revue Française d'Histoire d'Outre-Mer*, vol. 68, no. 1/4 (1981), p. 37-52.

248 **Slavery, Islam and the Jakhanke people of West Africa.** L. O. Sanneh. *Africa*, vol. 46, no. 1 (1976), p. 80-97.

An examination of the status of slaves in Islamic societies, and of the role of slavery among the Jakhanke, for whom slaves played a vital role as labourers or concubines. The paper also describes the effect on these clerics of the end of the slave trade.

249 **Le Soudan occidental au temps des grands empires xie-xvie siècles.** (Western Sudan in the time of the great empires, 11th-16th centuries.) Djibril Tamsir Niane. Paris: Présence Africaine, 1975. 271p.

Examines social, political economic and intellectual life in the great empires of the middle ages, which rose and fell in the area of Western Sudan, including present-day Senegal. The work is well illustrated with drawings and some excellent black-and-white plates.

250 **A tentative chronology of Futa Toro from the sixteenth through the nineteenth centuries.**
David Robinson, Philip Curtin, James Johnson.   *Cahiers d'Etudes Africaines*, vol. 12, no. 4 (1972), p. 555-92.
Attempts to make sense of the chronology of the Middle Valley of the Senegal river in the period up to 1901 by sifting through a mass of often contradictory evidence from oral, Arabic and archival sources.

251 **Theoretical issues in historical international politics: the case of the Senegambia.**
Lucie Gallistel Colvin.   *Journal of Interdisciplinary History*, vol. 8, no. 1 (1977) p. 23-44.
An overview of the study of international politics in Senegambia during the precolonial period, this paper argues that spiritual and cultural factors have often been neglected in favour of analyses of power.

252 **La traite atlantique des esclaves et ses effets économiques et sociaux en Afrique: la cas [sic] du Galam, royaume de l'hinterland sénégambien au dix-huitième siècle.** (The Atlantic slave trade and its economic and social effects in Africa: the case of Galam, a kingdom in the Senegambian hinterland in the 18th century.)
Abdoulaye Bathily.   *Journal of African History*, vol. 27, no. 2 (1986), p. 269-293.
Continuing the debate on the severity of the local effects of the slave trade, this paper looks at the case of Galam, which, during the 18th century, had an unusually large French population due to its role as an entrepôt in the slave trade, the stimulus for which came from European demand rather than local warfare. The conclusion is that the effects of the trade were more severe than is often presented, both in relation to the drain on the population and the impact on the food supply, due to the necessity of feeding the slaves awaiting transportation.

253 **The uses of oral tradition in Senegambia: Maalik Sii and the foundation of Bundu.**
Philip D. Curtin.   *Cahiers d'Etudes Africaines*, vol. 15, no. 2 (1975), p. 189-202.
This paper is a comparison and analysis of a large number of oral accounts, many collected by Curtin himself, of the life of the founder of the state of Bundu in eastern Senegal in the 1690s, and the common elements and discrepancies between them. Curtin argues that these accounts are more valuable for the light they shed on the legitimization of political power in the region than for their historical detail.

254 **The Western Atlantic coast 1600-1800.**
J. Suret-Canale. In: *History of West Africa*, vol 1. Edited by J. F. A.
Ajayi, Michael Crowder. London: Longmans, 1971. p. 387-440.
A broad survey of the impact of European trade on the region and the growth of
centralized states. It includes a detailed discussion of the early history of the Wolof-
Serer states, the Fuuta Toro, the Gambia river valley, Bundu and the Casamance, and
ends with an assessment of the often contradictory effects on local politics of the
European presence.

255 **The Wolof kingdom of Kayor.**
V. Monteil. In: *West African Kingdoms in the 19th century*. Edited by
D. Forde, P. Kaberry. London: Oxford University Press, 1967,
p. 260-81.
An outline of the history of the Wolof kingdom of Kayor, a vassal of Jolof until the
16th century, together with its political system and the position of the Damel or ruler.
The first sections of the paper describe royal rituals and the social structure of the
kingdom, including the positions of the slaves and the *tyeddo* or warrior class. The
later sections discuss the career of the 19th-century ruler Lat Dyor, his resistance to
the French railway (to which he had in fact secretly agreed), and the legends
surrounding his death.

Les Diakhanké: histoire d'une dispersion. (The Jakhanke: history of a
diaspora.)
See item no. 186.

The Jakhanke: the history of an Islamic clerical people of the Senegambia.
See item no. 187.

Le pouvoir politique en Sénégambie des origines à la conquête coloniale.
(Political power in Senegambia from its origins to the colonial conquest.)
See item no. 437.

**Pouvoir politique traditionnel en Afrique occidentale: essais sur les institutions
politiques précoloniales.** (Traditional political power in West Africa: essays
on precolonial political institutions.)
See item no. 438.

European settlements and companies

256 **L'administration du Sénégal de 1781 à 1784: l'affaire Dumontet.**
(The administration of Senegal from 1781 to 1784: the Dumontet
affair.)
Léon-Pierre Raybaud. *Annales Africaines*, vol. 15 (1968), p. 113-72.
The first part of a two-part paper, this is a lengthy and detailed study, based on
primary sources, of the administrative and commercial system of Senegal during the

governorship of A. Dumontet, a period marked by the exposure of irregularities, an investigation of the government and demands for reform.

257 **L'administration du Sénégal de 1781 à 1784: deuxième partie.**
(The administration of Senegal from 1781 to 1784: Part II.)
Léon-Pierre Raybaud. *Annales Africaines*, vol. 16 (1969), p. 173-210.
The second part of the paper (q.v.) deals with issues which developed during the administration of M. le Comte de Repentigny (1784-85): they relate to the problems, due to mismanagement and economic decline, of the Compagnie de la Guyane, which was responsible for administration, and the competition between the British and the French in the region, with the French succeeding in recovering the island of Gorée.

258 **Assimilation in eighteenth-century Senegal.**
John D. Hargreaves. *Journal of African History*, vol. 6, no. 2 (1965), p. 177-84.
A study based on archival and secondary sources of the *habitants*, free persons of African or part-African descent and influenced by French culture, and their assimilation into French colonial society in the 18th century through employment, trade, marriage, and as concubines. The paper focuses on assimilation through religion (most *habitants* were Roman Catholic, and remained so even under the period of British rule), involvement in civic affairs, and the conscious acceptance of European values.

259 **Commercial rivalries and French policy on the Senegal River, 1831-1858.**
Margaret O. McLane. *African Economic History*, vol. 15 (1986), p. 39-67.
The paper relates the expansion of French influence along the Senegal river valley to the competition between merchants from Bordeaux and Marseilles over control of the local trade, mainly in gum arabic. French involvement in the interior increased as Bordeaux merchants established posts further up river to outflank their trading rivals.

260 **La Compagnie du Sénégal.** (The Senegal Company.)
Abdoulaye Ly. Paris: Présence Africaine, 1958. 310p.
A very detailed account of the Senegal Company in the last quarter of the 17th century, which did much to lay the foundations for later French colonial control of the region. It deals with the structure of the Atlantic trade, the rise and fall of the Senegal Company itself, and with its internal organization and finances. Thère is a useful ten-page bibliography with details of French provincial archives.

261 **The establishment of protectorate administration in Senegal, 1890-1904.**
H. O. Idowu. *Journal of the Historical Society of Nigeria*, vol. 4, no. 2 (1968), p. 247-67.
A study of the different systems of administration which the French operated in the four communes, based on the ideology of assimilation, with the hinterland administered as a protectorate. One of the most contentious issues in this dual system of administration, which lasted until 1920, was finance: although separate, the finances of the communes were in effect subsidized by the protectorate.

262 **Les établissements français sur la côte occidentale d'Afrique de 1758 à 1809.** (French companies on the west coast of Africa from 1758 to 1809.)
Leonce Jore. Paris: Librairie G.-P Maisonneuve et Larose, 1963. 477p.

This work describes the history of French trading houses and establishments from the middle of the 18th to the beginning of the 19th century, following on from the account of Delcourt (item 264) for the earlier period. It deals with their government and organization during a period when ownership was contested with the British after the latter occupied Gorée and Saint-Louis during the Seven Years' War.

263 **La fondation de Dakar (1845-1857-1869).** (The foundation of Dakar, 1845-1857-1869.)
Edited by Jacques Charpey. Paris: Larose, 1958. 596p. (Collection des documents inédits pour servir à l'histoire de l'Afrique occidentale française, 1).

A large-scale compendium of archival documents, and the major source on the 19th-century history of the capital. The documents are organized chronologically into chapters relating initially to the villages of Cap-Vert (1845-56) and later to the development of the town (1862-66) and its port (1862-67). The volume is beautifully illustrated and contains nine maps depicting the growth of the town. It also contains a brief editorial introduction and lengthy appendices on the founders of the city (with biographical information), a chronology and general subject matter.

264 **La France et les établissements français au Sénégal entre 1713 et 1763: la Compagnie des Indes et le Sénégal: la guerre de la gomme.** (France and French companies in Senegal between 1713 and 1763: the Indies and Senegal Company: the gum war.)
André Delcourt. Dakar: IFAN, 1952. 432p. (Mémoires 17).

A major study of the French trading establishments in the 18th century, their impact on local politics and trade, and the competition with the British and the Dutch, concentrating on the Compagnie des Indes et le Sénégal. It includes appendices, maps and a wide-ranging bibliography.

265 **Gorée au XVIIIe siècle: l'appropriation du sol.** (Gorée in the 18th century: the appropriation of land.)
Marie-Hélène Knight. *Revue Française d'Histoire d'Outre-mer*, vol. 64, no. 234 (1977), p. 33-54.

After the French occupied Gorée in 1677 the area attracted an African population, but there were no procedures by which they could obtain land. Through an examination of the measures by which this situation was corrected in 1763 and 1776, this paper sheds light both on the relations between Africans and Europeans during this period, and also on the role of the wealthy and influential *signares*.

266 **Gorée: six siècles d'histoire.** (Gorée: six centuries of history.)
Jean Delcourt. Dakar: Clairafrique, [n.d.], 1982. 101p.
A well-illustrated popular history by a priest and archivist. The main sections deal with the position of the island on the spice routes to the east, the period of Portuguese and Dutch domination, and the long period of French control, with occasional intrusions by the British, until Gorée's decline with the rise of Saint-Louis and Dakar on the mainland. Delcourt's *La turbulente histoire de Gorée* (The turbulent history of Gorée), (Dakar: Clairafrique [1982]. 101p.), covers similar ground and includes a Senghor preface.

267 **Instructions générales donnés de 1763 à 1870 aux gouverneurs des établissements français en Afrique occidentale, tomes I & II.** (General directives given from 1763 to 1870 to the governors of the French establishments in West Africa, volumes 1 and 2.)
Christian Scheffer. Paris: Librairie Ancienne Honoré Champion, 1921. 2 vols.
These two massive volumes, forming one of the major sources on the company period in Senegal, contain descriptions of the general directives and official communications between the French government and the administration in Senegal and other territories. The first volume covers the period from 1763 to 1831, and the second from 1831 to 1870.

268 **Un navire de commerce sur la côte Sénégambienne en 1685.** (A trading ship on the coast of Senegambia in 1685.)
Abdoulaye Ly. Dakar: IFAN, 1964. 66p. (Catalogues et Documents xvii).
Abdoulaye Ly provides an introduction to the text taken from a ship's log belonging to the vessel *l'Amitié*, which sailed from France to the coast of Senegal and neighbouring countries in 1685. The text of the log is presented along with a commentary. The vessel was involved in trading on behalf of La Compagnie du Sénégal for gold and slaves.

269 **Saint-Louis du Sénégal, ville aux mille visages.** (Saint-Louis, Senegal: town with a thousand faces.)
Félix Brigaud, Jean Vast. Dakar: Clairafrique, 1987. 170p.
Another popular and well-illustrated history from the same stable as the Gorée volumes, this time with a preface by Abdou Diouf. The book chronicles the evolution of the small trading port into the national capital, and the later chapters deal with the history of the local churches.

270 **Saint-Louis du Sénégal au début du XIXe siècle: du comptoir à la ville.** (Saint-Louis, Senegal, at the start of the 19th century: from trading post to town.)
Alain Sinou. *Cahiers d'Etudes Africaines*, vol. 29, no. 115/6 (1989), p. 377-95.
An account of the rise of Saint-Louis, at the mouth of the Senegal river, which was for many years the administrative capital of Senegal until it was eclipsed by Dakar in the 20th century.

271 **The *signares* of Saint-Louis and Gorée: women entrepreneurs in eighteenth-century Senegal.**
George E. Brooks. In: *Women in Africa: studies in social and economic change.* Edited by Nancy J. Hafkin, Edna G. Bay. Stanford, California: Stanford University Press, 1976, p. 19-44.

An interesting study of the *signares*, the wealthy and influential women of African or mixed descent who formed social and economic relationships with European men in the 18th and early 19th centuries. They allowed their partners access to African commercial networks, and acted as interpreters, in addition to becoming wealthy traders and leaders of society in their own right.

272 **The trade in gum arabic: prelude to French conquest in Senegal.**
James L. A. Webb, Jr. *Journal of African History*, vol. 26, no. 2/3 (1985), p. 149-68.

A description of crises in the trade which was the mainstay of the coastal economy between the decline of the slave trade and the rise of the groundnut industry.

273 **La vie à Gorée de 1677 à 1789.** (Life on Gorée from 1677 to 1789.)
Marie-Hélène Knight-Baylac. *Revue Française d'Histoire d'Outre-Mer*, vol. 57, no. 209 (1970), p. 377-420.

A lengthy paper on life and society on the island during the late 17th and 18th centuries, describing the relative positions of the main social groups of Europeans, mulattos (including *signares*), free Africans and slaves awaiting export. Eventually the island's dependence on outside sources of food led the population to shift to the mainland, and to settle around Dakar.

274 **La vie quotidienne à Saint-Louis par ses archives (1779-1809).** (Daily life in Saint-Louis seen through its archives, 1779-1809.)
Françoise Deroure. *Bulletin de l'IFAN*, vol. 26(B), no. 3/4 (1963), p. 397-439.

Describes life in the town, based on archives and travellers' reports, during a period in which control switched from France to Britain (from 1809 to 1816) and back again. The paper deals with the port and trade, religion, Afro-European relations, slavery, leisure, and the town's defences.

Les débuts de l'enseignement en Afrique francophone: Jean Dard et l'Ecole Mutuelle de Saint-Louis de Sénégal. (The beginnings of education in French-speaking Africa: Jean Dard and the *Ecole Mutuelle at* Saint-Louis, Senegal.) *See* item no. 592.

The colonial period: the 19th century

275 **A propos de l'émancipation des esclaves au Sénégal en 1848.** (On the emancipation of the slaves in Senegal in 1848.)
Roger Pasquier. *Revue Française d'Histoire d'Outre-Mer*, vol. 54, no. 194/7 (1967), p. 87-150.

An important study of the effects on Senegalese society and economy of the abolition of slavery, within the context of the decline of the trading-post system and the changing power relations between the mulatto *habitants* who had hitherto dominated the economy, and the Europeans who were to dominate it in future. As a sequel to Pasquier's 1967 paper, see: 'L'abolition de l'esclavage au Sénégal: l'attitude de l'administration française (1848-1905)' (The abolition of slavery in Senegal: the attitude of the French administration, 1848-1905), by François Renault, *Revue Française d'Histoire d'Outre-Mer*, vol. 58, no. 210 (1971), p. 5-81. Renault's paper describes the survival of slavery in one guise or another after its legal abolition, as the 19th-century wars generated new prisoners. De facto abolition came only with the turn of the 20th century.

276 **L'affaire Chautemps (avril 1904) et la suppression de l'esclavage de case au Sénégal.** (The Chautemps affair of April 1904 and the suppression of household slavery in Senegal.)
M'Baye Guèye. *Bulletin de l'IFAN*, vol. 27(B), no. 3/4 (1964), p. 543-59.

Chautemps was a French administrator who brought a group of local chiefs to trial for selling children, only to be assassinated for his pains. This paper, based on archival sources, describes the events surrounding his death, which helped bring about the abolition of slavery in Senegal.

277 **Assimilation in 19th century Senegal.**
H. Oludare Idowu. *Cahiers d'Etudes Africaines*, vol. 9, no. 2 (1969), p. 194-218.

A survey of the legislation in the late 18th and early 19th centuries which formed the basis for the assimilation policy, and of the period from 1871 when it was put into operation, with the establishment of the *Conseil général*. The requirement that councillors had to be literate in French was restrictive, and in general very few Senegalese became assimilated at all.

278 **Chiefs and clerics: Abdul Bokar Kan and Futa Toro 1853-1891.**
David Robinson. Oxford: Clarendon Press, 1975. 238p.

A major historical study of the social and political upheavals which occurred among the Tukulor of Fuuta Toro, northern Senegal, between the establishment of an Islamic state at the end of the 18th century and French military intervention from the 1860s onwards. It centres around the career of Abdul Bokar Kan, who attempted to restore autonomy in the region, despite the encroachment of Umar Tal from the east and Faidherbe and the French from the west. The appendices include data on population and population movements, the texts of treaties, a chronology of the main events, and lists of office holders.

279 **La colonie du Séñgal au temps de Brière de l'Isle (1876-1881).** (The colony of Senegal in the time of Brière de l'Isle, 1876-1881.)
Francine N'Diaye. *Bulletin de l'IFAN*, vol. 30(B), no. 2 1968, p. 463-512.

This paper gives an account of the colony and its administration during a time of great fluctuations in power. It focuses on the the political in-fighting involving the governor in conflict with the local trading establishment, whose confidence he gradually lost. After a virulent press campaign attacking him for failing to put an end to slavery, he was finally recalled to France.

280 **The conquest of the Western Sudan: a study in French military imperialism.**
A. S. Kanya-Forstner. Cambridge, England: Cambridge University Press, 1969. 297p.

Standard history of French military expansion in the region, the early chapters of which deal with events in and around Senegal, including the careers of Faidherbe and Umar Tal, and the debate over the construction of the Senegal-Niger railway.

281 **Conquête et résistance des peuples de Casamance, (1850-1920).** (Conquest and resistance among the peoples of the Casamance, 1850-1920.)
Christian Roche. Dakar: Nouvelles Editions Africaines, 1976. 391p. maps. bibliog.

The major history of the Casamance area during the period of colonization, this is a lengthy study of the European impact and different patterns of resistance among the local peoples, the Muslim Malinke, the Joola and Balant of the forest areas and the Peul. It discusses life in the region up to the mid-19th century, early Casamance resistance to colonial expansion, the career of Muusa Moola, and the impact of the First World War. Well illustrated with maps, the book also contains a sixteen-page bibliography with a lengthy list of archival sources, and nine appendices. This work also appeared as *Histoire de la Casamance: conquête et résistance: 1850-1920* (History of the Casamance: conquest and resistance 1850-1920) (Paris: Editions Karthala, 1985. 401p.).

282 **The establishment of elective institutions in Senegal, 1869-1880.**
H. O. Idowu. *Journal of African History*, vol. 9, no. 2 (1968), p. 261-77.

A study of the unique political institutions which developed in Senegal in the late 19th century: municipal government, with an elected general council and representation in the French parliament.

283 **France in Senegal in the nineteenth century: coastal trade in the four communes.**
Rita Cruise O'Brien. *Tarikh*, vol. 2, no. 4 (1969), p. 21-31.

A concise and informative account of the histories of the four 'communes', Gorée, Saint-Louis, Rufisque and Dakar during the 19th century, and the way in which they adapted to changes in the regional economy.

284   **French 'Islamic' policy and practice in late 19th-century Senegal.**
David Robinson.   *Journal of African History*, vol. 29, no. 3 (1988),
p. 431-35.
A re-examination of French policy towards Muslims in Senegal between 1850 and
1900. The French consistently opposed militant Islamic states whose policies conflicted
with their own interests, but were much more tolerant of older states with which they
had coexisted for a long time, and on which they relied for cadres of administrative
chiefs.

285   **Islam and imperialism in Senegal: Sine-Saloum, 1847-1914.**
Martin A. Klein.   Edinburgh: Edinburgh University Press, 1968. 285p.
A major study of the incorporation of the Sine-Saloum area and particularly the Serer
people into the French colony during the second half of the 19th century, by one of the
most important writers in English on Senegalese history. It contains detailed
discussions of the local political structure of the area, the development of European
involvement, the careers of Faidherbe and Ma Ba, and the scaling down of the French
colonial effort after 1870. These efforts revived, and book ends with an account of the
final French military annexation, the extension of the railway and the rationalization of
the colonial administrative order. At the end are extensive notes, a glossary and a
useful thirteen-page bibliography. Klein has published a number of papers covering
similar ground including 'Chiefship in Sine-Saloum (Senegal), 1887-1914', in *Colonialism
in Africa 1870-1960 3: profiles of change*. Edited by Victor Turner (Cambridge,
England: Cambridge University Press, 1971, p. 49-73); and 'Colonial rule and
structural change: the case of Sine-Saloum', in *The political economy of underdevelopment: dependence in Senegal*. Edited by Rita Cruise O'Brien (Beverly Hills, California;
London: Sage Publications, 1979, p. 65-99) (Sage Series on African Modernization and
Development 3).

286   **The merchants and General Faidherbe: aspects of French expansion in
Senegal in the 1850s.**
Leland Conley Barrows.   *Revue Française d'Histoire d'Outre-Mer*,
vol. 61, no. 223 (1974), p. 236-83.
An account of the links between the merchants of Bordeaux and French political
expansion in West Africa. Faidherbe's appointment as governor in 1854 came after
Bordeaux merchants had petitioned the Senegalese governor to use the military to
protect both French traders and peanut farmers from attack, and during his
administration mercantile interests were well served. Faidherbe's career is discussed
further in 'Faidherbe and Senegal: a critical discussion' *African Studies Review*, vol. 19,
no. 1 (1976). p. 95-117, also based on the author's doctoral research.

287   **Métis et colons: la famille Devès et l'émergence politique des Africains
au Sénégal 1881-97.** (Creoles and settlers: the Devès family and the
political emergence of Africans in Senegal 1881-97.)
François Manchuelle.   *Cahiers d'Etudes Africaines*, vol. 24, no. 4
(1984), p. 477-504.
Examines economic rivalry and political intrigue in Senegal in the latter part of the
19th century, focusing on the fortunes of a Creole family at a time when the Creole
communities of Saint-Louis and Gorée were deeply divided, and in which their
dominant position in the colony was threatened by the arrival of French immigrants.

288 **Le mise en valeur du Sénégal de 1817 à 1854.** (The development of
Senegal from 1817 to 1854.)
Georges Hardy.   Paris: Emile Larose, 1921. 376p.
Provides a detailed account, based on a wide range of sources, of a neglected period of
Senegalese history from the French takeover in 1817 to the arrival of Faidherbe. It
concentrates on the careers and work of Julien Schmaltz and Jean-François Roger,
both of whose plans for developing the region, through colonization or the
development of agriculture, were ultimately unsuccessful. For a while the role of the
colony was simply as a trading post, until an economic and political crisis in the 1850s
launched the career of Faidherbe. Despite its age this remains the standard history of
this period. In addition to the lengthy bibliography there is an index of names.

289 **A nineteenth century Fulbe state.**
Charlotte A. Quinn.   *Journal of African History*, vol. 12, no. 3 (1971),
p. 427-40.
Based on archival sources and oral history, this work describes the Fulbe Firdu state
created in the region between the Gambia river and the Fouta Djallon by Alfa and
Musa Molo, in the late 19th century. It describes Musa Molo's adaptations to the
advent of colonial rule, eventually through settling in The Gambia.

290 **Ouali N'Dao: the exile of Alboury N'Diaye.**
Eunice A. Charles.   *African Historical Studies*, vol. 4, no. 2 (1971),
p. 373-82.
This paper is based on the recollections of Ouali N'Dao, who had accompanied
Alboury, the ruler of the Jolof until 1890, into exile. Alboury, an able ruler who
early in his career had cooperated with the French, later opposed them, and migrated
with his followers to the east to escape their advance. He died in exile in Niger.

291 **La politique coloniale française à l'égard de la bourgeoisie commerçante
sénégalaise (1820-1960).** (French colonial policy with regard to the
Senegalese merchant middle class [1820-1960].)
Samir Amin.   In: *The development of indigenous trade and markets in
West Africa.* Edited by Claude Meillassoux.   London: Oxford
University Press for the International African Institute, 1971, p. 361-76.
A concise summary of the history of the commercial classes in Senegal, which argues
that, although until 1900 the French colonial authorities had supported the growth of
an African merchant class, in the 20th century they undermined the merchants'
position in favour of colonial firms, the Lebanese and the 'petty whites'. Amin's
conclusion is that the processes of capital accumulation which operate in Senegal have
allowed a transfer of wealth to the developed economies and have prevented a strong
local commercial class from developing. Amin covers similar ground elsewhere,
including 'La bourgeoisie d'affaires sénégalaise' (The Senegalese business classes),
Homme et Société, vol. 12 (1969), p. 29-41.

292 **La représentation du Sénégal au Parlement français sous la Seconde République (1848-1851).** (The representation of Senegal in the French Parliament under the Second Republic, 1848-1851.)
Saliou Mbaye. *Bulletin de l'IFAN*, vol. 38(B), no. 3 (1976), p. 515-51.

A study, based on Senegalese archives, of the careers and times of two largely forgotten figures, Durand Barthélemy Valantin, and John Sleighth, the first deputies from Senegal, elected in 1848 and 1851 respectively.

293 **Senegal: a study in French assimilation policy.**
Michael Crowder. London: Methuen 1967. 2nd ed. 104p.

A concise and still valuable study of French assimilation policies and African reactions to them. Chapters on assimilation in practice and French reactions to it are followed by an account of political reforms in French West Africa after 1945 and the development by African intellectuals and leaders, such as Senghor, of concepts such as negritude. The book ends with accounts of the transition to independence and the failure of the Mali Federation, the status of the French in Senegal, and inter-ethnic relations among the Senegalese Africans in the aftermath of independence.

294 **Le Sénégal: la France dans l'Afrique occidentale.** (Senegal: France in West Africa.)
Louis Léon César Faidherbe. Nedeln: Kraus Reprint, 1974. 2nd ed. 501p.

The major source on the French expansion into the West African interior by the man who orchestrated the colonial development. Faidherbe was governor of Senegal from 1854 to 1861, and again between 1863 and 1865. This work dates from later in his career (1889) when he was a member of the French Senate. The book is divided into two parts, the first dealing with the period of the trading companies and the slave trade, and the second with the period from the suppression of slavery in the French colonies in 1848, through the periods of Faidherbe's governorships, French penetration and the military campaigns in the interior, up to the late 1880s. Within each part, the narrative is continuous, but a lengthy table of contents at the end provides a summary.

295 **Le Sénégal sous le Second Empire: naissance d'un empire colonial (1850-1871).** (Senegal under the Second Empire: birth of a colonial empire [1850-1871].)
Yves-Jean Saint Martin. Paris: Editions Karthala, 1989. 607p.

This important work is based on Saint-Martin's doctorat d'Etat thesis presented in 1980. The period 1850 to 1871, dominated by the personality of Governor Faidherbe, saw the territory of Senegambia transformed under the influence of the early European colonial missions and the development of a French colonial empire with discrete boundaries. Primarily a political and military history, the book describes the Senegambia region in 1850, and the French attempts to create a French Senegambia. Political and economic interests in metropolitan France supported such developments, particularly as French trading companies benefited from growing commercial links. The book describes the circumstances which undermined French political ambitions and the policies which subsequently laid the foundations for the present-day nation of Senegal.

296 **Senegambia – Mahmadou Lamine.**
B. Olatunji Oloruntimehin. In: *West African resistance: the military response to colonial occupation.* Edited by Michael Crowder. London: Hutchinson University Library for Africa, 1978, 2nd ed., p. 80-110.
An account of the struggle by the Sarakole of south-eastern Senegal, led by Lamine, to free the area from political domination by the Tukulor empire to the east and the French to the west. Lamine's success in organizing the local people led to an alliance between the Tukulor and the French, and his defeat at Toubakouta in 1887.

297 **Shaikh Amadu Ba and jihad in Jolof.**
Eunice A. Charles. *International Journal of African Historical Studies*, vol. 8, no. 3 (1975), p. 367-82.
An account of the career of the Islamic leader who contributed much to the Islamization of the Wolof by conquering the kingdom of Jolof in a holy war in 1870. He died in another war five years later, defeated by an alliance of other rulers in the region who feared his power.

298 **Slavery and emancipation in Senegal's peanut basin: the 19th and 20th centuries.**
Bernard Moitt. *International Journal of African Historical Studies*, vol. 22 (1989), p. 27-50.
An important study of the end of slavery in Senegal at the start of the colonial period. The paper discusses institutions of slavery in the precolonial period, the origins of slaves and the routes within the region along which they were transported, French policy towards slavery and emancipation, and the options open to freed slaves, some of whom joined the Mouride brotherhood, and some of whom became migrant labourers.

299 **Slavery, emancipation and labour migration in West Africa: the case of the Soninke.**
François Manchuelle. *Journal of African History*, vol. 30, no. 1 (1989), p. 89-106.
Discusses changes in the organization of labour among the Soninke during the 19th century. Slavery was gradually replaced by wage labour migration, preparing the way for the development of the groundnut industry.

300 **Slavery, groundnuts, and European capitalism in the Wuli kingdom of Senegambia, 1820-1930.**
Peter Maurice Weil. *Research in Economic Anthropology*, vol. 6 (1984), p. 77-119.
A study of social stratification, focusing on changes in, and the eventual decline of slavery during the 19th and early 20th centuries in Wuli, a Mandinka state on the Gambia river, now divided between Senegal and The Gambia. The paper contains a useful overview of social stratification in the region, and a useful bibliography.

301 **Une source de l'histoire coloniale du Sénégal: les rapports de situation politiques (1874-1891).** (A source for Senegalese colonial history: the reports on the political situation, 1874-1891.)
Yves Saint Martin. *Revue Française d'Histoire d'Outre-Mer*, vol. 52, no. 187 (1965), p. 153-224.

A discussion of the potential usefulness for historians of the reports on the local political situation which were sent by Governors of Senegal to the French Ministry of the Navy and the Colonies during the late 19th century, and which are preserved in the Dakar archives. The paper contains a description of the reports and the ministerial responses to them, sketches of governors of the period, and case studies in which they are used to shed light on the histories of Walo, Kayor, Jolof and Fuuta Toro in the 1870s. There are also two maps, four charts and extensive notes.

302 **Les troupes du Sénégal de 1816 à 1890. Tome I. Soldats au Sénégal du Colonel Schmaltz au Général Faidherbe (1816-1865).** (The troops of Senegal from 1816 to 1890. vol 1. Soldiers in Senegal from Colonel Schmaltz to General Faidherbe, 1816-1865.)
Pierre Gentil.   Dakar: Les Nouvelles Editions Africaines, 1978. 187p.

A large-scale study of 19th-century Senegalese military history by a former colonial administrator, based on a doctoral thesis. This first volume presents a detailed account of the use of African troops by the French up to and including the Faidherbe governorship. A second volume deals with the period from Colonel Pinet Laprade to Colonel Dodds (1856-90).

The colonial period: the 20th century

303 **Beyond resistance and collaboration: Amadu Bamba and the Murids of Senegal.**
David Robinson.   *Journal of Religion in Africa*, vol. 21, no. 2 (1991), p. 149-71.

An account of the career of Amadu Bamba, the founder of the Mouride order who, paradoxically, is remembered both for his resistance to, and collaboration with, the French colonial government. Robinson argues that the image of resistance was largely created by the French themselves by repeatedly exiling the religious leader. Collaboration with the régime came later and was developed further by Amadu Bamba's successors.

304 **Colonial conscripts: the *Tirailleurs Sénégalais* in French West Africa, 1857-1960.**
Myron Eschenberg.   London: James Currey; Portsmouth, New Hampshire: Heinemann, 1991. 236p.

This is a social history of the men who served in the Tirailleurs Sénégalais regiments of the French colonial army, and the author examines the contradictory position in which these men often found themselves. Partly based on surveys and interviews conducted by the author with veterans and ex-servicemen from various former French colonies (the regiment was not exclusively made up of Senegalese) the book sets their experiences within the wider social and political context of labour, migration and history.

305 **Dakar pendant la deuxième guerre mondiale: problèmes de surpeuplement.** (Dakar during the Second World War: problems of overpopulation.)
Denise Bouche. *Revue Française d'Histoire d'Outre-Mer*, vol. 65, no. 3 (1978), p. 423-38.

A review of the history and development of Dakar, and the problems of disease, shortage and overcrowding encountered during the Second World War.

306 **Double impact: France and Africa in the age of imperialism.**
Edited by G. Wesley Johnson. Westport, Connecticut; London: Greenwood Press, 1985. 407p.

This fascinating volume investigates the influences of France and Africa on each other with respect to their social, cultural, political, economic and artistic lives. There are contributions from some of the most eminent West Africanists, and many of the chapters relate to Senegal. They cover subjects such as the African influence on French colonial railways, the political role of Léopold Senghor in Paris, the impact of Senegalese educated élites on the French, the French impact on Senegalese goldsmiths, and the main currents in Franco-African literature.

307 **The emergence of black politics in Senegal: the struggle for power in the four communes 1900-1920.**
G. Wesley Johnson, Jr. Stanford, California: Stanford University Press, 1971. 260p.

The standard account of the origins of African nationalism in Senegal in the struggles for political power between the urban Africans, the French and the Creoles. The first part contains useful background chapters on the history of the colony, the evolution of local government, French colonial rule and African political rights. The second part deals with the successive attempts of the French and Creoles to dominate local politics, and with the 'African awakening' expressed in the growth of Islamic radicalism, and the ambitions of Senegal's educated Africans. The later chapters centre around the career of Blaise Diagne, who won the election to the deputyship in 1914. Johnson concludes that the African's success in their quest for political power and recognition was an important step toward the political independence of all French-speaking Africa. This is also dealt with in the author's paper 'The ascendancy of Blaise Diagne and the beginning of African politics in Senegal', *Africa*, vol. 36, no. 3 (1966), p. 235-52.

308 **Fantasia of the *Photothèque*: French postcard views of colonial Senegal.**
David Prochaska. *African Arts*, vol. 24, no. 4 (1991), p. 40-7, 98.

A beautifully illustrated overview of the postcard industry in Senegal, which accounted for over two-thirds of the nearly 9,000 cards issued in West Africa during the colonial period. The article describes the market for the cards, the firms which produced them, and the main genres: ethnic and racial types, views of places, women, the world of work, social life, and political or historical events.

309 **French West Africa and decolonization.**
Yves Person. In: *The transfer of power in Africa: decolonization,
1940-1960.* Edited by E. Prosser Gifford, William Roger Lewis. New
Haven, Connecticut: Yale University Press, 1982. p. 141-72.
A concise survey of the decolonization process in the region from 1945 to 1960, dealing
with the post-war political order, the emergence of new political parties, and the
failure of attempts at federation.

310 **French-speaking tropical Africa.**
Ruth Schachter Morgenthau, Lucy Creevy Behrman. In: *The
Cambridge history of Africa: Volume 8, from c. 1940 to c. 1975.* Edited
by Michael Crowder. Cambridge, England: Cambridge University
Press, 1984. p. 615-73.
This chapter gives a general account of French withdrawal from its African colonies,
and the period immediately after independence. It deals with formal decolonization,
the development of political parties leading to independence, political difficulties in the
new states, social, economic and cultural change, and international relations. As the
final section makes clear, French economic hegemony in the new states was not
seriously challenged, and yet by the mid-1970s new patterns of regional cooperation
were beginning to emerge.

311 **From adversaries to comrades-in-arms: West Africans and the French
military 1885-1918.**
Charles John Balesi. Waltham, Massachusetts: Crossroads Press,
African Studies Association, 1979. 182p.
An account of the recruitment of West Africans by the French army during the early
colonial period, written by a French soldier who later became a historian. The book
focuses on the recruitment of African troops after pacification, and their role in the
First World War during which 250,000 Africans fought in France.

312 **Le Front Populaire au Sénégal (mai 1936-octobre 1938).** (The Popular
Front in Senegal, May 1936-October 1938.)
Yves Person. *Mouvement Social,* no. 107 (1979), p. 72-102.
An account of the effects of the rise of a populist government in France on politics in
the French colonies, particularly in the privileged 'four communes' in Senegal where
the colonial élite was strongly entrenched. Although the reforms achieved little at the
time, Person argues that they helped pave the way for the more radical changes of the
postwar period.

313 **Galandou Diouf et le Front Populaire.** (Galandou Diouf and the
Popular Front.)
Iba Der Thiam. *Bulletin de l'IFAN,* vol. 38(B), no. 3 (1976),
p. 592-618.
An examination of the career of the populist Senegalese politician who lived from 1875
to 1941. The paper discusses Diouf's political support among the masses and his role in
politics between 1936 and 1941.

314 **The guns of Dakar: September 1940.**
John Williams. London: Heinemann, 1976. 201p.

A lively account of the dispatch of 7,000 British and Free French troops to Dakar in 1940, in an attempt to establish Free French control over the region at the expense of the Vichy régime, and the reasons for its failure.

315 **L'impact des intérêts coloniaux: SCOA et CFAO dans l'ouest africain, 1910-1965.** (The impact of colonial interests: SCOA and CFAO in West Africa, 1910-1965.)
Catherine Coquery-Vidrovitch. *Journal of African History*, vol. 16, no. 4 (1975), p. 595-621.

A historical study of the strategies and fortunes of the two giant French trading companies, Société Commerciale de l'Ouest African, and the Compagnie Française d'Afrique Occidentale, which had a near-monopoly in many sectors of the market in French West Africa, the latter being responsible for most of the groundnut trade with Senegal. The profits from the trade reached a high point in 1952, and thereafter declined. Since independence the firms have, rather belatedly, modernized their structures, diversified their activities and internationalized their investments.

316 **Quatorze millions de français dans la fédération de l'Afrique occidentale française?** (Were there 14 million Frenchmen in the French West African Federation?)
Denise Bouche. *Revue Française d'Histoire d'Outre-Mer*, vol. 69, no. 2 (1982), p. 97-113.

A critical discussion of the degree of the integration of French and Senegalese culture and Senegalese identification with France by the outbreak of World War II. The conclusion is that it had reached only a tiny élite, and that 'assimilation' was therefore something of a myth.

317 **The Second World War: prelude to decolonisation in Africa.**
Michael Crowder. In: *The Cambridge history of Africa: Volume 8, from c. 1940 to c. 1975.* Edited by Michael Crowder. Cambridge, England: Cambridge University Press, 1984, p. 8-51.

This chapter gives a concise survey of the effects of the war on the colonial powers, and its impact on Africans, either through recruitment into the European armies, or through the economic activity stimulated by the war. These, together with the administrative and political reforms which they provoked, made the war a watershed in African history.

318 **La tuerie de Thiès de septembre 1938. Essai d'interprétation.**
(The slaughter at Thiès in September 1938: an interpretive essay.)
Iba Der Thiam. *Bulletin de l'IFAN*, vol. 38(B), no. 2 (1976), p. 300-38.

Based on both the official account, and accounts from strikers and other sources, this paper is a reconstruction of the events at Thiès of 27 September 1938, when many striking railroad workers were killed or wounded during a confrontation with the police and the military.

Le Sénégal: organisation politique, administration, finances, travaux publics. (Senegal: political organization, administration, finance, public works.) *See* item no. 21.

Saint-Louis du Sénégal. Evolution d'une ville en milieu africain. (Saint-Louis, Senegal. Evolution of a town in an African setting.) *See* item no. 39.

Atlas des colonies françaises, protectorats et territoires sous mandat de la France. (Atlas of French colonies, protectorates and mandated territories.) *See* item no. 75.

Les grandes missions françaises en Afrique occidentale. (The great French missions to West Africa.) *See* item no. 91.

Voyage au Soudan Occidentale (1863-1866). (Voyage to Western Sudan, 1863-1866.) *See* item no. 118.

The Senegalese general strike of 1946 and the labor question in post-war French Africa. *See* item no. 412.

Political parties in French-speaking West Africa. *See* item no. 439.

Politics and government in former French West and Equatorial Africa: a critical bibliography. *See* item no. 440.

Senegal. *See* item no. 441.

Senegal: the elections to the Territorial Assembly, March 1957. *See* item no. 442.

De la chefferie traditionnelle au canton: évolution du canton colonial au Sénégal 1855-1960. (From the traditional chiefdom to the canton: evolution of the colonial canton in Senegal, 1855-1960.) *See* item no. 462.

France and Islam in West Africa, 1860-1960. *See* item no. 566.

L'Islam et l'histoire du Sénégal. (Islam and the history of Senegal.) *See* item no. 569.

The origins of clericalism in West African Islam. *See* item no. 575.

Social and economic factors in the Muslim revolution in Senegambia. *See* item no. 579.

Peste et société urbaine à Dakar: l'épidémie de 1914. (The plague and urban society in Dakar: the epidemic of 1914.)
See item no. 619.

Post-independence

319   **The making of a liberal democracy: Senegal's passive revolution, 1975-1985.**
Robert Fatton, Jr.   Boulder, Colorado; London: Lynne Riener, 1987. 189p.

One of the standard accounts in English of recent Senegalese politics, focusing on the transition from a one-party to a tripartite system following the political reforms of 1976. Further liberalization followed the accession of President Diouf in 1981 and the elections of 1983. After introductory and theoretical chapters, the central section of the book deals with the economic crisis, patron-client ties in Senegalese politics, and the process of transition. Fatton concludes that even though democratization in Senegal is limited and fragile, due to the weakness of the bourgeoisie and the power of the bureaucracy, the system of government is better than that of most other African régimes. The author has covered some of this ground in 'Gramsci and the legitimization of the state: the case of the Senegalese passive revolution', *Canadian Journal of Political Science*, vol. 19, no. 4 1986, p. 729-50; 'Clientelism and patronage in Senegal', *African Studies Review*, vol. 29, no. 4 (1986), p. 61-78; and 'Democratization of Senegal (1976-1983): "passive revolution" and the democratic limits of liberal democracy', *Review* (Fernand Braudel Center), vol. 10, no. 2 (1986), p. 279-312.

320   **The politics of independence: 1960-1986.**
Mohamed Mbodj.   In: *The political economy of Senegal under structural adjustment*. Edited by Christopher L. Delgado, Sidi Jammeh.   New York: Praeger, 1991, p. 119-26.

A concise survey of the main periods of national politics since independence, and the underlying economic factors, including poor rainfall and low producer prices in the 1960s and drought in the 1970s. Changes in government policy were unable to cope with these, and so on its accession in the 1980s, the Diouf régime was faced with mounting problems which have reinforced the country's dependency.

Le Parti Démocratique Sénégalaise. Une opposition légale en Afrique. (Senegalese Democratic Party: a legal opposition in Africa.)
See item no. 448.

Un parti politique africain: l'Union Progressiste Sénégalaise. (An African political party: the Senegalese Progressive Union.)
See item no. 449.

Les partis politiques sénégalais. (Senegalese political parties.)
See item no. 450.

Political opposition in Senegal: 1960-67.
See item no. 452.

Senegal.
See item no. 453.

Senegal.
See item no. 454.

Sénégal: l'état Abdou Diouf ou le temps des incertitudes. (Senegal: Abdou Diouf's state or the time of uncertainty.)
See item no. 455.

The foreign policy of Senegal.
See item no. 493.

From French West Africa to the Mali Federation.
See item no. 499.

Dream of unity: pan-Africanism and political unification in West Africa.
See item no. 501.

The Senegambian Confederation.
See item no. 506.

La politique française de coopération en Afrique: le cas du Sénégal. (The French policy of cooperation in Africa: the case of Senegal.)
See item no. 517.

Relations between France and Senegal: 1960-1969.
See item no. 518.

Africa contemporary record.
See item no. 855.

Europa World Year Book.
See item no. 860.

The Economy

General

321 **L'Afrique étranglée: Zambie, Tanzanie, Sénégal, Côte-d'Ivoire, Guinée-Bissau, Cap-Vert.** (Strangled Africa: Zambia, Tanzania, Senegal, Ivory Coast, Guinea-Bissau, Cape Verde.) René Dumont, Marie-France Mottin. Paris: Editions du Seuil, 1980. 265p.

Chapter six contains a lengthy discussion of economic exploitation and desertification in Senegal. The same authors address similar issues in *Le défi sénégalais: reconstruire les terroirs, libérer les paysans* (The Senegalese challenge: reconstruct the land, liberate the peasants) (Dakar: ENDA, 1982. 68p.).

322 **L'économie sénégalaise.** (The Senegalese economy.) Paris: Ediafric, 1970. 214p. (La documentation africaine).

A general survey of the economy a decade after independence, with a general introduction (including some thoughts from Senghor on African socialism), followed by sections of facts and figures on agriculture, livestock production and fishing; industry, energy and mines; foreign trade; transport; and finance and credit. It ends with an analysis of the results of the first two economic plans (1961-64 and 1965-69), and outlines of the options and priorities of the third plan (1969-73). Also available from the same publisher are: *Mémento de l'économie africaine* (Summary of African economy), (11th ed., 1985), which has data under similar headings in a thirty-four-page section on Senegal (country sections numbered separately); *Les plans de développement des pays d'Afrique noire* (Development plans of Black African countries), (4th ed., 1977), containing a ten-page country section data on the fourth five-year plan (1973-77) and the fifth four-year plan (1978-81).

323 **Evaluating structural adjustment policies for Senegal.**
Gilles Duruflé. In: *Political dimensions of the international debt crisis.*
Edited by Bonnie K. Campbell. London: Macmillan, 1989. p. 92-128.
An analysis of the origin of structural imbalances in the Senegalese economy from 1960
to 1980, the nature of the intervention by international lending agencies such as the
IMF and World Bank, and the impact of adjustment programmes on the Senegalese
economy. It reviews the prospects for adjustment policies in the agricultural and
industrial sectors, and their limitations. The author has discussed these issues at greater
length in *L'ajustement structurel en Afrique (Sénégal, Côte d'Ivoire, Madagascar)*,
(Paris: Karthala, 1988), of which pages 21-85 deal specifically with Senegal.

324 **Mécanismes de l'exploitation en Afrique: l'exemple du Sénégal.**
(Mechanisms of exploitation in Africa: the example of Senegal.)
Monique Anson-Meyer. Paris: Editions Cujas, 1974. 170p.
This study traces the continuing dependency on the world economy and its implications
for Senegal, dealing with flows of trade and capital, and argues that 'neutral' systems of
planning evaluation and accounting themselves work to the benefit of international
capital and against the interests of developing countries.

325 **Neo-colonialism in West Africa.**
Samir Amin. Harmondsworth, England: Penguin, 1973. 298p.
A pioneering study of the economies of West Africa and their continuing
subordination to the interests of the industrialized countries by one of the most
important Marxist writers on Africa. The first chapter is a case study of the groundnut
economy of Senegal, arguing that this specialization is due to the interests of the
French and not the natural potential of the country. The sixth chapter examines
Senegal's economic stagnation, arguing that it is a result of the net transfer of resources
out of the country through foreign trade.

326 **The political economy of risk and choice in Senegal.**
Edited by Mark Gersovitz, John Waterbury. London: Frank Cass,
1987. 363p.
An important volume consisting of an introduction and nine papers on sources of
uncertainty in agriculture (including the climate), the peasantry, the cooperative
movement, finance, state intervention in agriculture, agricultural prices, and relations
with the international financial markets.

327 **The political economy of Senegal under structural adjustment.**
Edited by Christopher L. Delgado, Sidi Jammeh. New York:
Praeger, 1991. 219p.
The chapters in this major work, written by established authorities, deal with the
economy since independence and the prospects for growth; agricultural policies from
animation rurale to the new agricultural policy of the 1980s; the relationships between
structural adjustment and politics; the impact of economic reforms on the people of
Dakar; and the history of the Senegambian Federation.

328 **The political economy of underdevelopment: dependence in Senegal.**
Edited by Rita Cruise O'Brien. Beverly Hills, California; London:
Sage Publications, 1979. 277p. (Sage Series on African Modernization
and Development, 3).

This wide-ranging volume consists of an introduction and seven critical papers by
leading authorities on various aspects of the country's economy and dependence on
France.

329 **Les problèmes économiques du Sénégal.** (The economic problems of
Senegal.)
Yves Péhaut. *Cahiers d'Outre-Mer*, vol. 19, no. 75 (1966), p. 234-72.

A useful critical evaluation of the first national development plan, and a summary of
the aims of the second.

330 **Senegal, The Gambia, Guinea-Bissau, Cape Verde. Country Report.**
London: Economist Intelligence Unit. quarterly.

Published quarterly, this is an authoritative source of up-to-date information, with
summaries of the political and economic structure of each country, short digests of the
latest political and economic news, graphs, and, at the end, tables listing the quarterly
figures for major economic indicators.

331 **Le Sénégal: une réussite politique et une incertitude économique.**
(Senegal: a political success and an economic uncertainty.)
Emile Arrighi de Casanova. *Revue de Défence National*, no. 6 (1972),
p. 893-901.

An article which touches on the central problem of modern Senegal: why is a country
which is apparently a political success so unsuccessful economically?

332 **Senegal: tradition, diversification and economic development.**
Washington, DC: International Bank of Reconstruction and
Development, 1974. 341p.

This World Bank Report on Senegal describes the situation of the economic
development and growth in the country up to the early 1970s. As well as a review of
the main issues and the major economic sectors of agriculture, livestock, fisheries,
industry and tourism, it contains four appendices on agriculture, manufacturing,
taxation and planning, and ninety pages of statistical tables.

333 **Structural changes and colonial dependency: Senegal 1885-1945.**
Sheldon Gellar. Beverly Hills, California; London: Sage Publications,
1976. 80p. (Sage Research Papers in the Social Sciences, 5).

A concise account of the integration of the region into the colonial, political and
economic system and the creation of the present relations of economic dependency.
Some development did take place during the colonial period, but it was concentrated
in the Dakar region and those sectors of the economy in which European interests
already dominated.

Etude sur Le Sénégal. (Study of Senegal.)
See item no. 4.

Sénégal-Soudan: agriculture, industrie, commerce. (Senegal-Sudan: agriculture, industry, commerce.)
See item no. 22.

Integration, development and equity: economic integration in West Africa.
See item no. 494.

The politics of West African economic co-operation: CEAO and ECOWAS.
See item no. 496.

Quelle stratégie pour le Sahel? La difficile harmonisation de la stratégie du CILSS et du Club du Sahel avec les plans de développement nationaux des pays Saheliens. (What strategy for the Sahel? The difficulty of reconciling the strategy of the CILSS and the Club of Sahel with the national development plans of the Sahelian countries.)
See item no. 497.

La politique française de coopération en Afrique: le cas du Sénégal.
(The French policy of cooperation in Africa: the case of Senegal.)
See item no. 517.

Relations between France and Senegal: 1960-1969.
See item no. 518.

Agriculture, Fisheries, Pastoralism and Trade

Agriculture

334 **Agricultural sector study: main report.**
Dakar: Ministry of Rural Development, 1986. 163p.
A report which resulted from collaboration between the Ministry of Rural Development in Dakar and the Food and Agriculture Organisation of the United Nations, which presumably explains its publication in English. It provides a survey of the Senegalese economy, agricultural problems in the main regions, and a review of the New Agricultural Policy of the 1980s. It ends with sections on pricing and credit, education and extension services, and the supply of inputs for agriculture such as seed and fertilizer.

335 **Aspects techniques et sociaux de l'agriculture en pays bassari.**
(Technical and social aspects of agriculture among the Bassari.)
Georges Dupré. *Bulletin et Mémoires de la Société d'Anthropologie* (Paris), Series 11, vol. 8, no. 1/2 (1965), p. 75-159.
A lengthy study with detailed case material of the complex agricultural systems (compared with those of their neighbours) of the Bassari along the border with Guinea. The paper discusses the agricultural technology, soil and tools, the yearly cycle of farming activity, and the system of crop rotation. This is followed by a general account of Bassari social organization and its relations with land tenure, and of the organization of work groups.

336 **California cowpeas and food policy in Senegal.**
R. James Bingen (et al.). *World Development*, vol. 16, no. 7 (1988), p. 857-65.
An account of the attempts to develop cowpea cultivation as an alternative to groundnuts from 1985 onwards in Senegal, initially by importing 700 tons of a Californian variety. The paper argues that despite the rapid increase in production

which followed, and the dramatic improvement in the food situation of some farmers, there remained difficulties in developing the crop: inadequate supplies of good seed, shortages of equipment, and inefficiencies in storage and marketing; an area in which the government was much less successful than the private traders.

337 **L'état et la production paysanne ou l'état et la révolution au Sénégal 1957-1958.** (The state and peasant production, or the state and the revolution in Senegal, 1957-1958.)
Abdoulaye Ly. Paris: Presénce Africaine, 1958. 79p.
A brief study of the relations between the peasant and the state and between France and Senegal during three historical periods: at the time of the companies and trading posts; during the French Third Republic; and before independence. It was written at a time when the economic and constitutional position of the French West African colonies was under review, and so it ends with a clarion call for progressive socialism in the new political order.

338 **Food aid to Senegal: disincentive effects and commercial displacement.**
Simon Maxwell. Brighton, England: Institute of Development Studies, University of Sussex, 1986. 43p. (Discussion Paper 225).
An evaluation of whether or not food aid to Senegal in the wake of the droughts has acted as a disincentive to local production. Maxwell concludes that it has not. In fact, the author believes that food aid could be expanded to ease the balance of payments situation, and supplies should be targeted at those whose consumption has been most sharply reduced by the drought.

339 **Fraternité d'hivernage: le contrat de navétanat. Théorie et practique.**
(The brotherhood of the rainy season: the contract of the migrant farm worker. Theory and practice.)
Philippe David. *Présence Africaine*, vol. 31 (1960), p. 45-57.
A detailed discussion of the contracts between landlords and migrant workers in the groundnut industry in the 1950s. The landowner supplied housing, food and a piece of land for the worker to cultivate for himself. In return he generally received work for four mornings a week. The labourer received no pay, but could sell the crops he produced himself.

340 **From Senegambia to Senegal: the evolution of peasantries.**
Jean Copans. In: *Peasants in Africa: historical and contemporary perspectives*. Edited by Martin A. Klein. Beverly Hills, California: Sage Publications, 1977, p. 77-104.
A critical account by a Marxist anthropologist of the history of peasant production, subsistence, marketing and international trade in the region. Copans argues that despite changes in the regional economy, the position of the peasant farmers remains in many ways unchanged, in that they continue to be exploited. This exploitation is now organized through a national apparatus which controls agriculture and imposes new technologies from above.

341 **Gender, class and rural transition: agribusiness and the food crisis in Senegal.**
Maureen Mackintosh.   London: Zed Books, 1989. 218p.
A major study of the impact of commercial farming on local agricultural relations of production in the area between Dakar and Thiès. The book considers the effects of the arrival in the area of Bud Senegal, an offshoot of an American firm growing vegetables for export. It evaluates the loss caused by the project to the local farmers in terms of land, trees and income through their own vegetable farming. The second half of the book describes the situation of migrant labourers on a second estate, their wage work and the decline of farming in Cap-Vert, the impact of wage labour on gender relations, and the general position of commercial farming in relations between Europe and Africa.

342 **Maintenance sociale et changement économique au Sénégal. I. Doctrine économique et pratique du travail chez les Mourides.** (Social continuity and economic change in Senegal. Vol. I. Economic doctrine and work practices among the Mourides.)
J. Copans, Ph. Couty, J. Roch, G. Rocheteau.   Paris: ORSTOM, 1972. 274p.
A volume containing a series of papers which, taken together, provide an important source of information on the organization of production and labour among Wolof and Serer farmers belonging to the Mouride brotherhood. The chapters include both general accounts of the Serer and Wolof economies, and of Mouride agriculture, and detailed case studies of production. It is profusely illustrated with tables, maps and photographs, and ends with a glossary but is without a consolidated bibliography.

343 **Les marabouts de l'arachide: la confrérie mouride et les paysans du Sénégal.** (The holy men of the groundnut industry: the Mouride Muslim brotherhood and the peasants of Senegal.)
Jean Copans.   Paris: Le Sycomore, 1980. 242p.
An account of the rise of the Mouride brotherhood, which was entrained by a crisis in traditional Wolof society, the colonial conquest and the development of the groundnut industry. The two final sections of the book deal with the organization of labour by the Mouride producers and the role of the state in Senegalese agriculture. The author is critical of earlier studies of the Mourides, and an earlier lengthy critique of O'Brien is to be found in 'Paysannerie et politique au Sénégal' (Peasantry and politics in Senegal), *Cahiers d'Etudes Africaines*, vol. 18, no. 1/2 (1978), p. 241-56.

344 **Organisation coopérative et modification des rapports de production et des formes de propriété en milieu rural africain.** (Cooperative organization and modification of relations of production and of forms of ownership in a rural African setting.)
Georges Festinger.   *L'Homme et la Société*, vol. 6 (1967), p. 141-9.
A case study of a cooperative on the Petite Côte which did achieve a rapid increase in agricultural production, perhaps because it was the political élite who had both access to the new techniques and control of the land.

345 **Les paysans du bassin arachidier: conditions de vie et comportements de survie.** (The peasants of the groundnut basin: living conditions and survival strategies.)
Abdoulaye Bara Diop. *Politique Africaine*, vol. 45 (March 1992), p. 39-61.

A useful account of the options open to farmers in the groundnut industry, given the continuing low level of returns from agriculture. The paper deals with agricultural and non-agricultural sources of income; the rising cost of living, and the ways in which the farmers try to cope, through migration or alternative kinds of work.

346 **Les paysans du Sénégal: les civilisations agraires du Cayor à la Casamance.** (The peasants of Senegal: the agrarian civilizations from Kayor to the Casamance.)
Paul Pélissier. Saint-Yrieix, Haute Vienne, France: Imprimerie Fabrègue, 1966. 939p.

Probably the most important single study of Senegalese agriculture, this monumental book, based on both fieldwork and archival sources, focuses on the adaptive ingenuity of the African peasant within the environmental constraints of the region. The account is arranged geographically, around the three main regions of the country. The first part deals with the groundnut basin, including a chapter on its soils and vegetation, Wolof history and land tenure systems, Wolof agriculture, the Serer peasantry, and Serer agriculture. It ends with a chapter on the exploitation of new territories by the Mourides. The second part deals with the Sudan savannah zones, between Saloum and the Gambia river, and in the upper Casamance with its Peul and Tukulor inhabitants. The third part deals wih the riverine areas in the south of the country, in the lower Casamance, and in particular with Diola rice cultivation, the influence of Mande culture and Islam, and with the range of cultural and ecological variation. The book is well illustrated with excellent black-and-white plates throughout, and at the end is an important eight-page bibliography.

347 **Problèmes agricoles au Sénégal: la vallée du Sénégal, agriculture traditionnelle et riziculture mécanisée.** (Agricultural problems in Senegal: the Senegal valley, traditional agriculture and mechanized rice growing.)
Louis Papy. Saint-Louis, Senegal: Centre IFAN, 1952. 48p (Etudes Sénégalaises no. 2).

A study of agriculture in the Senegal river valley. A similar study by Paul Pélissier deals with groundnut production further south: *L'arachide au Sénégal: rationalisation et modernisation de sa culture* (The groundnut in Senegal: rationalization and modernization of its cultivation) (Saint-Louis, Senegal: Centre IFAN, 1952. 80p.).

348 **Quelques observations sur les blocages de la croissance dans l'agriculture sénégalaise.** (Some observations on the obstacles to growth in Senegalese agriculture.)
J. Brochier. *Tiers-Monde*, vol. 8, no. 30 (1967), p. 455-68.

An analysis of production and investment during the period of the first national plan (1961-65), in the groundnut basin of Senegal. The author concludes that levels of investment of earnings in the industry were high, but that the equipment purchased was often unproductive because of the farmers' lack of experience with the technology.

349 **Rice in West Africa: policy and economics.**
Scott R. Pearson, J. Dirk Stryker, Charles P. Humphreys (et al.).
Stanford, California: Stanford University Press, 1981. 482p.

The definitive study in its field, this book looks at rice policy and production in the Ivory Coast, Liberia, Sierra Leone, Senegal and Mali. After a discussion of methods, there are two chapters on each country discussing policies and production in turn. The study and economic evaluation of the varied techniques of rice production is particularly useful. The conclusion is that, with the exception of Mali, investment in rice production is not cost effective, which leaves the question of why so many governments in the region encourage it.

350 **Ruling class and peasantry in Senegal, 1960-1976: the politics of a monocrop economy.**
Donal B. Cruise O'Brien. In: *The political economy of underdevelopment: dependence in Senegal.* Edited by Rita Cruise O'Brien. Beverly Hills, California; London: Sage Publications, 1979, p. 209-27. (Sage Series on African Modernization and Development 3).

An important and concise discussion of the effects of continuing Senegalese dependence on France, military, political and economic, and the ways in which the ruling groups have sought to protect their positions. As a result, among the peasantry the Mouride brotherhood has emerged as what O'Brien describes as a 'bizarre and theatrical form of trade unionism', as the only organization apparently capable of protecting peasant interests.

351 **Supply and demand of millet and sorghum in Senegal.**
Amadou D. Niane. East Lansing, Michigan: African Rural Economy Program, Department of Agricultural Economics, Michigan State University, 1980. 80p. (Working Paper 32, sponsored by the US Agency for International Development, Bureau for Development Support, Office of Agriculture, Washington DC 20523).

Originally an MSc dissertation, this paper investigates the supply and demand for millet and sorghum. It concludes that supply is positively related to the previous year's prices for millet and sorghum and negatively related to the past year's prices for groundnuts and rice.

352 **La traite des arachides dans le pays de Kaolack, et ses conséquences économique, sociales et juridiques.** (The groundnut trade in the area of Kaolack, and its economic, social and legal consequences.)
Joseph Fouquet. Saint-Louis, Senegal: Centre IFAN, 1958. 261p. (Etudes Sénégalaises, 8).

This study of the development of the groundnut trade in the area around the town of Kaolack, situated in the peanut-growing basin of Sine-Saloum, central Senegal, is now of most interest for its analysis of the conditions of production, the soil, climate and demography and the organization of agricultural labour in the colonial period.

353 **Usages alimentaires dans la région de Khombole (Sénégal).** (Food uses
in the Khombole region, Senegal.)
Igor de Garine. *Cahiers d'Etudes Africaines*, vol. 3, no. 2 (1962),
p. 65-84.

A wide-ranging study of food production and consumption in an area in which the
population is divided between rural Serer, and groups of rural and semi-urbanized
Wolof. It contains information on diet, food preparation, differences in residential
organization, weaning, and the effects of groundnut cultivation. It also contains details
of expenditure on food among each of the three groups, and relates the symbolic
importance of food to its relative price: low in the rural areas and high in the city.

354 **A village level study of producer grain transactions in rural Senegal.**
Clark G. Ross. *African Studies Review*, vol. 25, no. 4 (1982),
p. 65-84.

This paper, based on research from the Diourbel-Thiès region of the country, provides
useful data on village and household grain transactions, compound production and
consumption, grain distribution and marketing in three villages. The policy
implications are that there is little justification for a state organization to purchase
millet, and that stimulating greater maize consumption in the rural areas should be a
major priority, partly to replace imported rice.

**Louga et sa région (Sénégal): essai d'intégration des rapports ville-campagne
dans la problématique du développement.** (Louga and its region, Senegal:
rural-urban links from the perspective of development.)
See item no. 37.

La moyenne vallée du Sénégal: étude socio-économique. (The middle Senegal
valley: a socio-economic study.)
See item no. 38.

Sob: étude géographique d'un terroir sérèr (Sénégal). (Sob: a geographical
study of a Serer region in Senegal.)
See item no. 40.

Sécheresses et famines du Sahel. (Droughts and famines of the Sahel.)
See item no. 70.

Kanel: l'exode rural dans un village de la vallée du Sénégal. (Kanel: rural
exodus in a village in the Senegal valley.)
See item no. 127.

Migration et production domestique des soninké du Sénégal. (Migration and
domestic production among the Soninke of Senegal.)
See item no. 129.

Paysans migrants du Fouta Toro (Valleé du Sénégal). (Migrant farmers of the
Fuuta Toro, Senegal River valley.)
See item no. 131.

Agriculture, Fisheries, Pastoralism and Trade. Agriculture

Urban migration, cash cropping, and calamity: the spread of Islam among the Diola of Boulouf (Senegal), 1900-1940.
See item no. 134.

Le long voyage des gens du Fleuve. (The long voyage of the people of the River region.)
See item no. 137.

The 'patriarchal ideal' of Soninke labor migrants: from slave owners to employers of free labour.
See item no. 138.

Power, prayer and production: the Jola of Casamance, Senegal.
See item no. 153.

Une société rurale au Sénégal. Les structures foncières, familiales et villageoises des Sérèr. (A rural society in Senegal: the structures of land tenure, family and the village among the Serer.)
See item no. 169.

The Wolof of Saloum: social structure and rural development in Senegal.
See item no. 174.

La terre et les gens du Fleuve. Jalons, balises. (The land and the people of the River region: milestones and beacons.)
See item no. 185.

Anciens et nouveaux droits fonciers chez les Diola au Sénégal et leurs conséquences pour la répartition des terres. (Old and new property rights among the Diola of Senegal and their consequences for land distribution.)
See item no. 472.

Capitalism and legal change: an African transformation.
See item no. 473.

Customary land tenure and land reform: the rise of new inequalities among the Diola of Senegal.
See item no. 475.

Essai sur quelques problèmes relatifs au régime foncier des Diola de Basse-Casamance (Sénégal). (Essay on some problems related to the land tenure system of the Diola of the Lower Casamance, Senegal.)
See item no. 477.

Les rapports du système foncier Toucouleur de l'organisation sociale et économique traditionnelle. Leur évolution actuelle. (The links between Tukulor land tenure and traditional social and economic organization, and their present development.)
See item no. 481.

Du régime des terres de la vallée du Sénégal au Fouta antérieurement à l'occupation française. (On the land system of the Senegal valley in Fuuta before the French occupation.)
See item no. 483.

La diffusion du progrès technique en milieu rural sénégalais. (The diffusion of technical progress in the context of rural Senegal.)
See item no. 604.

Manuel de la culture de l'arachide au Sénégal, à l'usage de vulgarisation. (Manual on groundnut cultivation, intended for popularization.)
See item no. 605.

Manuel de la culture de mils et sorghos dans le bassin arachidier sénégalaise, à l'usage de vulgarisation. (Manual on millet and sorghum cultivation in the Senegalese groundnut basin, intended for popularization.)
See item no. 606.

Manuel de l'utilisation des matériels agricoles dans les exploitations sénégalaises, à l'usage de la vulgarisation. (Operation manual for agricultural materials in Senegalese farming, intended for popularization.)
See item no. 607.

L'administration locale du développement rural au Sénégal. (Local administration of rural development in Senegal.)
See item no. 625.

Agricultural development and policy in Senegal: annotated bibliography of recent studies, 1983-89.
See item no. 626.

Animation rurale: **education for rural development.**
See item no. 628.

Associations rurales et socialisme contractuel en afrique occidentale: étude de cas: le Sénégal. (Rural associations and contractual socialism in West Africa: a case study of Senegal.)
See item no. 629.

Development of irrigated agriculture in Senegal: general overview and prospects: proposals for a second programme 1980-1985.
See item no. 631.

Le développement à la base au Dahomey et au Sénégal. (Grass-roots development in Dahomey and Senegal.)
See item no. 632.

L'évolution des structures agricoles du Sénégal: déstructuration et réstructuration de l'économie rurale. (The evolution of the agricultural structures of Senegal: taking apart and rebuilding the rural economy.)
See item no. 633.

Irrigated agriculture as an archetypal development project: Senegal.
See item no. 634.

Nation et développement communautaire en Guinée et au Sénégal. (National
and community development in Guinea and Senegal.)
See item no. 635.

L'organisation coopérative au Sénégal. (The organization of cooperatives in
Senegal.)
See item no. 636.

Politics, bureaucracy and rural development in Senegal.
See item no. 638.

The Senegal River valley: what kind of change?
See item no. 640.

The state and rural development 1960-85.
See item no. 641.

**Structural change and managerial inefficiency in the development of rice
cultivation in the Senegal River region.**
See item no. 642.

Fisheries

355 **Cayar: village de pêcheurs-cultivateurs au Sénégal.** (Cayar: a village of
fishermen-cultivators in Senegal.)
Eliane Sy. *Cahiers d'Outre-Mer*, vol. 18, no. 72 (1965), p. 342-68.
A description of a village between Dakar and Saint-Louis, which was founded by
Lebu in the 19th century, and which now has a mixed population of Wolof, Lebu,
Tukulor, Peul and Moors. The residential structure of the village is described, and
there is a detailed discussion of the organization of fishing, the techniques and the
division of labour between men and women, and wet- and dry-season agriculture.

356 **De la pêche comme activité nouvelle, de la mer comme nouvelle frontière
dans les pays du Tiers Monde, l'exemple du Sénégal, pays pêcheur sur
un continent terrien. 1re partie.** (Fishing as a new activity, and the sea
as a new frontier in the countries of the Third World, the example of
Senegal, a fishing country on a land-oriented continent. Part One.)
Jean Rieucau. *Afrique Contemporaine*, vol. 24, no. 136
(Oct.-Dec. 1985), p. 3-24.
In this general account of sea-fishing off Senegal and of the coastal communities, the
author argues that Senegal's waters are being over-exploited by foreign industrialized
fishing fleets, and that these resources could be developed locally with fish providing a
much-needed source of protein for the local people. Further articles in the same

journal provide more valuable information on the fishing industry, 'La pêche maritime: un moteur de l'économie sénégalaise, II (1)' (Maritime fishing: a motor of the Senegalese economy, part II (1)) by Bernard Lléres, *Afrique Contemporaine*, vol. 25, no. 137 (Jan.-March 1986), p. 56-74, which contains a useful bibliography, and 'Le Sénégal et la coopération internationale: l'exemple des ressources vivantes de la mer, II (2)' (Senegal and international cooperation: the example of sea-life resources, part II (2)), Jean Rieucau, *Afrique Contemporaine*, vol. 25, no. 138 (April-June 1986), p. 34-43, which reviews the progress of international development programmes.

357 **Deux expériences de développement de la pêche maritime au Sénégal.**
(Two experiences of development in sea fishing in Senegal.)
Jean Domingo. *Cahiers d'Outre-Mer*, vol. 35, no. 1 (1982), p. 35-62.
A comparison between two projects to develop fishing in Senegal: a programme to develop tuna fishing using advanced technology, an attempt which failed by the end of the 1970s; and a more modest programme of motorizing the traditional dug-out canoes, which proved more successful.

358 **L'économie maritime et rurale de Kayar, village sénégalais. Problèmes de développement.** (The maritime and rural economy of Kayar, a Senegalese village. Problems of development.)
Régine Nguyen Van Chi-Bonnardel. Dakar: IFAN, 1967. 257p.
bibliog. (Mémoires de l'IFAN, 76).
This socio-economic study focuses primarily on the maritime fishing village of Kayar, situated on the coast to the north of Dakar, and deals with the physical environment, the economy based on sea-fishing and agriculture, and with lifestyles and social organization. It includes thirty-two plates and a large bibliography.

359 **Entre terres et eaux: pêche maritime et évolution des systèmes de production en Casamance.** (Between lands and waters: maritime fishing and the evolution of production systems in Camasance.)
Marie-Christine Cormier-Salem. *Cahiers d'Etudes Africaines*, vol. 29, no. 3-4 (1989), p. 325-38.
An account of the way in which the Diola people of the lower Casamance River, although reputedly averse to maritime fishing, adopted this practice during the 1970s as a response to the Sahelian drought which undermined their economy based on rice cultivation and river fishing.

360 **L'essor de l'économie de pêche artisanale et ses conséquences sur le littoral sénégalais.** (The expansion of the economy of a non-industrial fishing economy and its consequences on Senegal's sea coast.)
Régine Nguyen Van Chi-Bonnardel. *Cahiers d'Etudes Africaines*, vol. 20, no. 3 (1980), p. 255-304.
An important study of the social organization of different forms of fishing on the Senegalese coast: a family-based form which the fishermen practise in their own villages, and in which the profits are shared by members of the kin group; and individual fishing by migrants. The paper also discusses problems of modernization, capital accumulation and competition from Dakar trawlers and factory ships from further afield.

361 **Market development, government interventions and the dynamics of the small-scale fishing sector: an historical perspective of the Senegalese case.**
Jean-Pierre Chauveau, Alassane Samba. *Development and Change*, vol. 20, no. 4 (1989), p. 599-620.

A useful historical acount of the small-scale 'artisanal' sector of Senegal's fishing industry, which describes the changing policies of the state from increasing intervention in the 1950s, to disengagement in the 1980s, a decade during which the artisanal sector reached the limits of its own self-financing capacity. It includes a short bibliography of works on Senegalese fisheries.

362 **Particularisme et évolution: les pêcheurs lébou.** (Particularism and evolution: fishermen of the Lebu.)
G. Balandier, P. Mercier. Saint-Louis, Senegal: Centre IFAN Senegal, 1952. 216p. (Etudes Sénégalaises, 3).

The Lebu inhabit the coastal areas of Senegal immediately to the north and south of the city of Dakar. This comprehensive ethnography typical of its period works systematically through the history and traditions of the area, socialization, sexuality, world views, ritual, social organization and economic activity, including a thirty-page section on fishing. At the end is an interesting collection of plates, unfortunately of rather poor quality.

363 **Peasant fishermen and capitalists: development in Senegal.**
Klaas de Jonge. *Review of African Political Economy*, vol. 15/16 (1979), p. 105-23.

A study of the nature of relations between peasants, capitalism and the state, illustrated by the case of part-time shrimp fishermen in the Casamance, an industry dominated by foreign companies. The paper outlines the structure of the industry, presents case material on conflict between the shrimp fishers, the companies and officials, and explains why the shrimp fishers, in spite of their apparent weakness, are sometimes able to get their way in an industry dominated by European companies.

364 **Les pêcheries des côtes du Sénégal et des rivières du sud.** (The fisheries of the coasts of Senegal and the southern rivers.)
A. Gruvel. Paris: Augustin Challamel for the Gouvernement Général de l'Afrique Occidentale Française, 1908. 245p.

An early and detailed monograph on fishes and fishing in Senegal consisting of a geographical and hydrographic survey of Senegal, a chapter on climate, a survey of fishing techniques in the Saint-Louis, Dakar, 'Petite Côte' and the southern river areas, and a catalogue of the main species. The final chapters are on the economic use of fishing products in Senegal, administration of the industry, and the country's salt marshes. The book is illustrated with numerous line drawings, maps and historically interesting plates of fishes, fishing and fishing locations.

365 **Vitalité de la petite pêche tropicale. Pêcheurs de Saint-Louis du Sénégal.**
(The vitality of small-scale tropical fishing. Fishermen of Saint-Louis, Senegal.)
Régine Bonnardel. Paris: Editions du CNRS, 1985. 104p. (Collection Mémoires et Documents de Géographie).
A well-illustrated account of the small-scale sector of the fishing industry in Senegal, which provides employment for 35,000 fishermen, in addition to the women who prepare dried fish. It covers techniques of fishing from motorized canoes, and the effects of out-migration by fishermen on Guet Ndar, a district of Saint-Louis, where the research was carried out.

Poissons de mer du Sénégal. (Saltwater fish of Senegal.)
See item no. 63.

Pastoralism

366 **Cattle and inequality: herd size differences and pastoral production among the Fulani of Northeastern Senegal.**
John W. Sutter. *Africa*, vol. 57, no. 2 (1987), p. 196-218.
An important empirical study of Fulani (Fulbe or Peul) pastoralists and farmers in the Ferlo region, based on research in 1981-82, and containing data on herd size, household revenues and expenditure, cattle prices, herd composition and take-off rates. The conclusion is that the pastoral population is increasingly polarized between households with small herds, some of whom are forced out of pastoralism completely, and households with larger herds, able to accumulate stock and maximize returns.

367 **The pastoral environment of northern Senegal.**
Oussouby Touré. *Review of African Political Economy*, vol. 42 (1988), p. 32-9.
A critical account of the effects of French colonialism and capitalism on pastoralism among the Peul (Fulbe) in the Ferlo region, and their transformation from transhumant herders and farmers into settled cattle ranchers. The ecological effects have been disastrous, leading to increasingly frequent droughts, but the effects on the local social structure have been more complex and difficult to evaluate in simplistic terms.

Raison pastorale et politique de développement: les Peul sénégalais face aux aménagements. (Pastoral reasoning and development policy: the Peul of Senegal facing change.)
See item no. 639.

Trade

368 **A la recherche de nouveaux 'poissons'. Stratégies commerciales mourides par temps de crise.** (In search of new 'fish': commercial strategies of the Mourides in a time of crisis.)
Victoria Ebin. *Politique Africaine*, vol. 45 (March 1992), p. 86-100.
A description based on case material of the move into market trade by some of the Mouride families as a way of coping with the economic crisis, and the international networks which were developed as a result. The author concludes that methods need to be found to enable the dynamism of the informal sector to meet the needs of the state.

369 **Du clandestin à l'officieux: les réseaux de vente illicite des médicaments au Sénégal.** (From the clandestine to the official: the network of illicit sales of medicines in Senegal.)
Didier Fassin. *Cahiers d'Etudes Africaines*, vol. 25, no. 2 (1985), p. 161-77.
A fascinating tale of crime, religion and political patronage, focusing on the illegal medicinal drugs trade which flourishes in Dakar and the towns around, as in many Third World urban areas. Fassin argues that, apart from occasional crackdowns, the trade is generally tolerated by the authorities, partly because the state is unable to satisfy the demand for drugs itself, and partly because the supply networks are controlled by the politically powerful Mouride brotherhood.

370 **Les femmes commerçantes au détail sur les marchés dakarois.** (Women retail traders in Dakar markets.)
D. van der Vaeren-Aguessy. In: *The development of indigenous trade and markets in West Africa*. Edited by C. Meilllassoux. London: Oxford University Press for the International African Institute, 1974, p. 244-55.
A study of the social and economic characteristics of market women who in the early years of independence made up sixty per cent of the retail traders in the Dakar markets, together with the associations which they had formed to defend their interests.

371 **Les marchés hebdomadaires de la région de Kédougou (Sénégal oriental).** (Weekly markets of the Kédougou region, Eastern Senegal.)
Alexandre Albenque. *Bulletin de l'IFAN*, vol. 32(B), no. 2 (1970), p. 558-87.
A description of the origins and the social and economic functions of markets in seven villages in the Kédougou department, an area in which the Fulbe (Peul) are the largest ethnic group.

372 **La petite production marchande et l'emploi dans le secteur informel.**
Le cas africain. (Petty production for the market and employment in
the informal sector. The African situation.)
P. Hugon, N. L. Abadie, A. Morice.   Paris: Université de Paris I,
Institut d'Etude du Développement Economique et Social, Group de
Recherche, [n.d.] 2 vols.

This work is a detailed analysis of petty market production and employment in the
informal sector of the Senegalese economy. It deals with a whole range of industries,
both traditional and modern, and describes their organization and development
potential.

373 **Pricing and selling decisions in a labor surplus economy.**
Curtis M. Jolly.   *Journal of Asian and African Studies*, vol. 24, no. 3/4
(1989), p. 188-98.

This paper presents a statistical analysis of the determinants of prices among market
vegetable traders in the Casamance. It concludes that the apparent irrationality of the
market results from the fact that it is in constant flux, and that many of the traders are
temporary workers, who are not always able to maximize profits.

374 **Les restauratrices de la zone industrielle de Dakar, ou la guerre des
marmites.** (The women food-sellers of the industrial zone of Dakar, or
the cooking-pot war.)
Made Bandé Diouf.   *Cahiers d'Etudes Africaines*, vol. 21, no. 1/3
(1981), p. 237-250.

An account of the links between the formal and informal sectors of the urban
economy, in the form of the industrial workers and the women (*gargotières*) who
provide them with cheap meals. The paper presents data on their origins and
demographic characteristics, marital status, occupation of spouse, and the wages they
pay their employees.

375 **Vie de relations au Sénégal: la circulation des biens.** (Life of
relationships in Senegal: the circulation of goods.)
Régine Nguyen Van Chi-Bonnardel.   Dakar: IFAN, 1978. 927p.
(Mémoires, 90).

An enormous study (around 750,000 words) of trade and distribution in Senegal, based
on the author's 1976 doctoral thesis, which is also one of the single most important
sources of general information on the Senegalese economy. The first part contains
chapters dealing with production (agricultural, mineral and industrial) and with the
economic role of Dakar. The second part contains surveys of the transport system and
the structure of rural credit, while the third part is a study of the marketing system
itself, the urban and rural markets, and the various roles of European, Lebanese and
African companies, merchants and traders. The final section summarizes the
transformation in the distribution system since independence. Profusely illustrated with
maps and diagrams throughout, the book ends with a twenty-seven-page bibliography,
and forty pages of black-and-white plates. Perhaps unsurprisingly, there is no index.

Agriculture, Fisheries, Pastoralism and Trade. Trade

Adjustment to West African realities: the Lebanese in Senegal.
See item no. 190.

Lebanese entrepreneurs in Senegal: economic integration and the politics of protection.
See item no. 192.

La politique coloniale française à l'égard de la bourgeoisie commerçante sénégalaise (1820-1960). (French colonial policy with regard to the Senegalese merchant middle class.)
See item no. 291.

Industry and the Labour Market

376 **Industrial labor in the Republic of Senegal.**
Guy Pfefferman. New York: Praeger, 1968. 325p.
This is the main study of the Senegalese formal sector labour market for the early years of independence, centring on the question of why, given that both the government and the unions were committed to expanding employment, so few jobs were actually created. The author blames the importation of French models inappropriate for African conditions; employers and unions for the slow pace of Africanization; and government for failing to assert its independence from France. There are sections on the labour market, the unions, labour legislation, training, the role of government in fixing wages, policy alternatives, and the constraints imposed by membership of the franc zone. There are also some useful appendices which include information on real wages, and the tabulated responses to the author's questionnaire.

377 **The industrial labor market and economic performance in Senegal: a study in enterprise ownership, export orientation, and government regulation.**
Katherine Terrell, Jan Svejnar. Boulder, Colorado: Westview Press, 1989. 129p.
A detailed overview of the labour market and industrial relations system, which concludes that the industrial sector has performed poorly, despite a relatively mature base at independence, considerable investment since then and preferential trade agreements. It blames this on factors internal to the economy, rather than the structure of dependency and external linkages which Marxist scholars have tended to stress.

378 **Les industries du Sénégal.** (The industries of Senegal.)
Jean Bernard Mas. Paris: Ministère de la Coopération, 1965. 69p.
Senegal at independence had perhaps the most developed industrial base in all of West Africa. This study, based on data collected in 1963, contains a general survey, surveys by sector, and tables giving information on factories and workshops, sales, consumption, imports and exports.

Industry and the Labour Market

379 **Manufacturing industries and their labour in the Dakar area.**
     A. Hauser. *Bulletin of the Inter-African Labour Institute*, vol. 5, no. 4
     (1958), p. 8-39.
A description of industrial production in the Dakar area in the late colonial period,
when it supported more industry than the rest of French West Africa. The paper gives
information on types of industry, zoning, taxation policies, working conditions, social
composition of the work force, and attempts at Africanization.

380 **The political economy of industrial wages in Senegal.**
     Maureen Mackintosh.   In: *The political economy of
     underdevelopment: dependence in Senegal.* Edited by Rita Cruise
     O'Brien.   Beverly Hills, California; London: Sage Publications, 1979,
     p. 156-76. (Sage Series on African Modernization and Development, 3).
A discussion of the level of minimum wages, the low wage policies of most industrial
firms, and the main features of union organization which allow the low wage policy to
be perpetuated. The final part of the paper discusses the reasons why wages remain
low, even in the more dynamic export production sector, irrespective of rises in
productivity.

381 **Politics under the specter of deindustrialization: 'structural adjustment'
     in practice.**
     Catherine Boone.   In: *The political economy of Senegal under
     structural adjustment.* Edited by Christopher L. Delgado, Sidi
     Jammeh.   New York: Praeger, 1991, p. 127-49.
A study of the constraints on government industrial policy, focusing on the textile
industry which developed rapidly during the 1950s, but which by the late 1970s had
nearly collapsed due to competition from illegal imports from The Gambia. The
industry was then taken over by local businessmen with state finance, a solution which
the author sees as government commitment to the bourgeoisie rather than the urban
poor.

382 **Quelques aspects du chômage à Dakar.** (Some aspects of unemployment
     in Dakar.)
     Y. Mersaudier.   *Notes Africaines*, vol. 97 (1963), p. 1-5.
Presents the results of a survey carried out among 400 unemployed, more than half of
whom were Wolof under thirty years of age.

383 **Sénégal: le secteur informel de Dakar.** (Senegal: the informal sector of
     Dakar.)
     Meine Pieter van Dijk.   Paris: Editions l'Harmattan, 1986. 164p.
This, the second volume of a two-part study of the informal sectors of Ouagadougou
and of Dakar, is based on a survey of 467 informal sector entrepreneurs in Dakar in
1977. After general sections on Senegal and the Dakar setting, the book contains an
occupation-by-occupation description of the main activities in the sector; discussions of
levels of income, investments and relations with customers; and of the general factors

114

which encourage or inhibit growth in the sector. The final chapter is a list of political recommendations.

384 **Small-scale manufacturing and repairs in Dakar: a survey of market relations within the urban economy.**
Chris Gerry. In: *Casual work and poverty in Third World cities.*
Edited by Ray Bromley, Chris Gerry. Chichester, New York: John Wiley & Sons, 1979, p. 229-50.

A study of small-scale producers in Dakar, namely furniture makers, leatherworkers, tailors, mechanics and metalworkers. It examines the organization of employment, the mode of acquisition of skills and basic equipment by each group, and their respective clientele. The author discusses similar themes in *Urban poverty, underdevelopment and recuperative production in Dakar, Senegal* (Swansea, Wales: University College Centre for Development Studies, 1977. 9p. [Occasional Paper, 1]); and 'The crisis of the self-employed: petty production and capitalist production in Dakar', in *The political economy of underdevelopment: dependence in Senegal.* Edited by Rita Cruise O'Brien (Beverly Hills, California; London: Sage Publications, 1979, p. 126-55. [Sage Series on African Modernization and Development, 3]).

385 **Le travail des cadres moyens africaines au Sénégal. I. Exigences, aptitudes et formations.** (The work of African middle managers in Senegal. I. Requirements, aptitudes and training.)
R. Descloitres, J.-C. Reverdy, R. Volante. Dakar; Aix en Provence, France: Centre Africain des Sciences Humaines Appliquées, 1962/3. 39p.

A study of the skills and training required by African middle managers in companies and administrative structures in Senegal, and the ways in which they can be developed through training programmes.

Dakar: métropole ouest-africaine. (Dakar: a West African metropolis.)
See item no. 34.

The uprooted of the Western Sahel: migrants' quest for cash in the Senegambia.
See item no. 133.

Gender, class and rural transition: agribusiness and the food crisis in Senegal.
See item no. 341.

Femmes prolétaires du Sénégal, à la ville et aux champs. (Proletarian women in Senegal, in the town and in the fields.)
See item no. 533.

Transport and Communications

386 **Dakar: station-service de l'Atlantique.** (Dakar: service station of the Atlantic.)
   Journal de la Marine Marchande, no. 1748 (18 June 1953). 103p. (special issue).

A glossy public relations exercise aimed at the international shipping community, this book consists of a series of short articles, lavishly illustrated with black-and-white photographs, on various aspects of the work of the port of Dakar.

387 **Dakar and West African economic development.**
   Richard J. Peterec.   New York: Columbia University Press, 1967. 206p.

A study of the changing role of the port of Dakar after independence, the reduced size of its hinterland, and the prospects for the increased traffic in groundnuts and phosphates offsetting some of these losses.

388 **Les escales du fleuve Sénégal.** (The ports of call on the Senegal river.)
   Assane Seck.   *Revue Géographique Africaine Occidentale*. no. 1/2 (1965), p. 71-112.

This paper describes the development of trade along the Senegal river, with sections on the main ports: Bakel, Matam, Kaédi, Dagana, Podor, Rosso and Boghé. The development of the rail and road network has lessened the river's importance, a trend which has been intensified by the high levels of emigration from the Senegal river valley.

389 **'Paris-Dakar'. . . En chemin de fer!** (Paris-Dakar . . . By rail!)
   Monique Lakroum.   *Histoire*, vol. 82 (1985), p. 66-75.

A short paper which gives an account of the many different schemes, all ultimately unsuccessful, for building a railway across the Sahara to link Europe with Dakar.

390   **Les salaires dans le port de Dakar.** (Wages in the port of Dakar.)
      Monique Lakroum.   *Revue Française d'Histoire d'Outre-Mer*, vol. 63,
      no. 3/4 (1976), p. 640-53.

A study of the impact on both European and African workers of the depression of the
early 1930s and the fall in the volume of sea traffic. The paper analyses the relationship
between pay and living costs for the main groups of workers during the 1930s.

391   **Les vélos de Kaolack.** (The bikes of Kaolack.)
      Alain Morice.   *Cahiers d'Etudes Africaines*, vol. 21, no. 1-3 (1981),
      p. 197-210.

An account of the transport industry in Kaolack, where mopeds are used as 'taxis'. It
describes the leasing arrangements between the drivers who operate the service and
the businessmen who own the machines.

Bulletin Statistique.
See item no. 418.

Banking and Finance

392 **L'aide au développement du Canada au Sénégal. Une étude indépendante. Canadian development assistance to Senegal: an independent study.**
Réal Lavergne, E. Philip English.   Ottawa: L'Institute Nord-Sud, 1987. 185p. (French edition), 173p. (English edition).
One of a series on Canada's foreign aid programmes to Third World countries, this book examines the context of aid, foreign aid programmes, the general characteristics of Canadian aid, the aid programmes in the fields of education and fisheries, and other forms including emergency aid channelled through NGOs. It ends with a discussion of the Canadian context of the aid programme, and contains an appendix on construction costs and a lengthy bibliography, a useful source of information on unpublished documents.

393 **Les 'anciennes contributions directes' au Sénégal.** (The 'old direct taxation' in Senegal.)
P.-A. Denis.   *Annales Africaines*, no. 1 (1961), p. 129-249.
The major account of the financial system in Senegal at the end of the colonial period, much of which is devoted to a description of the various categories of taxes in operation, including taxation of buildings and other property, land taxes, taxation through licences, tax on personal estates and the poll tax.

394 **Capital-market controls and credit rationing in Mali and Senegal.**
Susan Hickok, Clive S. Gray.   *Journal of Modern African Studies*, vol. 19, no. 1 (1981), p. 57-73.
A technical study of interest rates and forms of saving based on research carried out in 1980, which took into account not only the formal financial sector, but also other forms of savings by the local people, for example, in cattle and buildings. The paper argues that by keeping interest rates artificially low, the state was depressing the level of

savings through banks, and therefore of investment capital, and it considers the beneficial effects which would follow from a reversal of the policy.

395 **Condensé du régime fiscal du Sénégal.** (Digest of the fiscal regime of Senegal.)
Dakar: Chambre de Commerce d'Agriculture et d'Industrie, 1962. 232p.

A description and statistical analysis of public finance in Senegal to September 1962, including forms of indirect taxation and investment codes. Also relevant are the *Comptes économiques* (Economic accounts), published by the Direction de la Statistique, Dakar (1959-), which feature information on services and production, administration, finance and banking, and foreign trade.

396 **La crise de l'ajustement.** (The adjustment crisis.)
Makhtar Diouf. *Politique Africaine*, vol. 45 (March 1992), p. 62-85.

A survey of the effects on the population of the various phases of the structural adjustment programme implemented from 1979 onwards, which considers both the economic and social effects. The latter include rising unemployment, deteriorating terms of trade for producers, falling standards in education and training, poorer health and increased poverty. The author takes issue with a USAID report which concludes that, in the case of Senegal at least, the poorest people have not been the worst affected by the programmes.

397 **The decline of the franc zone: monetary politics in francophone Africa.**
Nicholas van de Walle. *African Affairs*, vol. 90, no. 360 (1991), p. 383-407.

An account of the developing crisis in the Franc Zone in the 1980s, due to the collapse of commodity prices and the appreciation of the French franc against the dollar, and also to increasing political instability in some member states. The author argues that the existence of the zone has supported patrimonial politics and urban bias in the economies of these states and helped delay significant political reform.

398 **Finances publiques sénégalaises.** (Senegalese public finances.)
Mamadou Diop. Dakar: Les Nouvelles Editions Africaines, 1977. 271p.

This is a legal rather than an economic text, examining the legal and administrative structure of public finance in Senegal. It is in two parts, the first on the general legal structure, and the second on particular topics such as taxation and revenue. A series of appendices contain legislative extracts. As with many of these legal texts, this is very much an overview of how the system should work, rather than how it does work.

399 **Public international development financing in Senegal.**
Robert F. Meagher. New York: Columbia University School of Law (mimeo), 1963. 150p.

This study by an American lawyer deals with external aid to Senegal in the early years of independence. After general chapters on the economy, planning and financial institutions, there is an account of aid programmes and case studies of the development of roads and housing.

400 **La zone franc est-elle le bouc-émissaire de l'échec du développement?**
(The franc zone, a scapegoat for development failures?)
Claude Freud. *Cahiers d'Etudes Africaines*, vol. 31, no. 1/2 (1991),
p. 159-74.

A defence of the franc zone against World Bank criticisms that, by maintaining an
overvalued currency in its member states, it has slowed down economic growth. Freud
argues that the zone has been a source of financial stability, and that the experience of
countries outside it shows that devaluation does not necessarily produce growth.

401 **Zone franc et développement africain.** (The franc zone and African
development.)
Patrick Guillaumont, Sylviane Guillaumont. Paris: Economica, 1984.
337p.

A description of the workings of the franc zone, consisting of France and thirteen
former colonies, which sheds light on the changes that have taken place since
independence. Originally conceived as a zone to protect the currencies of the newly
independent states, it later gave them a degree of monetary stability in an increasingly
unstable international environment. The book also considers the problems of
conducting monetary policy in view of the financial difficulties many of the member
states have faced over recent years, and it examines the consequences of the franc zone
for the development strategies of member countries.

Food aid to Senegal: disincentive effects and commercial displacement.
See item no. 338.

International Trade and Commerce

402 **Business opportunities in the 1980s: Francophone West Africa:**
Cameroon, Gabon, Ivory Coast, Guinea, Senegal, Benin, Togo.
[Paul Clifford]. London: Metra Consulting Group, 1984. 340p.
Pages 238-80 of this publication deal with business opportunities in Senegal, with
information on imports and exports; development (health, education and infrastructure); energy; agriculture; mining; industrial processing and manufacture; trade
policy, exchange controls, etc; and investing in Senegal.

403 **Doing business in Senegal: information guide.**
New York: Price Waterhouse, 1982. 76p.
One of a series of Price Waterhouse guides to the countries of the world aimed at
assisting those involved in foreign trade and investment, this volume on Senegal covers
local business practices, financial regulations, systems of accounting and taxation
structures.

404 **Senegal: the market for selected manufactured products from developing**
countries.
Geneva: International Trade Centre, 1969. 161p.
Now a fascinating period piece, this mimeographed manual was one of a series
compiled by the United Nations Conference on Trade and Development (UNCTAD)
to stimulate trade between developing countries, intended to provide practical
information for new exporters to Senegal. For statistical details of Senegalese imports,
see also: *Importations: commerce spécial* (Imports: foreign trade), published by the
Direction de la Statistique, Dakar, monthly from 1962 then half-yearly from 1970. This
is a sister volume to *Exportations: commerce spécial* (Exports: foreign trade) from the
same source.

405 **Le Sénégal à la dérive des marchés mondiaux.** (Senegal adrift from the world markets.)
Diego Perez de Arce. *Tiers-Monde*, vol. 27, no. 105 (1986), p. 163-77.

A study by a consultant to the French government of the dependency of the Senegalese economy. It discusses the complexity and instability of the world markets in food oils and rice, which Senegal can do nothing to control, and suggests that the problems can be partly alleviated by import substitution, stabilizing the quantity of goods available for export. In Senegal's case, this fluctuates widely from year to year, and necessitates cooperation with other countries in the region to obtain better terms in trade negotiations with the rest of the world.

L'impact des intérêts coloniaux: SCOA et CFAO dans l'ouest africain, 1910-1965. (The impact of colonial interests: SCOA and CFAO in West Africa, 1910-1965.)
See item no. 315.

ECOWAS and the economic integration of West Africa.
See item no. 510.

L'integration économique de l'Afrique de l'Ouest confrontée aux solides liens de dépendance des états africains de l'extérieur. (The economic integration of West Africa in the face of the solid links of external dependence of African states.)
See item no. 511.

Liberalising trade.
See item no. 512.

The state of economic integration in north west Africa south of the Sahara: the emergence of the Economic Community of West African States (ECOWAS).
See item no. 513.

Industrial and Labour Relations

406 **Les débuts du syndicalisme au Sénégal au temps du Front Populaire.**
(The beginnings of trade unionism in Senegal during the Popular Front
period.)
Nicole Bernard-Duquenet. *Mouvement Social*, no. 101 (1977),
p. 37-59.
Based on both archival and oral material, this paper deals with conflict in the
Senegalese union movement after its legalization by the Popular Front government in
France during the 1930s. When discussions with the unions were offered by the
Socialist governor general, the union leaders were more anxious to accept than the
rank and file members, whose main concern was their standard of living.

407 **The determinants of industrial-sector earnings in Senegal.**
Jan Svejnar. *Journal of Development Economics*, vol. 15, no. 1/3
(1984), p. 289-311.
This econometric study is based on the 1976 Industrial Census in Senegal, and
compares the earnings of Senegalese, other Africans and Europeans. Its conclusions
are unsurprising: there are variations in earnings, and Senegalese earn less than other
Africans and much less than Europeans. African women appear to earn as much as
their male counterparts, but non-African women earn less than non-African men.

408 **Industrial relations and the political process in Senegal.**
George R. Martens. Geneva: International Institute for Labour
Studies, 1982. 122p.
An account of the organization and structure of the movement, and its links with
industry and government before and after the political reforms of the 1970s.

409 **Labor relations in Senegal: history, institutions and perspectives.**
     Peter C. Bloch. Ann Arbor, Michigan: Centre for Research on
     Economic Development, University of Michigan, 1978. 41p.

A short account of the development of Senegalese labour law which also deals with the
legal basis of the trade union system, its role in the political system, and the structure
and function of employers' organizations. The labour system's roots in French law are
emphasized, particularly in terms of standards and procedures, and the effects of these
on production, prices and demand are investigated. There is also information on
conditions of employment, including wages, child labour, worker's compensation
schemes, social security and fringe benefits.

410 **Le mouvement syndical sénégalais à la veille de l'indépendance: un lieu
     de formation des élites politiques.** (The union movement in Senegal on
     the eve of independence: a site for the formation of political élites.)
     Mar Fall. *Présence Africaine*, no. 131 (1984), p. 24-34.

A brief study of the development of unionism in Senegal, against the background of
the level of economic development and political dependency, in which the intellectuals
played an important role. A useful source of references on the development of the
movement in the country as a whole.

411 **Le refus du travail forcé au Sénégal oriental.** (The rejection of forced
     labour in eastern Senegal.)
     Oussouby Touré. *Cahiers d'Etudes Africaines*, vol. 24, no. 1 (1984),
     p. 25-38.

A description of forced labour and workers' living conditions with reference to a sisal
plantation and factory at Wasadu in eastern Senegal, which was only able to function
with the help of the colonial authorities, who provided conscript labour. After the
Second World War and the abolition of forced labour, production soon collapsed as
the aged machinery deteriorated and the workers left en masse.

412 **The Senegalese general strike of 1946 and the labor question in post-war
     French Africa.**
     Frederick Cooper. *Canadian Journal of African Studies*, vol. 24, no. 2
     (1990), p. 165-215.

An important archival study of a labour dispute which raised major questions both
about colonial labour policy and about colonialism itself. An African labour movement
had developed during the 1930s, but had been suppressed during the war. The lifting of
the ban led to increased political activity, demands by urban workers for increased
wages and a reduction in discrimination, eventually culminating in a strike by black
civil servants in Dakar which was soon joined by other workers.

413 **Strike movements as part of the anti-colonial struggle in French West
     Africa.**
     Jean Suret-Canale. *Tarikh*, vol. 5, no. 3 (1977), p. 44-56.

A summary article by a leading French Marxist historian of West Africa, who argues
that though strikes were relatively infrequent up to 1936, in the later colonial period
they were increasingly important in the independence movement.

414 **Trade unions and politics in French West Africa during the Fourth Republic.**
Guy Pfefferman. *African Affairs*, vol. 66 (1967), p. 213-30.
The author accounts for the lack of union involvement in politics in terms of the limited participation in politics of union leaders themselves, and their concern with economic and social rather than political issues.

415 **Le travail inégal: paysans et salariés sénégalais face à la crise des années trente.** (Unequal work: Senegalese peasants and wage-earners during the 1930s crisis.)
Monique Lakroum. Paris: Editions l'Harmattan, 1982. 187p.
An important study of the labour policy during the colonial period in Senegal, including the use of forced labour and the exploitation of the peasantry. The second part discusses the urban labour market: migration, under-employment and unemployment, the growth of militancy and unrest, and the evolution of a salaried workforce in advance of independence.

Statistics

416 **African statistical yearbook, 1987.**
Addis Ababa: Economic Commission for Africa, n.d. (c. 1991). 11th
ed. 4 vols.

Regularly updated, this is one of the fullest and most important source of statistical data on African countries, with over 2,000 tables, this publication contains country chapters with sections on population and employment, national accounts, agriculture, forestry and fishing, industry, transport and communciations, foreign trade, prices, finance and social statistics. Volume 2 deals with West Africa.

417 **Annuaire Statistique.** (Statistical Yearbook.)
Dakar: Ministère de l'Enseignement et de la Formation Professionelle, 1966/7.

This annual publication contains data on professional and technical training, including details on colleges, schools, their staff and classes. The Ministry of Education and Culture also publishes, somewhat irregularly, data on teaching at primary and secondary levels in *Statistiques de l'enseignement primaire et de l'enseignement secondaire* (Statistics on primary and secondary education).

418 **Bulletin Statistique.** (Statistical Bulletin.)
Dakar: Ministère de Transports et Télécommunications, 1960- .
quarterly.

A quarterly bulletin covering statistical analysis, particularly concerning port and railway traffic.

419 **Bulletin Statistique et Economique Mensuel.** (Monthly Statistical and Economic Bulletin).
Dakar: Grande Imprimerie Africaine, for the Ministère du Plan et de l'Industrie, Direction de la Statistique, 1960- . monthly.

This monthly publication gives statistical information on climate, demography, agriculture, industry, transport, commerce, imports and exports. It also provides details on the prices of construction materials, as well as the government's financial and budgetary position.

420 Compendium of social statistics and indicators, 1988.
New York: United Nations Publications, 1991. 4th ed. 685p.

A vast collection of statistics and indicators on global, regional, national and urban social conditions and social change, which draws on the resources of the UN Statistical Office, together with its affiliates (including. FAO, ILO, UNESCO, and WHO). One hundred and seventy-eight countries are detailed in fifty-five tables covering data on the whole range of demography, sociology, economics and health issues. Many of the tables give time-series data and projections for the future, and there are also helpful indexes. Other useful UN publications include *Compendium of housing statistics* (New York: United Nations Publications 1980. 3rd ed. 354p.). This covers the period 1975-77 (the first two editions cover the periods to 1971, and 1972-74), with information on global housing and related data, and summaries of national housing censuses. The data is unreliable and incomplete but this is the only source of global information; *Demographic yearbook* (New York: United Nations, 1982. 34th ed. 152p.) which contains international demographic statistics for 200 areas, including information on natality, household composition, various morality rates, nuptuality, divorce, and the composition of the population by marital status and sex; and *Statistical yearbook* (New York: UN Department of Economic and Social Information, 38th issue. 1993, 1109p.). This includes world and regional summaries, population and social statistics, and statistics on economic activity.

421 Development cooperation.
Washington, DC: Organization of Economic Cooperation and Development, 1992. 220p. annual.

This annual publication is the major source of information on financial flows to developing countries. Also available from the OECD is *Geographical distribution of financial flows to developing countries*. (Washington, DC: OECD Publications. annual). This publication deals with the volume and sources of external financial aid for 100 developing countries, and is an important source of highly technical information relating to debt.

422 Yearbook: trade.
Vol. 44, 1990. Rome: FAO, 1991, 339p.

This important series of standard statistical sources currently includes separate volumes on production, trade, fertilizer use, a commodity review and outlook, the state of food and agriculture, animal health, fisheries and forest products.

423 Government Finance Statistics Yearbook.
Washington, DC: International Monetary Fund Publications, 1976- .
Vol. 16, 1992. 711p. annual.

The basic source of information on government finance, including revenue expenditure, lending, financing and debt, at local, state and supranational levels. As with most of these volumes it is divided into world tables, facilitating comparisons between countries, and individual country profiles. Also published annually by the International Monetary Fund are: *International Financial Statistics Yearbook* (Washington, DC: International Monetary Fund, 1947-), a standard publication with a mass of statistical information divided into three parts: charts; world tables covering a range of economic indicators, and country tables. There are four-page entries showing performance on major financial indicators over a thirty-year period; *International Monetary Fund Annual Report* (Washington, DC: International Monetary Fund), an overview of the bank's activities includes tables showing the usage of bank resources by individual countries; and *Direction of trade statistics yearbook* (Washington, DC: International Monetary Fund), a major source of information for global imports and exports. It consists of a series of world and area tables, followed by country tables, listing the most important trading partners for each country.

424 **The new book of world rankings.**
New York: Facts on File, 1984. 490p.
Contains rankings of 190 countries in terms of 343 variables, grouped under: geography and climate; vital statistics; population dynamics and the family; race and religion; politics and international relations; foreign aid; military power; economy; finance and banking; trade; agriculture; industry and mining; energy; labour; transport and communications; consumption; housing; health and food; education; crime; media; cities; culture. The work is updated every four years and is the best available source of ranked data, for those who like league tables.

425 **Rapport annuel: tome I: partie administrative et statistique.** (Annual report: vol. 1: administrative and statistical part.)
Dakar: Ministère du Développement Industriel et de l'Environnement, Direction des Mines et de la Géologie, 1967- .
Annual report with statistical sections on mines, mining personnel, production, investment and explosives.

426 **Situation économique du Sénégal.**
Dakar: Sénégal, Ministère des Finances et Affaires Economiques, Direction de la Statistique, 1962- . annual.
The standard annual source of statistics on demography, health, education and the economy. The Société Africaine d'Edition, Dakar, also publishes *Le Sénégal en chiffres: annuaire statistique du Sénégal* (Senegal in figures: statistical yearbook of Senegal) (Société Africaine d'Edition, 1976- . annual), which contains sections on geography, population and the economy.

427 **The World Bank annual report 1991.**
Washington, DC: World Bank, 1991. 238p.
The official annual overview of the Bank. Unlike the World Tables (item 432) or the World Development Report (item 428) it does not give systematic data which can be compared over time, but it does contain a large amount of information on activities both in individual regions and countries. The 1991 edition includes sections on the Special Program of Assistance for Sub-Saharan Africa (p. 44-6), and a subregional perspective for West Africa (p. 111-12). At the end is a list of bank offices and an index. Other relevant annual World Bank publications include: *Commodity trade and price trends* (Washington, DC: World Bank Publications), on the value of imports and exports of the main commodities in developing countries; *World debt tables* (Washington, DC: World Bank Publications), a major source of information on medium- and long-term indebtedness, the core of which is the set of debt tables, including country-by-country information on 103 states.

428 **World Development Report 1991: the challenge of development.**
New York: Oxford University Press for the World Bank, 1978-
annual.

A standard source of statistics published annually since 1978, each volume consists of
general essays on trends and issues, followed by a select bibliography and, most
importantly, a statistical appendix. The 1991 issue includes country-by-country tables
on investment, savings and current account balance (Senegal has a 'severely indebted
middle income economy') and outstanding debt; world development indicators; and
details of a whole range of demographic, national and international economic and
other issues.

429 **World fertility survey.**
Voorburg, The Netherlands: World Fertility Survey, International
Statistical Institute, 1972- . irregular.

A huge international database consisting of six series of publications: comparative
studies, summaries of fertility surveys, occasional papers (including Senegal), scientific
reports, country reports (including Senegal) and technical bulletins. See also *World
Fertility Survey: major findings and implications*, (Voorburg, The Netherlands: World
Fertility Survey, 1984. 61p.).

430 **World handbook of political and social indicators.**
Charles Lewis Taylor, David A. Jodice. New Haven, Connecticut:
Yale University Press, 1983. 3rd ed. 2 vols.

A large-scale compendium of statistics and national rankings for a range of economic
and political variables. The first volume is mainly economic, with data on size of
government and allocation of resources, wealth production and population size,
inequality, literacy, education, and economic structure. The second volume is mainly
political, and includes data on protest demonstrations, political strikes, riots, armed
attacks, assassinations, deaths from political violence, political executions, national
elections, regular and irregular transfers of power. It ends with time-series profiles for
each country, relating these political events to government changes. Reliability of the
data is discussed and the appendices contain a lists of states and sources.

431 **World population, 1979: recent demographic estimates for the countries
and regions of the world.**
US Bureau of the Census. Washington, DC: US Government Printing
Office, 1980. 4th ed. 502p.

Based on US and United Nations data, this compendium includes world and regional
summary tables, in addition to country profiles. Useful features include the annotations
on sources and methods of estimation.

432 **World Tables 1992.**
Baltimore, Maryland: Johns Hopkins University Press for the World
Bank, 1992. 686p.

A standard World Bank source of statistics with useful and concise tables for each
country showing performance over the decade on a series of standard indicators,
including balance of payments, debt, foreign trade, revenue and expenditure. The final

part contains a series of tables on the main social indicators, including population, health and nutrition, education, employment and income, housing and consumption.

433 **Year Book of Labour Statistics.**
Geneva: International Labour Organization, 1935-36- . annual.
Vol. 52, 1993, 1,225p.
The most important source book on labour statistics available, with chapters dealing with the total and economically active populations, employment, unemployment, hours of work, wages, labour costs, consumer prices, occupational injuries, and industrial disputes. Senegalese coverage is, however, rather poor.

Les premiers recensements au Sénégal – le Sénégal centre-ouest et son évolution démographique (Siin, Saalum, Bawol, pays de l'ouest). Partie I: Présentation des documents. (The first census in Senegal: West Central Senegal and its demographic evolution in Siin, Saalum, Bawol and western regions. Part I: Presentation of documents.)
See item no. 144.

Recensement démographique de Dakar (1955). Résultats statistiques du recensement générale de la population de la commune de Dakar, effectué en avril et mai 1955. Fascicule 1. (Demographic census of Dakar. Statistical results of their general census of the population of the commune of Dakar, conducted in April and May 1995. Volume 1.)
See item no. 145.

Recensement général de la population d'avril 1976. Resultats définitifs, données corrigées. (General census of the population, April 1976: definitive results, corrected data.)
See item no. 147.

Senegal.
See item no. 148.

Politics and Government

General

434 **Forces politiques en Afrique noire.** (Political forces in Black Africa.)
Bakary Traoré, Mamadou Lô, Jean-Louis Alibert.   Paris: Presses
Universitaires de France, 1966. 312p. (Travaux et recherches de la
Faculté de Droit et des Sciences Economiques de Paris, série 'Afrique',
no. 2).

Contains three long essays on African politics, two of them directly relating to Senegal.
Traoré discusses the traditional system of politics and stratification, together with the
growth of political parties in the post-war period. Lô deals with the organization and
doctrines of the ruling party, the (then) Union Progressiste Sénégalaise, and includes
its by-laws as an appendix. The third essay is more general, on opposition groups in
Black African politics, including unions, students, and the military.

435 **Histoire politique du Sénégal: institutions, droit et société.** (Political
history of Senegal: institutions, law, and society.)
Gerti Hesseling, translated from the Dutch by Catherine Miginiac.
Paris: Editions Karthala, 1985. 437p.

The standard account of the Senegalese reception of French political institutions and
constitutional law. Although it stresses the importance of the French legacy, the author
argues that due to factors such as Senghorism, the political strength of the local élite,
and patron-client links based on Islam, Senegalese politics have developed their own
character. The chapters of the book give a detailed account of constitutional
developments from the precolonial period to Abdou Diouf, including informative
useful discussions of multi-party democracy, constitutional law and political rights.

436 **Saints and politicians: essays in the organisation of a Senegalese peasant society.**
Donal B. Cruise O'Brien. Cambridge, England: Cambridge University Press, 1975. 213p. (African Studies Series 15).
An important collection of essays, some of them reprints, which extend some of the themes of the author's earlier book *The Mourides of Senegal* (item no. 571) dealing with the style and personalities in Senegalese politics and the relationship between politics, economics and Islam in the 19th and 20th centuries.

Senegal: an African nation between Islam and the West.
See item no. 14.

Francophone sub-Saharan Africa 1880-1985.
See item no. 195.

Histoire du Sénégal. (History of Senegal.)
See item no. 196.

Historical dictionary of Senegal.
See item no. 198.

The Mourides of Senegal: the political and economic organization of an Islamic brotherhood.
See item no. 571.

Muslim brotherhoods and politics in Senegal.
See item no. 572.

Liberté. (Liberty.)
See item no. 723.

Ce que je crois. (What I believe.)
See item no. 724.

Léopold Sédar Senghor and African socialism.
See item no. 726.

Léopold Sédar Senghor and the politics of negritude.
See item no. 730.

Léopold Sédar Senghor: an intellectual biography.
See item no. 731.

Black, French and African: a life of Léopold Sédar Senghor.
See item no. 738.

Indigenous political systems

437 **Le pouvoir politique en Sénégambie dès origines à la conquête coloniale.**
(Political power in Senegambia from its origins to the colonial
conquest.)
M'Baye Guèye. *Revue Française d'Histoire d'Outre-Mer*, vol. 68,
no. 1/4 (1981), p. 380-7.
A brief overview of the effects of population movement, Islam and the slave trade on
Senegambian politics, resulting in more highly centralized states, the rulers of which
were increasingly involved in economic issues.

438 **Pouvoir politique traditionnel en Afrique occidentale: essais sur les
institutions politiques précoloniales.** (Traditional political power in West
Africa: an essay in precolonial political institutions.)
Pathé Diagne. Paris: Présence Africaine, 1967. 294p.
Three studies of precolonial politics in Senegal, which deal with the Serer of Sine-
Saloum, Kayor, and the relationship between Islam and politics among the Tukulor of
the Fuuta Toro. The author also discusses Serer politics and social stratification in
'Royaumes sérères: les institutions traditionnelles du Sine Saloum' (Serer kingdoms:
the traditional institutions of Sine-Saloum), *Présence Africaine*, vol. 54 (1965),
p. 142-72.

Genèse du pouvoir charismatique en Basse Casamance (Sénégal). (Genesis of
charismatic power in the Lower Casamance region of Senegal.)
See item no. 152.

**La société Wolof: tradition et changement. Les systèmes d'inégalité et de
domination.** (Wolof society: tradition and change. Systems of inequality and
domination.)
See item no. 172.

Albouri Ndiaye et la résistance à la conquête française du Sénégal. (Albouri
Ndiaye and the resistance to the French conquest of Senegal.)
See item no. 209.

Ancient Ghana and Mali.
See item no. 210.

**Aristocrats, slaves, and peasants: power and dependency in the Wolof states,
1700-1850.**
See item no. 211.

Bundu in the eighteenth century.
See item no. 212.

Chroniques du Fouta sénégalais. (Chronicles of the Senegalese Fuuta.)
See item no. 213.

Chronique du Wâlo sénégalais. (Chronicle of Walo, Senegal: 1186?-1855.)
See item no. 214.

Politics and Government. Indigenous political systems

Contribution à l'histoire de l'Empire du Mali (xiii-xvie siècles). (Contribution to the history of the Mali Empire, 13th-16th centuries.)
See item no. 216.

La dévolution du pouvoir au Fuuta-Tooro. (The devolution of power in the Fuuta Toro.)
See item no. 220.

The early states of the Western Sudan to 1500.
See item no. 221.

Economic change in precolonial Africa.
See item no. 222.

Essai sur l'histoire du Saloum et du Rip. (Essay on the history of Saloum and Rip.)
See item no. 223.

Le Grand Jolof (xiiie-xvie siècle). (The Grand Jolof kingdom, 13th-16th centuries.)
See item no. 224.

Histoire de Boundou. (History of Bundu.)
See item no. 225.

Histoire des Mandingues de l'Ouest. Le royaume du Gabou. (History of the Western Manding. The kingdom of Gabou.)
See item no. 227.

A history of the Upper Guinea Coast 1545 to 1800.
See item no. 230.

The Holy War of Umar Tal.
See item no. 231.

The impact of the Atlantic slave trade on the societies of the Western Sudan.
See item no. 232.

Islam and the state of Kajoor: a case of successful resistance to jihad.
See item no. 233.

The Islamic regime of Fuuta Tooro: an anthology of oral traditions transcribed in Pulaar and translated into English.
See item no. 234.

Jihad in West Africa: early phases and inter-relations in Mauritania and Senegal.
See item no. 235.

Mandingo kingdoms of the Senegambia: traditionalism, Islam and European expansion.
See item no. 236.

Politics and Government. Indigenous political systems

Les Maures et le Futa Toro au XVIIIe siècle. (The Moors and the Fuuta Toro in the 18th century.)
See item no. 237.

Ordres, castes et états en pays sérèr (Sénégal): essai d'interprétation d'un système politique en transition. (Orders, castes and estates in Serer country, Senegal: an interpretative essay on a political system in transition.)
See item no. 239.

Les portes de l'or. Le royaume de Galam (Sénégal) de l'ère musulmane au temps de négriers (VIII-XVIIIe siècle). (The golden gates. The kingdom of Galam, Senegal, from the Muslim era to the period of the slave traders, 8th-18th centuries.)
See item no. 240.

The pre-nineteenth century political tradition of the Wolof.
See item no. 242.

Le royaume du Waalo: le Sénégal avant la conquête. (The kingdom of Walo: Senegal before the conquest.)
See item no. 245.

La royauté *(mansaya)* **chez les Mandingues occidentaux d'après leurs traditions orales.** (Kingship, *mansaya*, among the western Mandinka as reflected in their oral traditions.)
See item no. 246.

La Sénégambie du xv au xixe siècle: traite négrier, Islam et conquête coloniale. (Senegal from the 15th to the 19th century: slave trade, Islam and colonial conquests.)
See item no. 247.

Le Soudan occidental au temps des grands empires xie-xvie siècles. (The Western Sudan in the time of the great empires, 11th-16th centuries.)
See item no. 249.

A tentative chronology of Futa Toro from the sixteenth through the nineteenth centuries.
See item no. 250.

Theoretical issues in historical international politics: the case of the Senegambia.
See item no. 251.

The Western Atlantic coast 1600-1800.
See item no. 254.

The Wolof kingdom of Kayor.
See item no. 255.

Pre-independence politics

439 **Political parties in French-speaking West Africa.**
Ruth Schachter Morgenthau.   Oxford: Clarendon Press, 1964. 725p.

A pioneering study which is still a standard text on political developments in French West Africa, mainly in Senegal, the Ivory Coast, Guinea and Mali, around the time of independence, based largely on material collected for an Oxford thesis in the mid-1950s. Much of the material was gathered from the African political leaders rather than from the French.

440 **Politics and government in former French West and Equatorial Africa: a critical bibliography.**
John A. Ballard.   *Journal of Modern African Studies*, vol. 3, no. 4 (1965), p. 589-605.

A concise summary of what was at that point a rapidly expanding literature, published in the wake of independence. It provides a useful overview on work in both English and French on the French policy of assimilation, colonial administration, postwar politics, and the early years of independence, and ends with a research agenda.

441 **Senegal.**
Ernest Milcent.   In: *African one-party states*. Edited by Gwendolen M. Carter.   Ithaca, New York: Cornell University Press, 1962, p. 87-148.

A standard account from the time of independence of the development of Senegalese nationalism. There are brief sections on the coming of the French, colonial rule, and the process of decolonization. The latter part of the paper provides a sketch of the Senegalese economy and of political processes and issues in the early years of independence.

442 **Senegal: the elections to the Territorial Assembly, March 1957.**
Kenneth Robinson.   In: *Five elections in Africa: a group of electoral studies*. Edited by W. J. M. MacKenzie, Kenneth Robinson.   Oxford: Clarendon Press, 1960, p. 281-7.

A detailed account of the Territorial Assembly elections held in Senegal in 1957, to elect African representatives for the assembly in France, a system discontinued after independence. The paper describes the historical background to the election, in Senegal's relations with France and the legal position of the four communes, the electoral system and the progress of the campaign itself.

French West Africa.
See item no. 5.

France and West Africa: an anthology of historical documents.
See item no. 194.

West Africa: the former French states.
See item no. 202.

La fondation de Dakar (1845-1857-1869). (The foundation of Dakar, 1845-1857-1869.)
See item no. 263.

La colonie du Sénégal au temps de Brière de l'Isle (1876-1881). (The colony of Senegal in the time of Brière de l'Isle 1876-1881.)
See item no. 279.

The conquest of the Western Sudan: a study in French military imperialism.
See item no. 280.

The establishment of elective institutions in Senegal, 1869-1880.
See item no. 282.

Islam and imperialism in Senegal: Sine-Saloum, 1847-1914.
See item no. 285.

Senegal: a study in French assimilation policy.
See item no. 293.

Le Sénégal: la France dans l'Afrique occidentale. (Senegal: France in West Africa.)
See item no. 294.

Une source de l'histoire coloniale du Sénégal: les rapports de situation politiques (1874-1891). (A source for Senegalese colonial history: the reports on the political situation, 1874-1891.)
See item no. 301.

Double impact: France and Africa in the age of imperialism.
See item no. 306.

The emergence of black politics in Senegal: the struggle for power in the four communes 1900-1920.
See item no. 307.

French West Africa and decolonization.
See item no. 309.

French-speaking tropical Africa.
See item no. 310.

Le Front Populaire au Sénégal (mai 1936-octobre 1938). (The Popular Front in Senegal, May 1936-October 1938.)
See item no. 312.

Galandou Diouf et le Front Populaire. (Galandou Diouf and the Popular Front.)
See item no. 313.

Quatorze millions de français dans la fédération de l'Afrique occidentale française? (Were there fourteen million Frenchmen in the French West African Federation?)
See item no. 316.

The Second World War: prelude to decolonisation in Africa.
See item no. 317.

Post-independence politics

443 **Après Senghor – a socialist Senegal?**
Pamela Cox, Richard Kessler. *African Affairs,* vol. 79, no. 316
(1980), p. 327-42.
A concise summary of the theory and practice of Senegalese socialism during the early
years of independence, which concludes that it remained largely political rhetoric, the
personal philosophy of Senghor which was never fully institutionalized.

444 **Casamance under siege.**
Peter da Costa. *West Africa* (26 Jan. – 3 Feb. 1991), p. 100-2.
An account of the Casamance emergency and the escalating death toll, in the wake of
the government's determination to crush the Movement des Forces Démocratiques de
Casamance (MFDC), by the appointment of a tough military governor. The article
discusses the Amnesty International report on the situation, the implications for
Senegal's relations with its southern neighbours, and the prospects for ending the
conflict.

445 **Le 'contrat social' sénégalais à l'épreuve.** (The Senegalese 'social
contract' on trial.)
Donal B. Cruise O'Brien. *Politique Africaine* vol. 45 (March 1992),
p. 9-20.
A discussion of the gradual breakdown of the historically close relationships between
political leaders and the Islamic brotherhoods in Senegal, which ends with speculation
about future developments. O'Brien envisages the possibility of the emergence of an
Islamic political party, but as this would become the arena for conflict between the
brotherhoods, it would probably not offer a serious threat to the government.

446 **L'évolution des dirigeants sénégalais de l'indépendance à 1975.**
(The evolution of Senegal's ruling class from independence to 1975.)
Gilles Blanchet. *Cahiers d'Etudes Africaines*, vol. 18, no. 1/2 (1978),
p. 49-78.
A useful source of information on Senegalese politics in the first fifteen years after
independence, this paper discusses changes both in the structure and the personnel of
government, as well as statistical data on the political leadership.

447 **Le Parti Africain de l'Indépendence: les dilemmes d'un mouvement communiste en Afrique occidental.** (The African independence party: the dilemma of a communist movement in West Africa.) William J. Foltz. *Revue Française d'Etudes Politiques Africaines,* vol. 45 (1969), p. 8-35.

A study of a radical political movement which began among African students in France, and which was imported to Senegal in 1957. It attracted some Senegalese intellectuals, but failed to secure wider support, eventually disintegrating during the 1960s.

448 **Le Parti Démocratique Sénégalais. Une opposition légale en Afrique.** (The Senegalese Democratic Party. A legal opposition in Africa.) Christine Desouches. Paris: Berger-Levrault, 1983. 241p.

A full-length account of the PDS, founded in 1974 by Abdoulaye Wade, just before Senegal's return to multi-partyism. It describes the origins of the party, its doctrines and programmes, and its organization and operations. The two final chapters deal with the impact of the party on Senegalese political life, and the implications of further political liberalization following Senghor's retirement. The appendices reproduce documents dealing with party policies, and there is a short bibliography.

449 **Un parti politique africain: l'Union Progressiste Sénégalaise.** (An African political party: the Senegalese Progressive Union.) F. Zuccarelli. Paris: Librairie Générale de Droit et de Jurispridence, 1970. 401p.

Clearly an 'authorized' account of the ruling party, published with government financial support and containing a foreword by Senghor. The four sections deal in turn with Senegalese political history up to 1966, including the breakup of the Mali Federation; the crisis of December 1962, and the party mergers of 1966; the structure and organization of the party; the theory and practice of African socialism; and the relationships between the ruling party and the state. At the end of the book there are some valuable appendices containing the statutes and rules of the party, details of party structure in the Cap-Vert region, the text of the communiqués announcing the fusion of political parties in 1966, and party accounts for 1965. There are also biographical sketches of party leaders, and a ten-page bibliography.

450 **Les partis politiques sénégalais.** (Senegalese political parties.) Jacques Marile Nzouankey. Dakar: Clairafrique, [1983]. 164p.

A study, by a professor of public law, of the rise, fall, and rebirth of party politics in Senegal. The first section deals with the history of political parties from 1946 onwards, including the period of one-party rule from 1960 to 1974, and the subsequent liberalization. The second section deals with party ideologies. The book ends with brief discussions of the aftermath of the 1983 elections, and the general significance of the Senegalese case.

451 **Political consolidation and center-local relations in Senegal.**
Clement Cottingham. *Canadian Journal of African Studies*, vol. 4,
no. 1 (1970), p. 101-20.
A discussion of the trend towards centralization in Senegalese politics in the first
decade of independence, based on case material from Kebemar. Political unrest in the
cities in 1968 led to the UPS (Union Progressiste Sénégalaise) attempting to strengthen
its influence in the rural areas through its control of patronage.

452 **Political opposition in Senegal: 1960-67.**
Donal B. Cruise O'Brien. *Government and Opposition*, vol. 2, no. 4
(1967), p. 557-66.
A study of the opposition parties in Senegal before and after independence, and the
ways in which Senghor and the UPS neutralized or incorporated them, effectively
creating a situation where there was no legal opposition.

453 **Senegal.**
Donal B. Cruise O'Brien. In: *West African states: failure and promise.*
Edited by John Dunn. Cambridge, England: Cambridge University
Press, 1978, p. 173-88.
A lively sketch of Senegalese politics after independence, which focuses on Senghor's
decision to return the country to a limited form of multi-partyism, and which contains
some fascinating observations on the relationship between regionalism and the sport of
wrestling.

454 **Senegal.**
Christian Coulon, Donal B. Cruise O'Brien. In: *Contemporary West
African states.* Edited by Donal B. Cruise O'Brien, John Dunn,
Richard Rathbone. Cambridge, England: Cambridge University
Press, 1989, p. 145-64.
Contains an important concise account of Senegalese politics by two of the leading
writers on Senegal, which asks whether the 'democratization' initiated by Senghor and
pursued by Diouf can respond to the rise of a militant Islam, to the development of a
regionalist movement in the Casamance, and to the discontent provoked by the IMF's
austerity measures. The notes (p. 209-11) contain many useful references.

455 **Sénégal: l'état Abdou Diouf ou le temps des incertitudes.** (Senegal:
Abdou Diouf's state or the time of uncertainty.)
Mar Fall. Paris: L'Harmattan, 1986. 87p.
Written by a Senegalese sociologist teaching in France, this book is a short critical
study of the country's economic problems in the mid-1980s. Fall argues that the despite
the succession of Diouf and the proliferation of opposition parties and newspapers, the
country remains in crisis, with declining groundnut revenues, no national political
consensus and with the government facing challenges both from Islamic movements
and separatism in the Casamance.

456 **Stability and stagnation: the state in Senegal.**
Jonathan S. Barker. *Canadian Journal of African Studies*, vol. 11, no. 1 (1977), p. 23-42.

This paper deals with the question of why Senegal combines political stability with striking economic failure, and argues that it is because the state helps a foreign capitalist class to accumulate a surplus from the Senegalese economy while supporting the local bureaucratic class. This is a clear and forceful statement on a common theme in the underdevelopment literature of the period. The author deals with related themes in an earlier paper, 'Political factionalism in Senegal', *Canadian Journal of African Studies*, vol. 7, no. 2 (1973), p. 287-303.

457 **State power and economic crisis in Senegal.**
Catherine Boone. *Comparative Politics*, vol. 22 (1990), p. 341-579.

This paper presents a concise and useful account of the Senegalese state and its increasing inability to distribute patronage in the face of the prolonged economic crisis in the region resulting from the burden of debt and the effects of the Sahelian drought.

458 **Who's who in Africa: leaders for the 1990s.**
Alan Rake. Metuchen, New Jersey; London: Scarecrow Press, 1992. 448p.

A country-by-country guide to the most important political figures in Africa. The section on each country begins with basic facts and figures (population, date of independence, head of state, type of government, political parties), followed by one-paragraph sketches and longer career histories of selected politicians. The section on Senegal (p. 269-77) includes Ousmane, Camara, President Abdou Diouf, Jean Collin, Cheikh Moustapha Niasse, Daouda Sow, Habib Thiam, and Abdoulaye Wade.

The making of a liberal democracy: Senegal's passive revolution, 1975-1985.
See item no. 319.

The politics of independence: 1960-1986.
See item no. 320.

The political economy of risk and choice in Senegal.
See item no. 326.

The political economy of Senegal under structural adjustment.
See item no. 327.

Ruling class and peasantry in Senegal, 1960-1976: the politics of a monocrop economy.
See item no. 350.

L'Islam au Sénégal: demain les mollahs? La 'question' musulmane et les partis politiques au Sénégal de 1946 à nos jours. (Islam in Senegal: tomorrow the Mullahs? The Muslim 'question' and the political parties in Senegal from 1946 to the present.)
See item no. 568.

Muslim brotherhoods and politics in Senegal in 1985.
See item no. 573.

Muslim politics and development in Senegal.
See item no. 574.

La question islamique au Sénégal. Le regain récent de l'Islam: un ménage pour l'état? (The Islamic question in Senegal. The recent revival of Islam: can the state cope?)
See item no. 577.

Administration and local government

459 **L'administration sénégalaise.** (The Senegalese adminstration.)
Jean-Claude Gautron. Paris: Editions Berger-Levrault, 1971. 95p.
(Encyclopédie administrative publiée par l'Institut International
d'Administration Publique).
A brief formal account of Senegalese administrative law and structure. The main
chapters deal with the legal administrative code, the national, territorial and local
administrative structures, and administrative practices.

460 **Autonomie locale et intégration nationale au Sénégal.**
Jean-Louis Balans, Christian Coulon, Jean-Marc Gastellu. Paris:
Pedone, 1975. 178p. (Bibliothèque Institut d'Etudes Politiques de
Bordeaux, Centre d'Etude d'Afrique Noire, Série Afrique Noire 5).
Presents three useful case studies of the relations between the national and local
political systems from the Fuuta-Toro (Coulon), the Niominka (Balans) and the Serer
of Mbayar (Gastellu). Each of them deals with the history of the group, local political
institutions and the distribution of power, and with relationships between the local
people and the Senegalese state.

461 **Bureaucrats and the Senegalese political process.**
Oladipo Adamolekun. *Journal of Modern African Studies*, vol. 9,
no. 4 (1971), p. 543-59.
A discussion of the political role of bureacrats under the Mamadou Dia and Senghor
administrations. Senegal has followed the French bureaucracy in allowing civil servants
to pursue political careers, and they are highly involved in Senegalese politics.

462   **De la chefferie traditionnelle au canton: évolution du canton colonial au
Sénégal 1855-1960.** (From the traditional chiefdom to the canton:
evolution of the colonial canton in Senegal, 1855-1960.)
François Zucarelli.   *Cahiers d'Etudes Africaines*, vol. 13, no. 2 (1973),
p. 213-38.

A valuable study of the evolution of the French administrative system, from the 1850s,
when French control began to extend beyond the coastal districts of Saint-Louis, to
independence. The extension of French control necessitated the involvement of
traditional chiefs in administration, and the paper describes their gradual evolution
into civil servants.

463   **Freedom and authority in French West Africa.**
Robert Delavignette.   London: Oxford University Press for the
International African Institute, 1950. 152p.

A survey of French colonial administrative practice in West Africa by a former official
in the French Cameroons, and a wonderful source of material for the study of imperial
ideologies. It contains chapters on the role of the commandant, colonial society, the
native territories, native policy, chiefs, law and custom, religion, the peasant
community and modernization. The author covers similar ground in his 'French
colonial policy in black Africa, 1945 to 1960' in *Colonialism in Africa 1870-1960,
volume 2. The history and politics of colonialism, 1914-1960*, edited by L. H. Gann,
Peter Duignan (Cambridge, England: Cambridge University Press, 1970, p. 251-85).

464   **The French tradition of administrative training in Africa: the Senegalese
experience.**
L. Adamolekun.   *Administration*, vol. 3, no. 2 (1969), p. 93-102.

A study of the training of senior civil servants and its dependence on French models.

465   **Les fonctionnaires de l'administration centrale sénégalaise.** (Civil
servants of the Senegalese central administration.)
Fatou Sow.   Dakar: IFAN, 1972. 226p.

Based on a survey of over 200 civil servants working in Senegal, this study investigates
the attitudes, lifestyles and socio-cultural position of this often reviled group. Sow
suggests that they operate in an ambiguous world, caught between the traditional and
the modern approach, Africa and the West, and that these ambiguities are reflected in
their daily lives. The study discusses the pre- and post-colonial administrative
structures and the officials' attitudes to political life and social mobility, their cultural
values, and their life-styles.

466   **Political space and the quality of participation in rural Africa: a case
from Senegal.**
Jonathan S. Barker.   *Canadian Journal of African Studies*, vol. 21,
no. 1 (1987), p. 1-16.

Based on the author's research in the Saloum town of Birkelane, from the 1960s to the
1980s, this paper reviews economic and political change over a twenty-year period, and
questions the received views of peasants both as recalcitrant conservatives and as the
victims of an urban bureaucracy. Increases in productivity are based on specific

Politics and Government. Administration and local government

patterns of interactions between the state and rural producers, and economic and political reforms need to be coordinated.

467 **Rulers of empire: the French colonial service in Africa.**
William B. Cohen. Stanford, California: Hoover Institution Press, 1971. 279p.

A broad survey of the region's colonial adminstrative structure and its functions, the methods of recruiting and of training its officials, and the way in which the colonial service adapted to changing world circumstances from the early 19th century through to the period after the Second World War. The work of the scholars and administrators who did so much for the study of the region and its peoples such as Louis Faidherbe, Henri Labouret, and Maurice Delafosse is discussed, and there is a large and valuable twenty-three-page bibliography which includes references to colonial memoirs and fiction as well as more scholarly work.

The establishment of protectorate administration in Senegal, 1890-1904.
See item no. 261.

Domaine national et développement au Sénégal. (National land and development in Senegal.)
See item no. 476.

Law

General

468 **Justice et développement au Sénégal.** (Justice and development in Senegal.)
Mamadou Diarra. Dakar: Nouvelles Editions Africaines, 1973. 269p.

In this legal history of the country, the first part traces the history of judicial institutions up to independence, showing in particular how they were adapted to the requirements of the colonial power. The second examines judicial institutions after 1960, and their influence on development. This is still a useful survey, despite the superficiality, by current standards, of the account of the relationship between law and the economy.

469 **Law and population in Senegal: a survey of legislation.**
Francis G. Snyder, Marie-Angélique Savané. Leiden, The Netherlands: Afrika-Studiecentrum, 1977. 242p.

This is a general reference work which summarizes the legislation enacted between 1960 and 1975 affecting mortality, migration and fertility among the population in Senegal. General topics dealt with include: health (the medical profession, drugs and pharmaceuticals, disease, food and environmental protection); the economy (employment and taxation); welfare (housing and education); nationality (immigration and emigration); demography and the family (the status of women, marriage, family planning, child welfare, and inheritance); and the state (military service and penal institutions). It contains extensive references to official and unofficial publications on Senegalese law, as well as to the secondary literature.

470 **Law reform in a developing country: a new code of obligations for Senegal.**
E. Allan Farnsworth. *Journal of African Law*, vol. 8, no. 1 (1964), p. 6-19.

An account of the moves in Senegal towards a more unified legal system, with the modification of the codes inherited from the French, the abolition of special customary courts, and the downgrading of customary law.

471 **Revue Sénégalaise de Droit.** (Senegalese Law Review.)
Dakar: Association Sénégalaise d'Etudes et de Recherche Juridiques. 1967- . biannual.

Published twice a year since 1967, this major academic journal is devoted to Senegalese legal issues.

Indigenous legal systems

472 **Anciens et nouveaux droits fonciers chez les Diola au Sénégal et leurs conséquences pour la répartition des terres.** (Old and new property rights among the Diola of Senegal and their consequences for land distribution.)
J. van der Klei, G. Hesseling. *African Perspectives*, no. 1 (1979), p. 53-66.

Based on fieldwork in the mid-1970s, the paper gives an account of the growing inequality in Diola property rights, following land reform in 1964, which established state control over land, and the land redistribution of 1978.

473 **Capitalism and legal change: an African transformation.**
Francis G. Snyder. New York; London: Academic Press, 1981. 334p.

A complex but important account of changing patterns of production and land tenure among the Banjal, a sub-group of the Diola who live in the Lower Casamance area in the extreme south-west of the country. It describes the systems of production, social organization and land tenure in the 19th century, followed by an account of their transformation following the penetration of capitalism. The work contains a substantial glossary of Banjal terms and a lengthy sixteen-page bibliography. The author has covered similar ground in a series of papers including: 'Labour power and legal transformation in Senegal', *Review of African Political Economy*, vol. 21 (1981), p. 26-43; 'Land law and economic change in rural Senegal: Diola pledge transactions and disputes', in *Social anthropology and law* edited by Ian Hamnett (London: Academic Press, 1977, p. 113-57); 'Customary law and the economy', *Journal of African Law*, vol. 28, no. 1/2 (1984), p. 34-43; and 'Colonialism and legal form: the creation of "customary law" in Senegal', *Journal of Legal Pluralism*, vol. 19 (1981), p. 49-90.

474 **La Chambre Spéciale d'Homologation de la Cour d'Appel de l'A.O.F. et les coutumes pénales de 1903 à 1920.** (The Special Approvals Tribunal of the Court of Appeal of French West Africa and customary punishments from 1903 to 1920.)
Dominique Sarr. *Annales Africaines*, no. 1 (1974), p. 101-15.
The paper, based on archival sources, discusses the work of the court created to supervise the administration of African customary law in French West Africa between 1903 and 1920. It focuses on the difficulties experienced by French officials in accepting customary law, as well as in applying French legal ideas to local cases. Gradually, customary law and penalties appear to have been modified in the direction of French law, so that the introduction of the French penal code after 1945 was relatively problem-free.

475 **Customary land tenure and land reform: the rise of new inequalities among the Diola of Senegal.**
J. van der Klei. *African Perspectives*, no. 2 (1978), p. 35-44.
This paper reconstructs Diola land tenure; patterns during the pre-colonial period and traces the changes since that time which have resulted in a new process of class formation.

476 **Domaine national et développement au Sénégal.** (National land and development in Senegal.)
Philippe Abelin. *Bulletin de l'IFAN*, vol. 41(B), no. 3 (1979), p. 508-38.
An account of the centralization of state control in Senegalese agriculture through legislation governing land use, and through agrarian and administrative reforms.

477 **Essai sur quelques problèmes relatifs au régime foncier des Diola de Basse-Casamance (Sénégal).** (Essay on some problems related to the land tenure system of the Diola of the Lower Casamance, Senegal.)
Louis-Vincent Thomas. In: *African agrarian systems*. Edited by D. Biebuyck. London: Oxford University Press for the International African Institute, 1963, p. 314-30.
An account of traditional patterns of Diola land tenure based on indigenous religious beliefs of the relationship between the lineage and the land. The author describes their modification due to demographic pressures, the spread of Islam, the cash economy and groundnut production, and the technical requirements of rice cultivation. He covers similar ground in 'L'organisation foncière des Diola (Basse-Casamance)' (The land tenure system of the Diola, Lower Casamance), *Annales Africaines*, vol. 1 (1960), p. 199-223.

478 **Jurisprudence des tribunaux indigènes du Sénégal (les causes de rupture du lien matrimonial de 1872 à 1946).** (The jurisprudence of the indigenous courts in Senegal: the causes of marital breakdown, 1872-1946.)
Dominque Sarr. *Annales Africaines*, vol. 22 (1975), p. 143-78.

An analysis of seventy-five divorce cases involving both traditional and Islamic law, dating from the colonial period. The paper distinguishes four types of action, involving adultery, desertion, ill-treatment and requests for annulment.

479 **Legal innovation and social change in a peasant community: a Senegalese village police.**
Francis G. Snyder. *Africa*, vol. 48, no. 3 (1978), p. 231-47.

A well-written case study of the impact of wider economic change on social control and authority relations within a Casamance village. In order to prevent stray domestic animals from damaging fields during a period of shortage, a young men's association extended its normal functions to include patrolling the fields, an innovation quickly abandoned when it generated considerable conflict within the local community.

480 **The Muslim judge and municipal politics in colonial Algeria and Senegal.**
Alan Christelow. *Comparative Studies in Society and History*, vol. 24 (1982), p. 3-24.

A comparative account of the role of the Islamic judge or *qadi* in two French colonies, and the change in French policy towards Islamic legal institutions (many of which deal with land holdings), from hostility and cooperation to final acceptance.

481 **Les rapports du système foncier Toucouleur de l'organisation sociale et économique traditionnelle. Leur évolution actuelle.** (The links between Tukulor land tenure and traditional social and economic organization, and their present development.)
Jean-Louis Boutillier. In: *African agrarian systems*. Edited by D. Biebuyck. London: Oxford University Press, 1963, p. 116-36.

A description of the organization of agriculture in parts of the lower Senegal River valley, where annual flooding means that some areas of land are more fertile and valuable than others. Two different land tenure systems have developed as a result. The conclusion is that disparities in the distribution of land and the resulting low yields have inhibited economic development in the area. Pages 133-6 give an English summary.

482 **Réforme foncière et stratégie du développement (réflexion à partir de l'exemple sénégalais).** (Agrarian reform and development strategy: reflecting on the example of Senegal.)
E. LeRoy. *African Perspectives*, no. 1 (1979), p. 67-81.

An analysis of the 1964 land reform in Senegal, which shows how, despite the 'African socialist' philosophy which lay behind it, it still allowed the development of a new capitalist class.

483 **Du régime des terres de la vallée du Sénégal au Fouta antérieurement à l'occupation française.** (On the land system of the Senegal valley in Fuuta before the French occupation.)
Henri Gaden. *Bulletin du Comité des Etudes Historiques et Scientifiques de l'Afrique Occidentale Française,* vol. 18, no. 4 (1935), p. 403-14.

Gaden's paper is a historical account of land holdings, rents and taxes among the Tukulor. This issue contains two other important studies: 'Etude sur la tenure des terres indigènes au Fouta' (A study of indigenous land tenure in Fuuta) by M. Vidal (p. 435-48) and 'Du régime des terres chez les populations du Fouta Sénégalais' (On the land system among the populations of the Senegalese Fuuta) by Abdou Salem Kane (p. 449-61). Vidal's paper describes the indigenous divisions of cultivable land in the river basin, concerning in particular those plots situated in the valuable flood-plain areas (*waalo*). Kane's paper is a detailed account of the system in operation in Fuuta Toro in the early part of this century, and describes the impact on it of French administrative policy.

484 **Régime des terres et stratégie de développement rural au Sénégal (un exemple de la résistance du droit coutumier africain).** (Land control and rural development strategy in Senegal: an example of the resistance of African customary law).
Mamadou Niang. *African Perspectives,* no. 1 (1979), p. 45-51.

The paper discusses the survival of African customary law, despite official changes, including the 1964 agrarian reform law which gave land titles to the occupant who had developed it. The case material is draw from an eight-year-long dispute between Peul pastoralists and Mouride farmers in the village of Cabugel, which ended in a compromise in 1976.

485 **Responsabilité, sanction et organisation judiciaire chez les Diola traditionnels de Basse-Casamance (Sénégal).** (Responsibility, sanction and judicial organization among the traditional Diola of the Lower Casamance, Senegal.)
Louis-Vincent Thomas. *Notes Africaines,* no. 104 (1964), p 106-12.

A study of Diola categories of evil, responsibility and sanctions, based on their religious beliefs, and the traditional procedures for settling disputes in which these elements occur.

Résidence, tenure foncière, alliance dans une société bilinéaire (Sérèr du Sine et du Baol, Sénégal). (Residence, land tenure and alliance in a bilinear society: the Serer of Sine and Baol, Senegal.)
See item no. 168.

Constitutional law

486   **Cadre constitutionnel et réalité politique de la République du Sénégal.**
(Constitutional framework and political reality in the Republic of
Senegal.)
Dimitri-Georges Lavroff.   *Afrika Spectrum*, no. 1 (1969), p. 5-17.

A summary account of the constitutional changes before and after independence. The
original constitution of 1959 was changed in 1960 after the breakup of the Mali
Federation; in 1963 after the political crisis of 1962; and again in 1967, with the powers
of the President being gradually strengthened. The author sees these developments as
attempts to overcome the major rifts in Senegalese society, between social classes, the
generations, and religious and ethnic groups.

487   **La République du Sénégal.** (The Republic of Senegal.)
Dmitri-Georges Lavroff.   Paris: R. Pichon & R. Durand-Auzias, 1966.
250p.

One of a series of texts on national constitutions, this standard account by a law
professor describes the Senegalese political system in the early years of independence.
A lengthy survey of the country and its history is followed by a section on the
institutions of the Republic: the principles of the constitution, the powers of the
President, the National Assembly, the judiciary and supreme court, and of the
economic and social council. The third part of the book deals with political
organizations, and the development of the Union Progressiste Sénégalaise, and the
opposition parties. At the end there is a summary bibliography and an administrative
map of the country, but no index.

Civil law

488   **Droit patrimonial de la famille au Sénégal (Régimes matrimoniaux –
libéralités – successions).** (Family property law in Senegal: rules of
marriage, gifts, succession.)
Serge Guinchard.   Paris: R. Pichon & R. Durand-Auzias, 1980. 669p.
(Bibliothèque Africaine et Malgache: Droit, Sociologie Politique et
Economie, 32).

A legal text which includes (on pages 67-75) a bibliography on African and Muslim
law. Book 1 deals with marriage and rights over matrimonial property, depending on
the type of marriage. Book 2 deals with gifts and bequests, and contains a section on
wills. The third book deals with succession, and includes sections on the determination
of heirs under customary and Islamic law. In the introduction the author makes the
point that there is often a difference between legal rules and what actually happens in
practice: this book concentrates upon the former.

Histoire politique du Sénégal: institutions, droit et société. (Political history of Senegal: institutions, law, and society.)
See item no. 435.

African boundaries: a legal and diplomatic encyclopaedia.
See item no. 489.

International Relations

General and regional

489 **African boundaries: a legal and diplomatic encyclopaedia.**
Ian Brownlie. London: C. Hurst; Berkeley, California: University of
California Press, for the Royal Institute of International Affairs,
London, 1979. 1355p.

A vast compendium of information and documentation relating to every frontier in
Africa. The sections relating to Senegal's frontiers are p. 213-29 (with The Gambia),
p. 314-20 (with Guinea), p. 350-8 (with Guinea-Bissau), p. 422-6 (with Mali), and
p. 431-5 (with Mauritania).

490 **Another week of terror.**
Mark Doyle, Chris Simpson. *West Africa* (8-14 May 1989), p. 725.

A detailed account of the communal disturbances in the towns of Senegal and
Mauritania in April 1989, following a border incident, together with the various
diplomatic moves by other African leaders to resolve the dispute. See also *The tragic
aftermath* by Mark Doyle, *West Africa* (15-21 May, 1989), p. 789-90; and *Troubled
waters* by Mark Doyle, *West Africa* (19-25 June 1989), p. 1007-9.

491 **Bilateral relations between Senegal and Nigeria, 1960-1980: cooperation
and conflicts.**
Bamitale Omole. *Geneva-Africa*, vol. 25, no. 2 (1987), p. 79-102.

A history of the varying fortunes of relations between the two states since
independence, with Senegalese worries that Nigeria would establish itself as the major
regional power. Relations were normalized after the succession of Abdou Diouf to the
Senegalese presidency and the re-establishment of military government in Nigeria,
both of which took place at the end of 1983.

492   **From federalism to francophonia: Senghor's African policy.**
Robert A. Mortimore.   *African Studies Review*, vol. 15, no. 2 (1972),
p. 283-306.
A critical analysis of President Senghor's foreign policy, dealing with Senegal's
membership of regional organizations.

493   **The foreign policy of Senegal.**
W. A. E. Skurnik.   Evanston, Illinois: Northwestern University Press,
1972. 308p.
The standard account of Senegal's foreign policy in the early years of independence,
and as yet the only full-length monograph in its field. Although much of the material is
now of historical rather than contemporary interest, there are interesting accounts of
links with France during the latter part of the colonial period, Senegal's involvement in
attempts to foster African unity, including the abortive Mali Federation, the structure
of the Senegalese foreign ministry and the recruitment of diplomats, and the effects on
foreign policy of ex-President Senghor's ideas and personality.

494   **Integration, development and equity: economic integration in West
Africa.**
Peter Robson.   London: George Allen & Unwin, 1983. 181p.
This book examines four organizations set up to promote economic integration in West
Africa, including the Communauté Economique de l'Afrique de l'Ouest (CEAO), the
Economic Community of West African States (ECOWAS) and (in chapter 7) the
Senegambian Confederation. The chapter reviews the historical background to the
confederation, the conditions of economic and monetary union, and the costs and
benefits such integration may entail.

495   **The Organisation of Senegal River States.**
Ronald Bornstein.   *Journal of Modern African Studies*, vol. 10, no. 2
(1972), p. 267-83.
A study of the regional grouping formed in 1968, which included Guinea, Mali,
Mauritania and Senegal, and which was intended to develop the Senegal river basin.
The paper deals with the structure of the organization, its history, and the troubled
relations between the leaders of the member states, particularly Senghor and Sekou
Touré of Guinea. The organization was dissolved in December 1971.

496   **The politics of West African economic co-operation: CEAO and
ECOWAS.**
Daniel C. Bach.   *Journal of Modern African Studies*, vol. 21, no. 4
(1983), p. 605-23.
A study of politics in West Africa leading up to the establishment of the Economic
Community of West African States in 1975, and the process by which the initial
opposition of the francophone countries to a Nigerian initiative gave way to
acceptance, and to growing cooperation between the two organizations. Neither has
had much impact on the existing international framework, or on the structure of the
region's economy.

497 **Quelle stratégie pour le Sahel? La difficile harmonisation de la stratégie du CILSS et du Club du Sahel avec les plans de développement nationaux des pays Saheliens.** (What strategy for Sahel? The difficulty of reconciling the strategy of CILSS and the Club du Sahel with the national development plans of the Sahelian countries.) Charles A. Jeanneret. *Canadian Journal of African Studies*, vol. 16, no. 3 (1982), p. 443-77.

An evaluation of the strategy, adopted in 1977, aimed at greater regional cooperation, the harmonization of national development plans, and food self-sufficiency by 2000, through the development of dryland and irrigated agriculture, fisheries and livestock production. The paper's conclusions are gloomy: not only have these objectives not been achieved, but the probability that they will be achieved is slight.

498 **The Senegal-Mauritania conflict of 1989: a fragile equilibrium.** Ron Parker. *Journal of Modern African Studies*, vol. 29, no. 1 (1991), p. 155-71.

An account of Senegal's troubled relations with its northern neighbour, focusing on the events of April 1989, in which competition for land, resulting from desertification, led to violence and eventually to pogroms in the cities of both countries. These in turn forced the return of some 75,000 Senegalese and 170,000 Mauritanians back to their respective countries.

Africa's shared water resources: legal and institutional aspects of the Nile, Niger and Senegal river systems.
See item no. 45.

The decline of the franc zone: monetary politics in francophone Africa.
See item no. 397.

La zone franc est-elle le bouc-émissaire de l'échec du développement? (The franc zone, a scapegoat for development failures?)
See item no. 400.

Zone franc et développement africain. (The franc zone and African development.)
See item no. 401.

Black Africa: the economic and cultural basis for a federated state.
See item no. 692.

The Mali Federation

499   From French West Africa to the Mali Federation.
William J. Foltz.   New Haven, Connecticut: Yale University Press,
1965. 235p.

Although theoretically dated, this remains the standard study of the events
surrounding the formation and rapid demise of the Mali Federation between Senegal
and Mali in 1960. The author deals initially with the political organization and
economic integration in French West Africa. This is followed by an account of the
transition to independence, and the differing attitudes of the new leaders to continued
regional cooperation which initiated the Federation's collapse.

500   Political integration in Africa: the Mali Federation.
Donn M. Kurtz.   *Journal of Modern African Studies*, vol. 8, no. 3
(1970), p. 405-24.

This paper examines the background to the Mali Federation, as well as the conditions
at the time of union, and the problems that Senghor and Modibo Keita, the Malian
leader, faced after they had decided to form the Federation. The author's conclusion is
that despite the two leaders' commitment to the union, neither of them was willing to
risk his own local power base in promoting it.

Senegambian unity

501   Dream of unity: pan-Africanism and political unification in West Africa.
Claude E. Welch Jr.   Ithaca, New York: Cornell University Press,
1966. 396p.

A general study of the problems of political unity in West Africa. Chapter 6 (p. 250-90)
discusses the situation up to the end of the first decade of independence in
Senegambia. It ends with an account of the United Nations report of 1964 which
discussed the options for future cooperation and recommended the establishment of a
federation.

502   Ethnic affinity, partition and political integration in Senegambia.
F. A. Renner.   In: *Partitioned Africans: ethnic relations across Africa's
international boundaries 1884-1984.* Edited by A. I. Asiwaju.   London:
C. Hurst, 1985, p. 71-85.

A historical study of the differences which have developed between the two countries
as a result of the colonial partition, and which have made the achievement of unity so
difficult despite the obvious advantages which it would bring.

503 **The problem of Senegambia.**
Peter Robson. *Journal of Modern African Studies*, vol. 3, no. 3
(1965), p. 393-407.
Discusses relations between the two countries, concentrating on the economic
differences between them, which have resulted in massive cross-border smuggling,
while legitimate trade remained negligible.

504 **Regional integration and the crisis in sub-Saharan Africa.**
Peter Robson. *Journal of Modern African Studies*, vol. 23, no. 4
(1985), p. 603-22.
A useful regional survey which sees the Senegambian Confederation as one of a very
large number of attempts at inter-state cooperation. Here, the usual problems of
cooperation have been compounded by the level of smuggling from The Gambia into
Senegal.

505 **Senegal: the birth of Senegambia and of multiparty democracy.**
Africa Contemporary Record, vol. 14 (1981-82), p. B.532-48.
This article should ideally be read in conjunction with another which appeared in the
same volume of *Africa Contemporary Record*: 'Constitutional developments: Senegambia' (p. C.54-56). These two articles from the leading African yearbook record the
Senegalese military intervention which crushed an attempted coup in The Gambia on
30 July 1981, and contain a summary of the Confederation agreement concluded
between Presidents Diouf and Jawara on 14 November which established the
confederation between the two countries, an arrangement which lasted until 1989.

506 **The Senegambian Confederation.**
Lucy Colvin Phillips. In: *The political economy of Senegal under
structural adjustment.* Edited by Christopher L. Delgado, Sidi
Jammeh. New York: Praeger, 1991, p. 175-93.
An account of the economic factors which lay behind the breakdown of the
confederation in 1989. The paper deals with the structure of regional trade, and the
incompatible economic policies of the two governments with regard to trade, which
have resulted in a massive re-export of goods from The Gambia to Senegal – a practice
which the Senegalese authorities regard as smuggling. There follows a detailed
description of the realities of trade, and of the political problems which have prevented
the construction of a bridge to improve communications with the Casamance, or the
establishment of a customs union. The author describes the negative effects of the
present stalemate for both countries, but concludes that, although pressure for
annexation as a way of resolving the issue is growing in Senegal, it is unlikely to be
attempted under the present leadership.

507 **Senegambia: possibilities for closer co-operation in the field of education.**
Carew Treffgarne. In: *Senegambia: proceedings of a Colloquium at
the University of Aberdeen, April 1974.* Edited by R. C. Bridges.
Aberdeen, Scotland: Aberdeen University African Studies Group,
1974, p. 133-8.
Following a cultural exchange agreement in the early 1970s aimed at promoting
English teaching in Senegal and French teaching in The Gambia, the author examines
prospects for further educational cooperation.

508 **Senegambia revisited or changing Gambian perceptions of integration
with Senegal.**
Arnold Hughes. In: *Senegambia: proceedings of a Colloquium at the
University of Aberdeen, April 1974.* Edited by R. C. Bridges.
Aberdeen, Scotland: Aberdeen University African Studies Group,
1974, p. 139-70.
A discussion of issues which are, after twenty years, still current: Gambian suspicions
of Senegal's long-term aims in relations between them, and the preference of many
people in The Gambia for a wider regional association. Similar themes are addressed
in later papers by the same author, for instance 'The limits of consociational
democracy in The Gambia', *Civilisations*, vol. 22, no. 2/vol. 23, no. 1 (1982/3), p. 65-
95, and 'From colonialism to confederation: the Gambian experience of independence,
1965-1982', in *African islands and enclaves*, edited by Robin Cohen (Beverly Hills,
California; London: Sage, 1983, p. 57-80).

509 **Senegambia: the logical bases for integration.**
Jeggan C. Senghor. *Africa Quarterly*, vol. 22, no. 1 (1983), p. 5-24.
A discussion of the rationale for unity between Senegal and The Gambia, and an
assessment of the obstacles to it, including different economic policies and different
political attitudes inherited from British and French colonialism.

Economic Community of West African States (ECOWAS)

510 **ECOWAS and the economic integration of West Africa.**
Uka Ezenwe. London: C. Hurst, 1983. 210p.
A general account of the historical development of ECOWAS (Economic Community
of West African States) which reviews the costs and benefits of economic integration,
and the performance of other regional organizations. The author considers economic
integration to be a pre-requisite for rapid industrialization in the region, but this will
entail the surrender of elements of political sovereignty on the part of post-
independence states.

511 **L'intégration économique de l'Afrique de l'Ouest confrontée aux solides liens de dépendance des états africains de l'extérieur.** (The economic integration of West Africa in the face of the solid links of external dependence of African states.)
M. Fall. *Africa Development*, vol. 9, no. 1 (1984), p. 40-55.

A critical study of the difficulties of economic integration in West Africa, in the context of continuing ties between individual countries and their former colonial powers. Flows of foreign aid tend to reinforce economic dependency and promote neither regional integration nor development. The paper contains tables on flows of foreign investment and aid between 1974/75 and 1980.

512 **Liberalising trade.**
Paxton Idowu. *West Africa*, no. 3851 (1-7 July 1991), p. 1075.

A concise account of the main issues and problems facing the ECOWAS: the threat of an integrated Europe, Africa's marginalization in the international economy, declining export earnings and large debts, and the failure of efforts to encourage trade within the region. It also surveys some of the main aims of the organization in the 1990s: the establishment of a single monetary zone, rights of residence for citizens of members states; the completion of the telecommunications and highway networks; the preparation of an industrial master-plan; and the implementation of a joint agricultural development programme.

513 **The state of economic integration in north west Africa south of the Sahara: the emergence of the Economic Community of West African States (ECOWAS).**
Aguibou Y. Yansane. *African Studies Review*, vol. 20, no. 2 (1977), p. 63-87.

This paper gives a brief survey of moves towards economic and political cooperation between African states in the years after independence, the origins of the ECOWAS treaty, and early problems in its implementation.

Integration, development and equality: economic integration in West Africa.
See item no. 494.

The politics of West African economic co-operation: CEAO and ECOWAS.
See item no. 496.

Relations with the developed countries

514 **Cartesian underpinnings in Mitterrand's Senegal policy.**
Terrel D. Hale. *Trans-Africa Forum*, vol. 3, no. 4 (1986), p. 37-44.
The paper argues that by emphasizing order, unity and reason in France's relations with Senegal, Mitterrand has in fact been able to reinforce Senegalese dependence. The author covers similar ground in a second paper, 'The Cartesian model and dependency in Mitterrand's African policy: the case of Senegal', *Civilisations*, vol. 37, no. 1 (1987), p. 39-53.

515 **Colonization to co-operation: French technical assistance in Senegal.**
Rita Cruise O'Brien. *Journal of Development Studies*, vol. 8, no. 1 (1971), p. 45-58.
A critical account of the large-scale French technical assistance programme in Senegal, which employed 1,200 people in 1971, mostly as advisers to the administration. The author argues that a programme on this scale cannot be justified in terms of its practical effects, but that it has resulted in the perpetuation of colonial attitudes and patterns of dependency. Similar issues are dealt with in the author's 'Some problems in the consolidation of national independence in Africa: the case of the French expatriates in Senegal', *African Affairs*, vol. 73, no. 290 (1974), p. 85-94.

516 **French ascendance in the economy and state: the French and Lebanese.**
Rita Cruise O'Brien. In: *The political economy of underdevelopment: dependence in Senegal.* Edited by Rita Cruise O'Brien. Beverly Hills, California; London: Sage, 1979, p. 100-25. (Sage Series on African Modernization and Development 3).
An important study of the processes by which the French and Lebanese became entrenched in strategic sectors of the Senegalese labour market, which the author argues has effectively blocked the development of an African commercial class and a skilled African workforce and an efficient administration.

517 **La politique française de coopération en Afrique: le cas du Sénégal.** (The French policy of cooperation in Africa: the case of Senegal.)
Albert Bourgi. Paris: R. Pichon & R. Durand-Auzias, Librairie Générale de Droit et de Jurisprudence, 1979. 373p. (Bibliothèque Africaine et Malgache: Droit, Sociologie Politique et Economie, 30).
A detailed study of the continuing links between France and Senegal, both through the legal agreements between them, and in the substantive areas of political, military, technical, and educational cooperation. Most importantly, there are chapters on financial aid and economic dependence, including the organization of the CFA franc zone. The appendices include a useful list of accords between France and Senegal, a list of France's military agreements with African countries, and statistical tables on French aid.

518 **Relations between France and Senegal: 1960-1969.**
E. B. Davis.   Ann Arbor, Michigan: University Microfilms, 1978. 2 vols.

The major study in English of Franco-Senegalese relations in the first decade of independence, showing the continued importance of the relationship after the end of formal colonial control, even though the characterization of the relationship is much less sharp than in the Marxist accounts. The second volume ends with forty lengthy appendices, containing the texts of key agreements, and with a substantial sixteen-page bibliography.

Sénégal: l'experience du précurseur. (Senegal: previous experience.)
See item no. 20.

Special report on Senegal.
See item no. 25.

Europeans: white society in Black Africa: the French of Senegal.
See item no. 191.

Mechanismes de l'exploitation en Afrique: l'exemple du Sénégal. (Mechanisms of exploitation in Africa: the example of Senegal.)
See item no. 324.

Neo-colonialism in West Africa.
See item no. 325.

Structural changes and colonial dependency: Senegal 1885-1945.
See item no. 333.

L'aide au développement du Canada au Sénégal. Une étude indépendante. Canadian development assistance to Senegal. An independent study.
See item no. 392.

Society and Social Conditions

General

519 **Modernisation des hommes: l'exemple du Sénégal.** (Modernization of mankind: the example of Senegal.)
Pierre Fougeyrollas.   Paris: Flammarion, 1967, 236p.
Study of modernization and urban life in Dakar and Thiès from the 1960s by one of the leading sociologists working in Senegal during this period. The theoretical framework of the study, with its emphasis on 'modernization', psychological factors and questionnaires is now very dated, but the book does provide quantitative information on subjects such as urban lifestyles and consumption patterns, student attitudes and the impact of television at around the time of independence.

Social structure: categories and classes

520 **Elites et changements en Afrique et au Sénégal.** (Elites and change in Africa and in Senegal.)
Gilles Blanchet.   Paris: ORSTOM, 1983. 408p.
A study of the role of élites in African society, the second part of which contains three chapters on Senegal. The first of these deals with the country's political structures. The second is an account of Senegal's political history in the early years of independence, covering administration, the political opposition, and the politically significant interest groups, such as traditional notables, businessmen, and the military. The third chapter is a summary of the political role of the élite and their degree of autonomy. At the end is an appendix containing some interesting tables on the social characteristics of members of the élite, and their representation in political institutions.

521 **Histoire des classes sociales dans l'Afrique de l'Ouest. Tome II.
Le Sénégal.** (History of the social classes in West Africa. Volume 2:
Senegal.)
Majhemout Diop. Paris: Maspero, 1972. 285p.

The second volume of a two-volume work (the first refers to Mali) which traces the
history of social stratification and class conflict in the region from the slave and caste
system of precolonial society, through the changes brought about by colonialism, to the
class structure of the present day within the neo-colonial state. The stability of the
Senegalese state is explained in terms of the relatively broad base of the bourgeoisie in
alliance with foreign capital, the control of the peasantry by the marabouts, and the
control of the workers by the unions.

522 **The impact of the reforms on the urban population: how the Dakarois
view the crisis.**
Carolyn M. Somerville. In: *The political economy of Senegal under
structural adjustment.* Edited by Christopher L. Delgado, Sidi
Jammeh. New York: Praeger, 1991, p. 151-73.

A discussion of the far-reaching effects of the economic changes on urban consumers,
involving as they do the removal of subsidies on consumer goods, retrenchment and
rising unemployment, and the reduction of workers' job security through changes in
labour law. The second part of the paper is a description based on a 1986 survey of the
attitudes of the people of Dakar towards these changes, and it reveals little confidence
in the government's ability to solve the problems.

523 **La lutte des pouvoirs publics contre les 'encombrements humains' à
Dakar.** (The struggle of the public authorities against the 'human
obstacles' in Dakar.)
René Collignon. *Canadian Journal of African Studies,* vol. 18 (1984),
p. 573-82.

A study of the history of the relations between urban government and the street
population of traders, beggars, the destitute and the mentally ill in Dakar, which
concludes that the problem is itself a result of the way in which Dakar has grown over
the years, and that the paradoxical result of the repression to which these people are
subjected is to make this population more adaptable and thus more difficult to remove.

524 **Traditional social structure, the Islamic brotherhoods, and political
development in Senegal.**
Irving L. Markovitz. *Journal of Modern African Studies,* vol. 8, no. 1
(1970), p. 73-96.

A study of the relationships between social class and political change in modern
Senegal, which also considers the traditional caste structure and the rise of the Islamic
brotherhoods. The writer's conclusion is that classes have long existed in the country,
and that the conservative groups in power are capable of adapting to changing
conditions so as to retain their privileges.

Family and kinship relations

525 **Analyse dynamique de la parenté sénégalaise.** (A dynamic analysis of Senegalese kinship.)
Louis-Vincent Thomas. *Bulletin de l'IFAN*, vol. 30(B), no. 3 (1968), p. 1005-61.

A general survey of kinship and family institutions throughout the country, and the major trends of change taking place under the impact of colonialism and the spread of the world religions. These include the move away from matrilineal towards patrilineal and bilateral kinship systems, the increasing importance of the nuclear family, and changes in marriage patterns.

526 **Budgets familiaux africains: étude chez 136 familles de salariés dans trois centres urbains du Sénégal.** (African family budgets: a study of 136 wage-earning families in three urban centres in Senegal.)
Y. Mersadier. Dakar: IFAN, 1957. 102p.

A survey based on data from families in Thiès, Dakar and Saint-Louis, which includes details on the size and composition of family and consumption groups, their incomes and expenses. Although dated, the study provides an instructive insight into household finances in urban Senegal just before independence.

527 **La conception de l'autorité et son évolution dans les relations parents-enfants à Dakar.** (The concept of authority and its development in parent-child relations in Dakar.)
N. Le Guerinel (et al.). *Psychopathologie Africaine*, vol. 5, no. 1 (1969) p. 11-73.

A wide-ranging study of socialization in urban Senegal which deals with the weakening of authority, the effects of the introduction of Western education, the declining force of religion and tradition, the changing behaviour of peer groups, and conflict between the generations.

528 **Mariage et divorce dans la banlieue de Dakar.** (Marriage and divorce in the suburbs of Dakar.)
Luc Thoré. *Cahiers d'Etudes Africaines*, vol. 4, no. 4 (1964), p. 479-551.

A report on marriage based on research carried out in Dagoudane-Pikine in 1960-61, which discusses the origins of spouses in terms of caste, religion and ethnic group, and whether marriages were arranged or based on free choice, and looks at the reasons for the high frequency of divorce.

529 **Stratégies familiales, stratégies résidentielles en milieu urbain.** (Family and residential strategies in an urban setting.)
Annik Osmont. *Cahiers d'Etudes Africaines*, vol. 21, no. 1/3 (1981), p. 175-195.

An important study of the role of the extended family in Senegal, which argues that it is not just a survival of tradition, but is itself a result of the urbanization process in

Africa. Extended family ties are important during family celebrations, in the allocation of names, in the arrangement of marriages, and in the movement of children. Family development over the generations is discussed and illustrated with genealogies and house plans.

L'agglomération dakaroise: quelques aspects sociologiques et démographiques. (The Dakar agglomeration: some sociological and demographic aspects.) *See* item no. 31.

Dakar en devenir. (The development of Dakar.) *See* item no. 33.

Daoudane-Pikine, étude démographique et sociologique. (Daoudane-Pikine, a demographic and sociological study.) *See* item no. 35.

Société toucouleur et migration: enquête sur l'immigraton toucouleur à Dakar. (Tukulor society and migration: an investigation of Tukulor immigration to Dakar.) *See* item no. 132.

Recensement démographique de Dakar (1955). Résultats définitifs (2e fascicule): Etude socio-démographique de la ville de Dakar. (Demographic census of Dakar (1955). Definitive results, 2nd volume. Socio-economic study of the town of Dakar.) *See* item no. 146.

Gender relations

530 **Les conséquences de l'introduction d'une culture de rente et d'une culture attelée sur la position de la femme wolof à Saloum.** (The consequences of the introduction of a cash-crop cultivation and team cultivation on the position of the Wolof woman in Saloum.)
Bernhard Venema. *Tiers-Monde*, vol. 23, no. 91 (1982), p. 603-16.
This paper, based on research carried out in 1979, considers changes in agriculture in the peanut basin resulting from population growth and their impact on the position of Wolof women. It concludes that they have been relatively successful in adapting to changing agricultural conditions.

531 **Fashion, anti-fashion and heteroglossia in urban Senegal.**
Deborah Heath. *American Ethnologist*, vol. 19, no. 1 (1992), p. 19-33.
A study of *sanse*, 'dressing up', among women in Kaolack and the other cities of Senegal, this paper deals with the role of cloth in gift-giving and exchange, dress at political rallies, the relations of women traders and the weavers, dress at religious

rituals, dress among the Muridiyya (Mourides), and embroidery, including the sexual imagery of underskirts. This article contains interesting material, despite the forbidding jargon of the title.

532 **Femmes dakaroises: rôles traditionnels feminins et urbanisation.** (Women in Dakar: traditional feminine roles and urbanization.) Colette Le Cour Grandmaison. Paris: CNRS, 1972. 249p. (Annales de l'Université d'Abidjan, Série F, Tome 4, Ethnosociologie).

This general study of Lebou women's lives in Dakar is based on 500 completed questionnaires, life histories and other material collected between 1964 and 1966 in the Plateau, Medina and SICAP villa areas of the city. After the introductory chapter on the Dakar setting and the history of the Lebu, the chapters in the first section deal with the individual and social roles, with a special section on women healers; urban marriage and women's strategies, and social life in the city, including associations and leisure. The second part concentrates on the economy, changing occupations, income, expenditure and capital accumulation. Although theoretically limited by current standards, this study remains important as the fullest academic account of urban women in Senegal in the early years after independence. Women's economic roles were covered by the same author in 'Activités économiques des femmes dakaroises' (Economic activities of women in Dakar), *Africa*, vol. 39, no. 2 (1969), p. 138-52.

533 **Femmes prolétaires du Sénégal, à la ville et aux champs.** (Proletarian women in Senegal, in the town and in the fields.) F. Kane. *Cahiers d'Etudes Africaines*, vol. 17, no. 1 (1977), p. 77-94.

A study of women workers on a rural plantation run by a multinational company in the 1970s, which compares their lives and working conditions with those of factory workers in the city. Although the conditions for the factory women are better in terms of wages, benefits and union protection, the two groups still have much in common.

Power, prayer and production: the Jola of Casamance, Senegal. *See* item no. 153.

The *signares* of Saint-Louis and Gorée: women entrepreneurs in eighteenth-century Senegal. *See* item no. 271.

Les femmes commerçantes au détail sur les marchés dakarois. (Women retailers in Dakar markets.) *See* item no. 370.

Les restauratrices de la zone industrielle de Dakar, ou la guerre des marmites. (The women food sellers of the industrial zone of Dakar, or the cooking-pot war.) *See* item no. 374.

Women, Islam and *baraka*. *See* item no. 585.

L'artisanat féminin dans la région du Fleuve Sénégal. (Female craft production in the Fleuve region of Senegal.) *See* item no. 780.

Ethnicity

534 **Ethnic group relations in Senegal.**
Fatoumata-Agnes Diarra, Pierre Fougeyrollas.   In: *Two studies on ethnic group relations in Africa.*   Paris: UNESCO, 1974, p. 9-104.
Although regularly cited as a basic source, this is a rather superficial study of ethnic relations based on 109 interviews with people from a variety of ethnic backgrounds, including French and Lebanese. Its main interest is probably as a compendium of popular ethnic stereotypes in the form of verbatim quotations from the interviewees.

535 **Relations inter-ethniques et changements socio-économiques dans l'agglomération de Nyéméniki-Sekguekho-Touba Diakha.** (Inter-ethnic relations and socio-economic change in the Nyéméniki-Sekguekho-Touba Diakha village group.)
P. Charest.   *Bulletin et Mémoires de la Société d'Anthropologie* (Paris), Series 12, vol. 5, no. 1/4 (1969), p. 101-229.
This study of the seven villages to the north-west of Kédougou, concentrates on the relations between the four main ethnic groups in the area (Peul, Malinke, Bassari and Jakhanke) and the historical and cultural differences between them. The Malinke presence dates back for centuries, but the other three groups are much more recent arrivals. The author describes the complex relationships between them in production, land tenure, the division of labour, marriage and ritual.

La ville de Thiès: étude de géographie urbaine. (The town of Thiès: a study in urban geography.)
See item no. 44.

Beyond migration and conquest: oral traditions and Mandinka ethnicity in Senegambia.
See item no. 183.

Casamance under siege.
See item no. 444.

Another week of terror.
See item no. 490.

The Senegal-Mauritania conflict of 1989: a fragile equilibrium.
See item no. 498.

Religion

General

536 **Colonisations et religions en Afrique noire: l'exemple de Ziguinchor.**
(Colonizations and religions in black Africa: the example of
Ziguinchor.)
Jacqueline Trincaz.   Paris: L'Harmattan, 1981. 360p.
A major study by a French sociologist based on research in the early 1970s of the co-
existence and inter-relationships between Christianity, Islam and the traditional
religions in the Casamance area of southern Senegal. Ziguinchor, the largest town in
the area, has an ethnically mixed population and the three religious traditions, after a
period of rivalry, now coexist. The third part of the book is a detailed study of religious
beliefs, healing and possession among the Mancagne, an ethnic minority originating
from Guinea. There is an eighteen-page bibliography and appendices which include the
text of the Franco-Portuguese treaty of 1886, material on economic activity in the
town, and official documents on education and the family.

Indigenous religion

537 **Animisme, religion caduque: étude qualitative et quantitative sur les
opinions et la pratique religieuse en Basse-Casamance (pays diola).**
(Animism, an obsolete religion. A qualitative and quantitative study of
religious opinions and practice in the Lower Casamance, Diola
country.)
Louis-Vincent Thomas.   *Bulletin de l'IFAN*, vol. 27(B), no. 1/2
(1965), p. 1-41.
A study of religious change among the Diola, and developments in the organization
and practice of traditional religion in the face of the spread of Islam and Christianity.

Religion. Indigenous religion

The data suggest that the young are less interested in traditional religion than the old, and the men less than the women. Thus the traditional Diola religion may be about to become extinct.

538   **Bukut chez les Diola-Nioumon.** (Bukut initiation among the Diola-Niouman.)
Louis-Vincent Thomas. *Notes Africaines*, no. 108 (1965), p. 97-118.

An account of the Bukut male initiation ceremony which, at the time, seemed likely to be the last to take place among this particular group of Diola, given the rapid decline of traditional religion. The paper gives a detailed account of the various stages of the ritual, the initial sacrifices, the circumcision itself, the confinement of the circumcised in a sacred enclosure for two months, while they received instruction, and their eventual emergence, dressed in masks.

539   **Chasse rituelle, divination et reconduction de l'ordre socio-politique chez les Sérèr du Sine (Sénégal).** (Ritual hunting, divination and renewal of the socio-political order among the Serer of Sine, Senegal.)
Marguerite Dupire. *L'Homme*, vol. 16, no. 1 (1976), p. 5-32.

An account of an annual ritual involving divination, a collective hunt and sacrifices, to ensure a good rainy season. This ritual provides the basis for a survey by Dupire of Serer religious categories and the main organizational principles and cleavages in Sine Serer society.

540   **Diffusion en milieu diola de l'association du Koump baïnouk.** (The spread of the Baïnouk Koumpo association among the Diola.)
Jean Girard. *Bulletin de l'IFAN*, vol. 27(B), no. 1/2 (1965), p. 42-98.

A detailed study of a male secret society which spread rapidly from the 1940s onwards among the Diola along the Casamance river, in an area in which seventy per cent of the population had become Muslims. The functions of the society in reinforcing Diola values are described, together with its masks. The paper also contains the texts of forty-one songs in French translation.

541   **La dimension thérapeutique du culte des rab.** *Ndoup, tuuru* et *samp.* **Rites de possession chez les Lébou et les Wolof.** (The therapeutic dimensions of the rab cult. *Ndop, tuuru* and *samp.* Possession rites among the Lebu and Wolof.)
A. Zempleni. *Psychopathologie Africaine*, vol. 2, no. 3 (1966), p. 295-439.

An account of forms of healing rituals which involve invoking ancestral spirits who are thought to cause illness, and which act to reintegrate the patient into a re-strengthened family and social environment.

542   **Le Diola et le temps.** (The Diola and time.)
Louis-Vincent Thomas, David Sapir. *Bulletin IFAN*, vol. 29(B), no. 1/2 (1967), p. 331-424.

A lengthy examination of the philosophical and linguistic aspects of traditional Diola concepts of time, their limited recognition of historical processes, and their modification due to the rise of the cash economy and their greater geographical mobility.

543 **L'enfant *nit-ku-bon*: un tableau psychopathologique traditionnel chez les Wolof et les Lébou du Sénégal.** (The *nit-ku-bon* child: a traditional psychiatric image among the Wolof and the Lebu of Senegal.) A. Zempleni, J. Rabain. *Psychopathologie Africaine*, vol. 1, no. 3 (1965), p. 329-443.

One of a series of detailed studies of socialization practices and associated beliefs, by two French psychiatrists, this paper deals with a concept also in existence in other parts of West Africa: that certain children have a special relationship with the spirit world, because they are either reincarnations of ancestors, or of children who have previously died. It discusses the ways in which these children can be recognized, and the efforts which are made to protect them.

544 **Eyes of the night: witchcraft among a Senegalese people.** William S. Simmons. Boston, Massachusetts: Little, Brown & Co., 1971. 169p.

In this study of social structure and witchcraft beliefs among the Badyaranke, the early chapters deal with the main features of the social structure and the outline of the belief system, while chapter six is a lengthy description and analysis of twenty-one cases of suspected witchcraft. Unusually, in only a few of these cases had there been previous bad relations between the parties involved.

545 **From symptom to sacrifice: the story of Khady Fall.** A. Zempleni. In: *Case studies in spirit possession.* Edited by V. Crapanzano, V. Garrison. New York: John Wiley, 1977. p. 87-140.

A fascinating account of the career of a woman healer in Dakar, and the way in which she gradually moved into this profession through a series of illnesses and misfortunes, together with a guided tour around her shrines. A wonderfully vivid introduction to the colourful world of syncretic urban religion in West Africa.

546 *Kujaama*: **symbolic separation among the Diola-Fogny.** J. David Sapir. *American Anthropologist*, vol. 72, no. 6 (1970), p. 1330-48.

Kujaama is a mystical power or spirit which affects people who break taboos and neglect rituals. More generally it is related to flows of blood, and of mixing categories which are regarded as separate. So the belief in *kujaama* turns up in many different, and at first seemingly unrelated contexts, and in underlying ideas about the separation of the sexes and the generations at mealtimes, at funerals and during the harvest.

547 **Langage et techniques thérapeutiques des cultes de possession des Lébou du Sénégal.** (Language and healing techniques of the possession cults of the Lebu in Senegal.) Ousmane Silla. *Bulletin IFAN*, vol. 31(B), no. 1 (1969), p. 215-38.

A description of the *tuuru* and *ndöp* possession and healing cults, and in particular of the part played by language and bodily movement in ritual performances, which are compared to those in other forms of group therapy. The paper also contains transcriptions, translations and analyses of sacred songs collected during cult performances.

548 **Leper, hyena, and blacksmith in Kujamaat Diola thought.**
J. David Sapir. *American Ethnologist*, vol. 8, no. 1 (1981), p. 526-43.

Hyenas killed by this group of Diola during hunting are given funerals similar to those of men, while lepers are buried hurriedly together with a sacrificed dog by blacksmiths imitating the noise of hyenas. Through an analysis of Diola ideas about leprosy, blacksmiths, hyenas and dogs, Sapir reveals the logic of the system of symbolism which underlies these practices.

549 **Mariage des femmes et initiation des hommes: Beliyan et Bédik du Sénégal oriental.** (Female marriage and male initiation: Beliyan and Bedik in Sénégal Oriental.)
Marie-Paul Ferry. *Journal des Africanistes*, vol. 55, nos. 1-2 (1985) p. 75-83.

In this comparison between marriage and initiation as rites of passage among the Bassari, Ferry concludes that one function of these rituals is to help Bassari men retain their control over production.

550 **Nomination, réincarnation et/ou ancêtre tutélaire? Un mode de survie: l'exemple des Sérèr Ndout (Sénégal).** (Name giving, reincarnation and/ or guardian ancestor? A mode of survival: the example of the Serer Ndut of Senegal.)
Marguerite Dupire. *L'Homme*, vol. 22, no. 1 (Jan.-March 1982), p. 5-31.

Like many other West African peoples, the Serer Ndut appear to believe in a form of reincarnation, with an ancestor 'returning' in a newborn infant, the identity of the ancestor being revealed through divination. For these people, therefore, giving a child a name is a ritual which helps to ensure its survival.

551 **Powerlessness, exploitation and the soul-eating witch: an analysis of Badyaranke witchcraft.**
William Simmons. *American Ethnologist*, vol. 7, no. 3 (1980), p. 447-65.

In this ingenious paper, Simmons argues that the continuance of witchcraft beliefs can be explained in terms of the political economy: the Badyranke involvement with the state generates resentment against outsiders which is then displaced and aimed at fellow villagers. However, where a community is able to overcome powerlessness and resist exploitation (as in a neighbouring Muslim community), beliefs in witchcraft subsides.

552 **La quête de l'enfant: représentation de la maternité et rituels de stérilité dans la société Diola de Basse-Casamance.** (The quest for children: the representation of maternity and rituals to deal with sterility in Diola society of the Lower Casamance.)
Odile Journet. *Journal des Africanistes*, vol. 51, no. 1/2 (1981), p. 97-115.

In rural Africa the birth and survival of children is an uncertain business. This paper is a detailed examination of Diola ideas about procreation and rituals to deal with the difficulties which it brings. In particular, it discusses the *kanyaleen* rite, in which, through undergoing ritual humiliation, the mother tries to draw evil on to herself rather than her child.

553 **Religion traditionnelle et techniques thérapeutiques des Lébou du Sénégal.** (Traditional religion and therapeutic techniques among the Lebu of Senegal.)
Ousmane Silla. *Bulletin de l'IFAN*, vol. 30(B) (1968), p. 1566-80.

An account of the main categories of spiritual beings used to explain misfortune in Lebu belief, and the rituals associated with them.

554 **Rites d'initiation et vie en société chez les Sérèrs du Sénégal.** (Initiation rites and social life among the Serer of Senegal.)
Henri Gravrand. *Afrique Documents* (Dakar), vol. 52 (1960), p. 129-44.

An account of the main elements in the circumcision/initiation rituals in Serer society, and of the religious beliefs, concerning the personality, the ancestors and God, on which they are based.

555 **Rituels villageois, rituels urbains: la réproduction sociale chez les femmes joola du Sénégal.** (Village rituals, urban rituals: social reproduction among Joola women of Senegal.)
Didier Fassin. *L'Homme*, vol. 27, no. 104 (1987), p. 54-75.

A study of the changes which take place in rituals, especially the *kanaalen* rite which safeguards procreation, among Joola (Diola) women who move from the villages to the towns. Owing to better medical conditions and lower infant mortality in towns, the significance of the ritual among urban women is reduced and its performance is simplified. These changes in turn affect the ritual life of the village.

556 **The supernatural world of the Badyaranké of Tonghia (Senegal).**
William Simmons. *Journal des Africanistes*, vol. 37, no. 1 (1967), p. 41-72.

A survey of ritual and belief among a small ethnic group of 5,000 people who live along the border between Guinea and eastern Senegal, covering the social structure, the organization of rites, circumcision and excision, beliefs about sickness and the taboo violations which cause them, the role of the marabout, amulets, sorcery, omens and dreams, and the various categories of spiritual being. It ends with a useful glossary.

557 **Un système philosophique sénégalais: la cosmologie des Diola.**
(A Senegalese system of philosophy: the cosmology of the Diola.)
Louis-Vincent Thomas. *Présence Africaine*, vol. 32/33 (June-Sept.
1960), p. 64-76.

A brief sketch of Diola cosmology and philosophy which deals with the main elements of the Diola world view, and the basic characteristics of Diola thought. Similar issues are dealt with in another paper by the same author, 'Brève esquisse sur la pensée cosmologique du Diola' (Brief outline of Diola cosmological thought), in *African systems of thought*, edited by M. Fortes, G. Dieterlen (London: Oxford University Press, 1965, p. 366-82).

558 **Les 'tombes de chiens': mythologies de la mort en pays sérèr (Sénégal).**
('Dogs' tombs': mythologies of death among the Serer of Senegal.)
Marguerite Dupire. *Journal of Religion in Africa*, vol. 15, no. 3
(1985), p. 201-15.

Among the prehistoric structures to be found in the Serer areas of Senegal are some tumuli, known as 'dog's tombs'. An enquiry into the origins of this name leads to an exploration of Serer myths of the origins of death and the ambiguous significance of the dog in Serer culture.

559 **Totems sereers et contrôle rituel de l'environnement.** (Serer totems and
ritual control of the environment.)
Marguerite Dupire. *L'Homme*, vol. 31, no. 118 (1991), p. 37-66.

An exploration of the links between history, myth, ritual and control of the environment among the Serer, this paper deals with the history of the arrival of the Serer Ndut, the origins of their clans and of their totems, and a structural analysis of their totemic myths and rituals. The author detects a relationship between the hierarchy of clans, the totems, and the main economic activities of the Serer (fishing, herding and farming), and compares the Ndut myths with those of the Serer-Sin.

Islam

560 *Ceerno* **Muhamadu Sayid Baa ou le Soufisme intégral de Madiina
Gunaas (Sénégal.)** (*Ceerno* Muhamadu Sayid Baa or the complete
Sufism of Madina Gunaas, Senegal.)
Yaya Wane. *Cahiers d'Etudes Africaines*, vol. 14, no 4 (1974),
p. 671-98.

The study of an isolated Tukulor and Peul village in the south-east of the country, eighty-five kilometres from Tambacounda in Sénégal oriental. Due to its distance from the administration, the social organization is dominated by marabouts belonging to the Tijaniyya brotherhood. The paper consists of a description of the village and its daily life, and the text of an interview with Muhamadu Sayid Baa, its religious leader or *ceerno*. A translation of one of his sermons and the personal testimony of a man who believed that the spiritual intervention of the marabout had saved him from prison in Zaïre are appended.

561 **Charisma comes to town: Mouride urbanization 1945-1986.**
Donal B. Cruise O'Brien. In: *Charisma and brotherhood in African Islam.* Edited by Donal B. Cruise O'Brien, Christian Coulon.
Oxford: Clarendon Press, 1988, p. 135-55.

With the migration of members of the Mouride brotherhood to towns, following the agrarian crises, two forms of urban Mouridism have developed: a 'closed' version represented by the merchants, and an 'open' version which has developed among the urban intelligentsia committed to Islamic reform. A power struggle between these two groups appears to be imminent.

562 **La confrérie sénégalaise des Mourides.** (The Mouride brotherhood in Senegal.)
Cheikh Tidiane Sy. Paris: Présence Africaine, 1969. 350p.

One of the standard studies of the brotherhood in French by a member of a leading Tijaniyya family in Senegal, this book is based on research dating from 1963-64, and covers similar ground to the studies in English by Behrman and O'Brien (see items 561, 571-574, 576, and 584). Where this study goes further than the other two is in its emphasis on the changes taking place within Wolof society, and the author makes linkages between brotherhood social organization and traditional Wolof social organization. The author has dealt with similar issues in 'Ahmadou Bamba et l'islamisation des Wolof' (Ahmadou Bamba and the Islamization of the Wolof), *Bulletin de l'IFAN*, vol. 32 (B), no. 2 (1970), p. 412-33.

563 **La confrérie 'Tijaniyya Ibrahimiyya' de Kano et ses liens avec la zâwiya mère de Kaolack.** (The 'Tijaniyya Ibrahimiyya' brotherhood of Kano and its links with the mother lodge at Kaolack.)
Kane Ousmane. *Islam et Sociétés au Sud du Sahara*, vol. 3 (1989), p. 27-40.

The Tijaniyya brotherhood is strong in Northern Nigeria, particularly in the city of Kano, and this paper discusses the links between Kano and Kaolack, developed under the leadership of Ibrahim Niasse until his death in 1975, and since then by his son and successor, Abdoulaye.

564 **Etudes sur l'Islam au Sénégal: vol. 1. Les personnes; vol 2. Les doctrines et les institutions.**
Paul Marty. Paris: E. Leroux, 1917. 2 vols. (Collection de la Revue du Monde Musulman).

With official encouragement, Marty was responsible for a major survey of Islam throughout French West Africa in the early colonial period, at a time when the colonial government was deeply suspicious of the religion and its leaders. As well as these two volumes on Senegal, he also completed four volumes on the Soudan (Mali) and one on Dahomey (Benin). The first of the Senegal volumes is mainly concerned with the Tijaniyya order among the Tukulor, Wolof, and Manding, while the second is a general survey of doctrines and institutions, including education and law.

565   **Fonctions et activités des dahira mourides urbains (Sénégal).** (Functions
and activities of the urban Mouride *dahira* in Senegal.)
Momar Coumba Diop.   *Cahiers d'Etudes Africaines*, vol. 21, no. 1/3
(1981), p. 79-91.
Based on a section of the author's doctoral thesis, this is a study of the multifunctional
associations which have been developed by members of the Mouride order living in
towns as a way of maintaining the economic and political relationships between the
marabouts and their disciples. The paper describes the origins of the associations in the
rivalry between the Tijaniyya and Mouride orders, and their functions in the urban
setting, in the organization of ceremonies and pilgrimage, and in fund-raising.

566   **France and Islam in West Africa, 1860-1960.**
Christopher Harrison.   Cambridge, England: Cambridge University
Press, 1988. 242p.
A general study of French policy towards Islam in French West Africa during the
colonial period, based on the author's doctoral thesis. It deals with the roots of the
French attitudes to Islam, shaped by their experience in Algeria, and the way in which
French fears of Islam were gradually tempered during the course of the colonial period
as 'Islam noir' was increasingly seen as both benign and useful to the administration.
The book contains valuable accounts of education policy, the careers of the scholar-
administrators Delafosse and Marty, and the development of relations between the
French administration and the Mourides.

567   **L'influence de l'Islam sur la littérature 'wolof'.** (The influence of Islam
on 'Wolof' literature.)
Amar Samb.   *Bulletin de l'IFAN*, vol. 30(B), no. 2 (1968), p. 628-41.
A summary of the effects of Islam and Arabic on Wolof language, thought and poetry.
Religious poetry has thus replaced secular and traditional forms in importance.

568   **L'Islam au Sénégal: demain les mollahs? La 'question' musulmane et les
partis politiques au Sénégal de 1946 à nos jours.** (Islam in Senegal:
tomorrow the Mullahs? The Muslim 'question' and the political parties
in Senegal from 1946 to the present.)
Moriba Magassouba.   Paris: Karthala, 1985. 219p.
The most recent of the series of major studies of Islam in Senegal, this work differs
from the others in that it is written by a journalist rather than an academic, in its
polemical tone, and in the fact that it was written against the background of the
resurgence of fundamentalist Islam world-wide in the 1980s. It raises the question of
whether, given the chronic economic and social crisis in the country, the future lies
with a secular, or with some form of Islamic, republic.

569   **L'Islam et l'histoire du Sénégal.** (Islam and the history of Senegal.)
Amar Samb.   *Bulletin de l'IFAN*, vol. 33(B), no. 3 (1971), p. 461-507.
A survey of the growing importance of Islam among the population of Senegal from
the 17th century onwards. The Muslims were in a majority by 1893, and by 1970 the
proportion of the population in Senegal professing Islam had risen to ninety-five per
cent.

570 **Islamic conversion and social change in a Senegalese village.**
William S. Simmons. *Ethnology*, vol. 18 (1979), p. 303-23.
An account of conversion to Islam among the Badyaranke of Tonghia village in the upper Casamance region, which was largely as a result of increasing links with the wider Senegalese society, and a growing ethnic diversity within the community itself.

571 **The Mourides of Senegal: the political and economic organization of an Islamic brotherhood.**
Donal B. Cruise O'Brien. Oxford: Clarendon Press, 1971. 321p.
The first part of this major study describes the history of Islam in Senegal, the foundation of the brotherhood by Amadu Bamba, and its expansion in the 20th century. The second part describes the organization of the order: followers; leaders; central organization; and a colourful splinter group known as the Bay Fall. The third part describes the important role of the order in Senegal's economics and politics: the *dara* or farming settlement; agriculture and land tenure; the role of the brotherhood in the cities; and its relations with politicians and the state. The conclusion reflects on the future of the order and threats to the authority of its leaders.

572 **Muslim brotherhoods and politics in Senegal.**
Lucy Creevey Behrman. Cambridge, Massachusetts: Harvard University Press, 1970. 475p.
One of a series of major studies of the Muslim brotherhoods in Senegal which was published in the 1970s, this book deals both with the conditions under which the brotherhoods attracted a mass following, and with the development of links between the brotherhoods, the political parties and the state, particularly through the government's use of the marabouts as agents in agricultural social reform.

573 **Muslim brotherhoods and politics in Senegal in 1985.**
Lucy E. Creevey. *Journal of Modern African Studies*, vol. 23, no. 4 (1985), p. 715-21.
The paper contains a useful, concise description of the development and the present political role of the three main Muslim brotherhoods; the Qadiriyya, Tijaniyya, and Muridiyya (Mourides), on whom the Diouf government has relied for support among the country's peasant farmers.

574 **Muslim politics and development in Senegal.**
Lucy Creevey Behrman. *Journal of Modern African Studies*, vol. 15, no. 2 (1977), p. 261-77.
A summary of the changing relationship between the politicians and the marabouts in the decade since the author's original research on the Mouride brotherhood was carried out. The author concludes that despite having their power base diminished through the processes of urbanization and secularization, the influence of the marabouts in politics remains strong, as the people rely on them as community spokesmen, and as the politicians depend upon them as a source of (mainly rural) support.

575 **The origins of clericalism in West African Islam.**
Lamin O. Sanneh. *Journal of African History*, vol. 17, no. 1 (1976),
p. 80-97.
A summary of the origins of the Jakhanké (Diakhanke), the Muslim clerical order which originated among the Serakhulle (Sarakole or Soninke), and spread throughout Senegambia and elsewhere in West Africa. Much of the paper is devoted to a consideration of the career and chronology of al-Hajj Salim Suware, the major figure in the group's early history.

576 **The political significance of the Wolof adherence to Muslim brotherhoods in the nineteenth century.**
Lucy Behrman. *African Historical Studies*, vol. 1, no. 1 (1968),
p. 60-78.
A brief history of the Muslim brotherhoods, which focuses on their role in political change, the reasons for their appeal in Senegal, and the consequences of Wolof conversion in the 19th century.

577 **La question islamique au Sénégal. Le regain récent de l'Islam: un ménage pour l'état?** (The Islamic question in Senegal. The recent revival of Islam: can the state cope?)
Mar Fall. *Cultures et Développement*, vol. 15, no. 3 (1983), p. 443-54.
A short survey of Islamic reform movements in Senegal from the mid-1930s to the present, but particularly in the period after independence, together with the reaction of the state to these developments.

578 **The Shaykh's men: religion and power in Senegambian Islam.**
Lucie G. Colvin. *Asian and African Studies*, vol. 20, no. 1 (1986),
p. 61-71.
A study of the process of conversion among the Wolof, whose society was composed of separate occupationally divided communities. Muslim clerics became identified as one of these occupational communities, and this limited their contact with the majority of the Wolof population. Islam was able to spread to the Wolof masses only after a class of Wolof clerics had developed.

579 **Social and economic factors in the Muslim revolution in Senegambia.**
Martin A. Klein. *Journal of African History*, vol. 13, no. 3 (1972),
p. 419-41.
An account of the way in which the struggles between the warrior élite and the Muslim peasants in 19th-century Senegambia resulted in a predominantly Muslim society in the present day.

580 **Le Tidjanisme au Sénégal.** (Tijaniyya Islam in Senegal.)
Ibrahima Marone. *Bulletin de l'IFAN*, vol. 32(B), no. 1 (1970),
p. 136-215.
A lengthy account of the growth of the brotherhood in Senegal, largely through the efforts of the *khalifa* El Hadj Malik Sy, who established his headquarters at

Tivaouane, and his descendants. The paper describes the organization of the order, its relationship with local religion and marriage practices, struggles for power within the order since the death of Malik Sy, and its involvement in national politics. At the end is a collection of transcribed and translated Wolof Tijani verse.

581   **The Torodbe clerisy: a social view.**
       John Ralph Willis.   *Journal of African History*, vol. 19, no. 2 (1978), p. 195-212.
An account of the rise of clericism in the Fuuta Toro of Senegal and the Fuuta Jallon of Guinea from the late 18th century onwards, which had a profound effect on the societies of the Senegal river valley as the clerics attempted to enforce *sharia* law in areas such as taxation and land tenure.

582   **Touba et son *magal*.** (Touba and its *magal*.)
       Amar Samb.   *Bulletin de l'IFAN*, vol. 31(B), no. 3 (1969), p. 733-53.
A description of the annual pilgrimage, involving about a quarter of a million people, to Touba, the sacred city of the Mouride order, in commemoration of the death of the Mouride founder, Ahmadu Bamba in 1927.

583   **Traditional society, change and organizational development.**
       Clement Cottingham.   *Journal of Modern African Studies*, vol. 11, no. 4 (1973), p. 675-81.
A useful review article of three of the major studies of the Mourides in Senegal, the books by Donal Cruise O'Brien, Lucy Behrman and Cheikh Tidiane Sy, all of which examine the remarkable capacity of the movement to affect both economic and political development.

584   **A versatile charisma: the Mouride brotherhood 1967-75.**
       Donal B. Cruise O'Brien.   *European Journal of Sociology*, vol. 18, no. 1 (1977), p. 84-106.
A study of the resilience and versatility of the Muslim movement since the late 19th century, the paper traces its evolution from a charismatic and nationalistic religious community, through a period from 1912 when it helped to organize land settlement, to an important force in party politics before and after independence. Now, O'Brien argues, it has become a peasants' trade union, through which the members can extract resources from the state.

585   **Women, Islam and *baraka*.**
       Christian Coulon.   In: *Charisma and brotherhood in African Islam*. Edited by Donal B. Cruise O'Brien, Christian Coulon.   Oxford: Clarendon Press, 1988. p. 113-33.
A study of the role of women in Senegalese Islam, and the ways in which they are able to inherit *baraka* or holiness within the family. The paper ends with an account of the career of Sokhna Magat Diop, the only Senegalese woman leader of a Muslim religious community.

Urban migration, cash cropping, and calamity: the spread of Islam among the Diola of Boulouf (Senegal), 1900-1940.
See item no. 134.

Esquisses sénégalaises (Walo, Kayor, Dyolof, Mourides, un visionnaire.) (Senegalese sketches: Walo, Kayor, Jolof, Mourides, a religious visionary.)
See item no. 149.

Muslim peoples: a world ethnographic survey.
See item no. 150.

Power, prayer and production: the Jola of Casamance, Senegal.
See item no. 153.

The Holy War of Umar Tal.
See item no. 231.

Islam and the state of Kajoor: a case of successful resistance to jihad.
See item no. 233.

Jihad in West Africa: early phases and inter-relations in Mauritania and Senegal.
See item no. 235.

Mandingo kingdoms of the Senegambia: traditionalism, Islam and European expansion.
See item no. 236.

Chiefs and clerics: Abdul Bokar Kan and Futa Toro 1853-1891.
See item no. 278.

French 'Islamic' policy and practice in late 19th-century Senegal.
See item no. 284.

Shaikh Amadu Ba and jihad in Jolof.
See item no. 297.

Beyond resistance and collaboration: Amadu Bamba and the Murids of Senegal.
See item no. 303.

Maintenance sociale et changement économique au Sénégal. I. Doctrine économique et pratique du travail chez les Mourides. (Social continuity and economic change in Senegal. Vol. 1. Economic doctrine and work practices among the Mourides.)
See item no. 342.

Les marabouts de l'arachide: la confrérie mouride et les paysans du Sénégal. (The holy men of the groundnut industry: the Mouride Muslim brotherhood and the peasants of Senegal.)
See item no. 343.

Ruling class and peasantry in Senegal, 1960-1976: the politics of a monocrop economy.
See item no. 350.

A la recherche de nouveaux 'poissons'. Stratégies commerciales mourides par temps de crise. (In search of new 'fish': commercial strategies of the Mourides in a time of crisis.)
See item no. 368.

Saints and politicians: essays in the organisation of a Senegalese peasant society.
See item no. 436.

Traditional social structure, the Islamic brotherhoods, and political development in Senegal.
See item no. 524.

Contribution à une étude de l'enseignement privé coranique au Sénégal. (Contribution to the study of private Koranic education in Senegal.)
See item no. 591.

L'école française et les Musulmans au Sénégal de 1850 à 1900. (French schooling and the Muslims of Senegal.)
See item no. 593.

Christianity

586 **The Catholic Mission and some aspects of assimilation in Senegal, 1817-1852.**
D. H. Jones. *Journal of African History*, vol. 21, no. 3 (1980), p. 323-40.
A study of the history of a group of Catholic missionaries in the early 19th century trying to establish their work in Senegal. Their problems were numerous: lack of political support; language difficulties which limited the opportunities for evangelism; and a shortage of money with which to develop elementary education. There was also the problem of the strength of Islam among the local populations, which had its own Koranic educational system.

587 **Le Christianisme au Sénégal.** (Christianity in Senegal.)
Hughes Jean de Dianoux. *L'Afrique et l'Asie Modernes*, no. 4, (1981), p. 3-22.
This paper contains a brief survey of Christian history since the 15th century, and an examination of the role of the Catholic Church during the Senghor presidency.

588 **The emergence of a Diola Christianity.**
Robert Martin Baum. *Africa*, vol. 60, no. 3 (1990), p. 370-398.

This paper, which is important both as a study of Christianity in Senegal, and as a contribution to wider debates about the nature of religious conversion, examines the processes of religious change among a group of Diola in the Casamance, and the interaction between Diola traditional beliefs and elements of the Christian faith. The author reviews the past century of the religious history of Diola-Esulalu, a community of around 15,000 people in the Casamance region of southern Senegal, and the tensions which have occurred during this period between the two religions. He concludes that traditional religion has not been swept away by the world religions, but has remained independent and dynamic, and has in turn influenced the development of local Christianity. Despite changes in the organization of Christianity since 1945, making it possible to adapt it more fully to Diola culture, it still does not meet the needs of many converts, and reconversion back to traditional beliefs remains a common occurrence.

589 **Missions catholiques et administration française sur la côte d'Afrique de 1815 à 1870.** (Catholic missions and French administration on the coast of Africa, 1815-1870.)
Paule Brasseur. *Revue Française d'Histoire d'Outre-Mer*, vol. 62, no. 3 (1975), p. 415-46.

A general account of the growth of Catholic missionary work in Western Africa, including Guinea, Senegambia and Gabon, against a background of French government expectation that the Church would exert a 'civilizing' influence in the region.

La Chrétienté africaine de Dakar. Partie descriptive et statistique. 1er, 2ième, 3ième cahiers. (African Christianity in Dakar. Descriptive and statistical section. 3 books.)
See item no. 142.

Notes d'instructions à une étude socio-religieuse des populations de Dakar et du Sénégal. (Instruction notes for a socio-religious study of the populations of Dakar and Senegal.)
See item no. 143.

Saint-Louis du Sénégal, ville aux mille visages. (Saint-Louis, Senegal: town with a thousand faces.)
See item no. 269.

Education, Research and Technology

Education

590 **Autrefois, notre pays s'appelait La Gaule. . . Remarques sur
l'adaptation de l'enseignement au Sénégal de 1817 à 1960.** (In the past,
our country was called Gaul. . . Remarks on educational adaptation in
Senegal from 1817 to 1960.)
Denise Bouche. *Cahiers d'Etudes Africaines*, vol. 8, no. 29 (1968),
p. 110-22.
Despite the stereotype that the French simply imported their educational system to
Africa with little change (which provides the joke underlying the title of the paper) the
reality, as the author makes clear, was more complex. The paper reviews attempts to
adapt the curriculum to local conditions dating back to 1850.

591 **Contribution à une étude de l'enseignement privé coranique au Sénégal.**
(Contribution to the study of private Koranic education in Senegal.)
Cheikh Amalla Diallo. *Revue Française d'Etudes Politiques
Africaines*, no. 76 (1972), p. 34-48.
According to surveys in the 1960s, one-third of all children in Senegal attended
Koranic schools. This paper gives an overview of the system as it evolved since the
1950s. The Koranic schools have provided access to education in areas where no state
schools are available, but, the author claims, at the cost of high rates of delinquency
and difficulties for the students in adapting to the modern world.

592 **Les débuts de l'enseignement en Afrique francophone: Jean Dard et l'Ecole Mutuelle de Saint-Louis de Sénégal.** (The beginnings of education in French-speaking Africa: Jean Dard and the *Ecole Mutuelle* at Saint-Louis, Senegal.)
Joseph Gaucher.   Paris: Le Livre Africain. 1968. 198p.

An account of the chequered career of Jean Dard, pioneer teacher and linguist, who was sent out to Senegal to start a school in Saint-Louis, a town recently repossessed by France at the end of the Napoleonic wars. The book reproduces many documents and letters from the period, both in the text and in the extensive appendices.

593 **L'école française et les Musulmans au Sénégal de 1850 à 1900.** (French schooling and the Muslims of Senegal, 1850-1920.)
Denise Bouche.   *Revue Française d'Histoire d'Outre-Mer*, vol. 61, no. 223 (1974), p. 218-35.

A study of the development of the dual education system in Senegal which has persisted to the present day. The Muslims had their own system of Koranic education, and French attempts to modify their educational system to accommodate Muslim needs met with little success.

594 **Education and class conflict.**
Olivier Le Brun.   In: *The political economy of underdevelopment: dependence in Senegal*. Edited by Rita Cruise O'Brien.   Beverly Hills, California; London: Sage, 1979, p. 175-208. (Sage Series on African Modernization and Development 3).

An important discussion of the evolution of the Senegalese education system and the results of its dependence on French models. Le Brun argues that the system is relatively efficient at reproducing the ruling class, but that the wider economy has grown too slowly to absorb all the graduates, so that the result is rising unemployment among the educated.

595 **L'éducation des adultes au Sénégal.** (Adult education in Senegal.)
P. Fougeyrollas, F. Sow, F. Valladon.   Paris: UNESCO (Institut International de Planification de l'Education), 1967. 46p.

The authors review the results of the plan by the IIPE to establish an educational programme for the teaching of French and English to adults. On the basis of interviews with educationalists and consultation of the relevant literature, the work assesses the requirements and problems of adult language teaching, as well as techniques for teaching French.

596 **History of Western education in French-speaking Africa: the example of Senegal.**
Michael Vandewiele.   *Psychological Reports*, vol. 53 (1983), p. 507-15.

This paper gives a concise and useful account of the development of education in Senegal, describing the present system as the result of a continuous attempt to adapt a foreign curriculum to local needs. Senegalese intellectuals regard the system as having worked fairly satisfactorily, but argue that the cultural focus should shift from Europe to Africa, and that more use should be made of Wolof and other local languages.

597 **Interwar schools and the development of African history in French West Africa.**
Gail P. Kelly. *History in Africa*, vol. 10 (1983), p. 163-85.

An account of the development of the teaching of African history in schools in French West Africa, and the ways in which perceptions of the past were structured by the colonial present. Despite the obvious biases which this created, there was innovation in the use of folklore and ethnographic materials which helped legitimize the use of these kinds of materials in historical research.

598 **Learning to be marginal: schooling in interwar French West Africa.**
Gail P. Kelley. *Journal of Asian and African Studies*, vol. 21, no. 3-4 (1986), p. 171-84.

An analysis of the ways in which schools in French West Africa under colonial rule managed to separate African students from their own cultures. The analysis is based on school texts which described Africa from the point of view of outsiders, and which presented a view of the student as different from other Africans; and on students' essays which reflected the same themes of identity and separation.

599 **Lycéens de Dakar: essai de sociologie de l'éducation.** (Secondary school students in Dakar: an essay in the sociology of education.)
Françoise Flis-Zonabend. Paris: François Maspero, 1968. 213p.

This study, based on interviews with 314 secondary school children in Dakar, discusses their social backgrounds, living conditions, the relationships between the *lycées* and other schools, the relationships of the students with their families, and with other students, and their leisure activities and career choices. The conclusions are critical of the wholesale adoption of a metropolitan system of education which often has little relevance to the lives of the African students. The appendices include a useful survey of the development and state of education in Senegal in the early years of independence, together with a brief survey of the social structure of Dakar.

600 **Non-formal education and education policy in Ghana and Senegal.**
Babacar Sine. Paris: UNESCO, [1979], 35p. (Educational Studies and Documents, 35).

A short comparative study which outlines the cultural and educational needs of selected urban and rural communities. The author highlights the contribution which non-formal education can make in meeting these needs, and calls for greater integration of such methods into the agendas of educational planners. The Senegalese part of the study focuses on Guédiawaye, a suburban area of Dakar, some ten kilometres from the city centre.

601 **Phenomène d'acculturation chez les étudiants de la cité universitaire de Dakar.** (Acculturation among the students of the Dakar university campus.)
Pierre Fougeyrollas. *Revue Française de Sociologie*, vol. 4, no. 4 (1963), p. 411-23.
A typical 1960s study of modernization based on interviews with 159 African students at the University of Dakar, investigating their attachment to traditional African values (such as community and culture), their attitudes towards the West and towards French as a national language, and their views on the suppression of the caste system, changes in marriage patterns, and politics.

602 **Senegal.**
In: *The World of Learning*. London: Europa Publications, 1992, 42nd ed. p. 1183-4.
An entry in the standard directory on research and higher education for the countries of the world, with information on the names, addresses and activities of learned societies, research institutes, museums, universities and colleges. The longest entry is on the Université Cheikh Anta Diop de Dakar (formerly the University of Dakar), and its affiliated institutes.

603 **Systèmes d'éducation et mutations sociales: continuité et discontinuité dans les dynamiques socio-éducatives. Le cas du Sénégal.** (Systems of education and social change: continuity and discontinuity in socio-educational dynamics. The case of Senegal.)
Roland Colin. Paris: Librairie Honoré Champion, 1980. 2 vols.
This thesis on the history of education in Senegal deals with education in precolonial society, focusing on initiation, the growth of the Western educational system during the colonial period, the introduction of more radical socialist policies under Mamadou Dia (1957-62), and the reversion to a more conservative policy after his fall. One strand in the wider political debate, therefore, was the clash between one view of education based on the European tradition, in which Senghor had been trained, and another based on the realities of the countryside. The study includes lengthy appendices containing the text of important archival material.

Enquête sur les langues parlées au Sénégal par les éléves de l'enseignement primaire. (Investigation of the languages spoken in Senegal by primary school pupils.)
See item no. 651.

Research and technology

604 **La diffusion du progrès technique en milieu rural sénégalais.**
(The diffusion of technical progress in the context of rural Senegal.)
J. Brochier. Paris: Presses Universitaires de France, 1968.
A major study of the rural economy of the Thiénaba *arrondissement,* fifteen kilometres east of Thiès. The three sections deal with the geography and economy of the area, the national agricultural programme after independence, its implementation in Thiénaba. The conclusion is that some technical improvements produced increased output and were accepted by the farmers, but that the results were meagre in comparison with the resources expended, and had little effect on the general living conditions in the area. The study is well documented with numerous tables. An extract from the book was published as 'Enquête sur le mouvement coopératif dans un arrondissement sénégalais' (An inquiry into the cooperative movement in a district of Senegal), *Civilisations,* vol. 21, no. 1 (1971), p. 19-37.

605 **Manuel de la culture de l'arachide au Sénégal, à l'usage de vulgarisation.** (Manual on groundnut cultivation, intended for popularization.)
Dakar: Ministère du Développement Rural/Société d'Aide Technique et de Coopération (SATEC), 1968. 106p.
The third of the SATEC manuals includes information on fertilizing and manuring, parasites, diseases, pests, fallowing, harvesting and the production of groundnuts for seed.

606 **Manuel de la culture de mils et sorghos dans le bassin arachidier sénégalaise, à l'usage de vulgarisation.** (Manual on millet and sorghum cultivation in the Senegalese groundnut basin, intended for popularization.)
Dakar: Ministère du Développment Rural/Société d'Aide Technique et de Coopération (SATEC), 1968. 97p.
The second of the SATEC manuals deals with types and characteristics of species of millet and sorghum, soil preparation, and cultivation. There are also notes on manuring, and on diseases, pests and parasites.

607 **Manuel de l'utilisation des matériels agricoles dans les exploitations sénégalaises, à l'usage de la vulgarisation.** (Operation manual for agricultural materials in Senegalese farming, intended for popularization.)
Dakar: Ministère du Développment Rural/Société d'Aide Technique et de Coopération (SATEC), 1968. 159p.
The first of a series of manuals prepared for officials involved in an education programme among farmers of the groundnut belt. It covers the principles of animal traction, including harnessing and yoking, and a long section on groundnut cultivation, including soil preparation, sowing, weeding, and harvesting.

608 **Senegal.**
In: *International research centers directory.* Edited by Darren L.
Smith. Detroit, Michigan: Gale Research, 1988-89, 4th ed. vol. 2,
p. 978-81.
Names and addresses of research organizations, with notes on the organization,
research descriptions, publications and information services. The Senegal section
includes information on eighteen institutions, most of them concerned with economic
development, agriculture or the environment.

609 **Sénégal: organisation et gestion de la recherche sur les systèmes de
production.** (Senegal: organisation and management of research into
systems of production.)
Jacques Faye, R. James Bingen. The Hague: International Service for
National Agricultural Research, 1989. 186p.
This report focuses on the 'organisation and management of on-farm client-oriented
research', and ways in which research can be made to benefit the poorer peasant. The
sections outline the Senegalese context, the history of agricultural research in Senegal,
mainly at the Institut Sénégalais de Recherches Agricoles founded in 1975, research
programmes in each of the main areas of the country, and an evaluation of their
impact. The interest of the report lies as much in the light it sheds on the difficulties of
this kind of research and in the relationships between the researchers and the farmers,
as in the actual results achieved, which appear to be modest.

610 **Le transfert d'un modèle d'enseignement technique supérieur du Québec
au Sénégal: le cas de l'Ecole Polytechnique de Thiès.** (The transfer of a
model of higher technical education from Quebec to Senegal: the case
of the Thiès Polytechnic College.)
Charles H. Davis, Marie-Paule Laberge. *Canadian Journal of African
Studies,* vol. 20, no. 1 (1986), p. 57-72.
This paper is an evaluation of a Canadian educational aid programme, in which the
Ecole Polytechnique de Montréal assisted the Ecole Polytechnique de Thiès in
developing its engineering teaching. A useful study of the predictable difficulties of
recruiting expatriate staff, adapting North American teaching to African conditions,
and of training a Senegalese teaching force. A study by the same authors of what the
Canadians gained from the project was published as 'Professional rewards in a Canada-
Senegal cooperative project in engineering education: the case of the Projet de l'Ecole
Polytechnique de Thiès', *Canadian Journal of Development Studies,* vol. 8 (1987),
p. 283-97.

Colonization to co-operation: French technical assistance in Senegal.
See item no. 515.

Social Policy and Planning

Health and medicine

611 **Les conditions de développement d'une psychiatrie sociale au Sénégal.**
(Conditions for the development of social psychiatry in Senegal.)
René Collignon. *Présence Africaine*, no. 129 (1984), p. 3-19.

A brief survey of the development of psychiatric services and psychiatric treatment in Senegal to meet the needs of African patients, and a useful source of references in this field.

612 **De la quête de légitimation à la question de la légitimité: les thérapeutiques 'traditionnelles' au Sénégal.** (In search of legitimation of the question of the legitimate: traditional therapies in Senegal.)
Eric Fassin, Didier Fassin. *Cahiers d'Etudes Africaines*, vol. 28, no. 2 (1988), p. 207-31.

A discussion of the search for legitimacy by traditional healers in Senegal, with reference to three case studies, from Pikine, Sine and Dakar, which questions the meaning of the term 'legitimacy' and points to the absurdity of a situation in which both the state and the medical establishment condemn traditional healing, while officials and doctors do not hesitate to consult them. Similar ground is covered in a brief paper in English by the same authors, 'Traditional medicine and the stakes of legitimation in Senegal', *Social Science and Medicine*, vol. 27, no. 4 (1987), p. 353-7.

613 **The ecology of malnutrition in the French-speaking countries of West Africa and Madagascar.**
Jacques M. May, Donna M. McMellan. New York: Haffner, 1968. 433p.

This study, the first chapter of which (p. 3-46) deals with Senegal, surveys the geography, history, government, agricultural and foreign policies of each country, before considering in detail its food resources, and their production, trade and supply.

There is information on urban and rural diets, together with an analysis of the nutritional disease patterns and consideration of the adequacy of levels of food consumption.

614   **Ethno-gynécologie et pathologie bedik.** (Bedik ethno-gynaecology and pathology.)
Jacques Gomila. *Journal des Africanistes*, vol. 49, no. 2 (1979), p. 137-42.

Gomila was both a doctor and an anthropologist. This paper, part of a longer manuscript which he had been working on with a colleague at the time of his death, is a brief outline of Bedik ideas of women's disorders related to reproduction, sterility and the menopause.

615   **Hygiène et assainissement de la ville de Dakar.** (Hygiene and sanitation in the city of Dakar.)
Dakar: Agence Economique de l'Afrique Occidentale Français, 1930. 16p.

A survey of Dakar's water resources and sanitation in the colonial period, with sections on drinking water, drains, rubbish disposal and sanitation.

616   **Intoxication par le chanvre indien au Sénégal.** (Indian hemp intoxication in Senegal.)
H. Collomb (et al.). *Cahiers d'Etudes Africaines*, vol. 3, no. 1 (1962), p. 139-44.

A survey of cannabis production, distribution and consumption. The authors found that the plant was grown nearly everywhere in Senegal, that there was a well-organized network of distribution, and that consumption was extremely widespread, particularly among the younger men.

617   **La lutte anti-lépreuse au Sénégal: médecine européenne et médecine africaine.** (The struggle against leprosy in Senegal: European medicine and African medicine.)
Yvette Parès. *Présence Africaine*, no. 124 (1982), p. 76-96.

A brief survey of the struggle against leprosy, which discusses bacteriological research, practical applications, medicinal plants, traditional therapy, and prospects for the future.

618   **Oedipe Africain.** (African Oedipus.)
Marie Cécile Ortigues, Edmond Ortigues.   Paris: Editions l'Harmattan, 1984. 3rd ed. 324p.

A classic attempt to apply psychoanalytical categories to psychiatric practice in West Africa, based on the authors' clinical experience between 1962 and 1964.

619 **Peste et société urbaine à Dakar: l'épidémie de 1914.** (The plague and urban society in Dakar: the epidemic of 1914.)
Elikia M'Bokolo. *Cahiers d'Etudes Africaines*, vol. 22, no. 1/2 (1982), p. 13-46.

The serious outbreak of plague in Dakar in 1914 was totally unexpected. It lasted for a year, and spread to the rural areas, despite attempts to isolate the city. This paper traces the progress of the epidemic, its spread and the extent of the mortality, as well as the opposition by the local people to the sanitary precautions imposed by the authorities, which were at times discriminatory and ran contrary to local beliefs.

620 **Republic of Senegal.**
Department of Health Data, Division of Preventive Medicine.
Washington, DC: Walter Reed Army Medical Center, 1965. 64p.
(Walter Reed Army Institute of Research Health Data Publication no. 26).

This report, prepared by the Department of Health Data primarily for the use of officers of the US Army Medical Service, was based on the information available up to 1965. It contains a brief survey of the country, public health and sanitation, and animal disease carriers, including insects; a catalogue of Senegalese diseases; and an account of medical institutions. The appendices contain lists of poisonous snakes, arthropods, and animal diseases, followed by lists of hospitals, health centres, maternity centres and leprosaria.

621 **La santé au Sénégal.** (Health in Senegal.)
Association des Travailleurs Sénégalais de Santé en France. *Présence Africaine*, no. 124 (1982), p. 118-129.

A brief survey of the main health problems in both the urban and rural areas of the country. It deals with problems of manpower, the integration of African and Western medicine, the African pharmacopoeia, and a survey of government health policy. It ends with both short-term and long-term recommendations for dealing with the situation.

622 **Santé et population en Sénégambie des origines à 1960.** (Health and population in Senegambia from its origins to 1960.)
Réne Collignon, Charles Becker. Paris: Institut National d'Etudes Démographiques, 1989. 554p.

An impressive and comprehensive medical and demographic bibliography for the region which lists 2,908 references. There are eighteen chapters, dealing with sources, general topics, hygiene and public health, geography and medical topography, preventions and vaccinations, demography, physical and biological anthropology, nutrition, parasitic disease, viral diseases, 'nuisances', tumour and cancers, healing, and contemporary historical works. Each reference is accompanied by a short summary, and there is an index of authors and materials.

623 **La santé publique sans l'état? Participation communautaire et comités de santé au Sénégal.** (Public health without the state? Community participation and health committees in Senegal.)
Didier Fassin, Eric Fassin. *Tiers-Monde*, vol. 30, no. 120 (1989), p. 881-91.

A study of community mobilization and public health improvements in Pikine, a city which grew from a small village outside Dakar in 1950 to a large satellite town, with poor services and infrastructure. The paper discusses contrasting views of community involvement, together with the formation of local bodies to deal with local problems, and ends with the question of whether it is possible to have public health without the state, given Senegal's economic problems.

624 **Vingt ans de travaux à la clinique psychiatrique de Fann-Dakar.**
(Twenty years of work at the Fann-Dakar psychiatric clinic.)
René Collignon. *Psychopathologie Africaine*, vol. 14, no. 2/3 (1978), p. 133-324.

A major overview, in the form of an annotated bibliography, of the work carried out by the members of a psychiatric team based at the Centre Hospitalier Universitaire de Fann-Dakar, during the period from 1956 onwards. It includes published articles; conference and seminar papers; theses and monographs based on research into psychiatry, psychology and sociology carried out at Fann; and later work by former participants in the programme. There are also indexes of authors, themes and sources.

Du clandestin à l'officieux: les réseaux de vente illicite des médicaments au Sénégal. (From the clandestine to the official: the network of illicit sales of medicines in Senegal.)
See item no. 369.

La lutte des pouvoirs publics contre les 'encombrements humains' à Dakar.
(The struggle of the public authorities against the 'human obstacles' in Dakar.)
See item no. 523.

From symptom to sacrifice: the story of Khady Fall.
See item no. 545.

Langage et techniques thérapeutiques des cultes de possession des Lébou du Sénégal. (Language and healing techniques of the possession cults of the Lebu in Senegal.)
See item no. 547.

Religon traditionnelle et techniques thérapeutiques des Lébou du Sénégal.
(Traditional religion and therapeutic techniques among the Lebu of Senegal.)
See item no. 553.

Rural planning and development

625 **L'administration locale du développement rural au Sénégal.** (Local administration of rural development in Senegal.)
R. Descloitres, J.-C. Reverdy, R. Volante. Dakar; Aix en Provence, France: Centre Africain des Sciences Humaines Appliquées, 1964. 209p.

An evaluation of the benefits of rural development administration in villagers' lives, which considers the relationships between regional and district administrators and officials, and between local committees and the higher echelons of administration. It also examines the role of technical assistants in agricultural cooperatives and makes a number of recommendations about the extent of the control exercised at all levels in the administrative structure.

626 **Agricultural development and policy in Senegal: annotated bibliography of recent studies, 1983-89.**
Eric W. Crawford (et al.). East Lansing, Michigan: Institute of International Agriculture, Michigan State University, 1990. 254p.

The most recent survey of the current literature, with 356 entries listed by author. There are indexes for titles and key words, and each of the references is also evaluated for 'relevance' (i.e. whether or not it was considered useful for the purposes of the USAID planners).

627 *Animation rurale*: **biography of an African administrative agency.**
Irving Leonard Markovitz. In: *The political economy of Senegal under structural adjustment.* Edited by Christopher L. Delgado, Sidi Jammeh. New York: Praeger, 1991, p. 69-84.

An account of the early successes and the subsequent disintegration of the *animation rurale* programme, which was responsible for the training of thousands of village-level *animateurs* in the 1960s but which by the mid-1980s had virtually ceased to function. Markovitz regards its history as reflecting a more general retreat by the government from the ideals which they held at the time of independence.

628 *Animation rurale*: **education for rural development.**
Jeanne Marie Moulton. Amherst, Massachusetts: Centre for International Education, 1977. 249p.

A study of the history of the concept of *animation rurale* and its application in the two Sahel states of Senegal and Niger. Though criticized for accepting wholeheartedly the rhetoric of African socialism, the book is a useful source of case material which helps to explain why the programme was often less than successful, mainly because of the imposition of the bureaucrats' categories and visions of development on a reluctant peasantry.

629 **Associations rurales et socialisme contractuel en Afrique occidentale:
étude de cas: le Sénégal.** (Rural associations and contractual socialism in
West Africa: a case study of Senegal.)
Pierre Laville. Paris: Editions CUJAS, 1972. 371p.

A study of the cooperative movement in Senegal before and in the early years after
independence, based on the author's 1967 doctoral thesis. The first part of the book
describes the structure of indigenous provident societies during the colonial period,
their finances and their role in agriculture, together with the early growth of the
cooperative movement. The second part describes the integration of the movement
into the national programme of rural development after independence.

630 **Coopératives ou autogestion: Sénégal, Cuba, Tunisie.** (Cooperatives or
self-management: Senegal, Cuba, Tunisia.)
Gabriel Gagnon. Montreal: Les Presses de l'Université de Montréal.
1976. 482p.

A large-scale comparative study of cooperative development in three Third World
countries, the first 149 pages of which, written together with Jules Savaria, are a
relatively self-contained study of Senegal. The general argument is that the cooperative
system cannot be considered as a specific and autonomous mode of production, and
that it is quickly neutralized when it puts at risk the power of the dominant classes.
This explains why the idea of 'rural animation' which could have given the
organizations another dimension, was given less emphasis.

631 **Development of irrigated agriculture in Senegal: general overview and
prospects: proposals for a second programme 1980-1985.**
Club de Sahel. Dakar: Permanent Interstate Committee for Drought
Control in the Sahel, 1979. 108p.

A mimeographed report based on the findings of a two-week mission from the Club de
Sahel, a consortium of aid donors, to Senegal in May 1979. It deals with the status of
irrigated farming in development planning, constraints – including physical, social and
management – with problems of finance, and with proposals for the 1980-85 period.
The seven appendices include an outline of Senegalese geography and the economy,
information on the activities of the Société d'Aménagement et d'Exploitation des
Terres du Delta (SAED), one of the major Senegalese organizations set up to oversee
rural development, and a collection of mimeographed maps showing the location of
some of the irrigation schemes.

632 **Le développement à la base au Dahomey at au Sénégal.** (Grass-roots
development in Dahomey and Senegal.)
Jean Serreau. Paris: Pichon et Durand-Auzias. 1966. 358p.
(Bibliothèque d'Economie Politique, 7).

A comparative account of the problems of, and potential for, economic development in
the two countries. The section on Senegal deals with the goals of the first plan (1961-5),
animation rurale, the *centres d'expansion ruraux* and the cooperative movement.

633 **L'évolution des structures agricoles du Sénégal: déstructuration et réstructuration de l'économie rurale.** (The evolution of the agricultural structures of Senegal: taking apart and rebuilding the rural economy.) V. C. Diarassouba. Paris: Editions CUJAS, 1968. 298p.

A study which is still important as a source of information on successive phases of state policy and the organizations set up to implement them during the colonial period and after independence. The general conclusion is that 1959 marked a turning point in the country's agricultural strategy, with the beginning of a programme to work out a better structure for the rural economy, mainly through *animation rurale* and rural cooperatives. Both, unfortunately, were comparative failures.

634 **Irrigated agriculture as an archetypal development project: Senegal.** Alfred S. Waldstein. In: *Anthropology and rural development in West Africa.* Edited by Michael M. Horowitz, Thomas M. Painter. Boulder, Colorado; London: Westview, 1986, p. 117-43.

An account of the problems of economic development in the Kassak zone of the Senegal River delta, where re-settled peasant farmers practise irrigated rice farming and other crop production under the direction of the Société d'Aménagement et d'Exploitation des Terres du Delta (SAED). It argues that this state organization, which controls all aspects of production, sale and distribution of crops, is insufficiently flexible, too autocratic, and not adapted to the economic conditions of the zone. The author proposes that development projects be smaller and less dependent on capital-intensive techniques.

635 **Nation et développement communautaire en Guinée et au Sénégal.** (National and community development in Guinea and Senegal.) Henry de Decker. Paris: Mouton, 1967. 470p.

Pages 217-414 of this work deal with Senegal and focus on the *animation rurale* (rural animation) programme, particularly the relations between the local population and the agents of development.

636 **L'organisation coopérative au Sénégal.** (The organization of cooperatives in Senegal.) Marguerite Camboulives. Paris: Pedone, 1967. 402p.

A history of the varied forms of cooperative organization that had developed in Senegal up to the mid-1960s, together with their legal basis, functions and management. It considers their role in agricultural development and diversification, as well as in the provision of credit. There is also an account of development and training agencies such as the Banque Nationale de Développement du Sénégal (BNDS), the Centres Régionaux d'Assistance pour le Développement (CRAD), and the Centres d'Expansion Rurale (CER) among many others.

637 **Paysanneries aux abois: Ceylan, Tunisie, Sénégal.** (Peasantries at bay: Ceylon, Tunisia, Senegal.) René Dumont. Paris: Seuil, 1972. 254p.

Presents three case studies of the forms of deception practised on the peasants by the state. In the case of Senegal, where groundnut production predominates, peasant farmers operate within types of social and administrative structures in the form of agricultural cooperatives, which effectively perpetuate colonial forms of exploitation.

638 **Politics, bureaucracy and rural development in Senegal.**
Edward J. Schumacher. Berkeley, California: University of California Press, 1975. 279p.

An important account of the one-party state and rural development policies in Senegal, based on research carried out from 1966 to 1968. The first six chapters deal with aspects of politics and administration: party organization and electoral mobilization; constitutional change and the growth of executive power; development administration in the post-colonial period; and the process of bureaucratic rationalization. The second half of the book is a critical account of state intervention in the economy, through cooperatives, marketing and rural development and credit schemes.

639 **Raison pastorale et politique de développement: les Peul sénégalais face aux aménagements.** (Pastoral reasoning and development policy: the Peul of Senegal facing change.)
Christian Santoir. Paris: ORSTOM, 1983. 185p. maps. (Travaux et Documents, 166).

An important study of the effects of irrigation schemes and settlement upon the Peul (Fulbe) of Senegal. The first part describes the effects on the Peul of agricultural development in Jolof, the rise of the groundnut industry and sedentarization. The second part deals with developments in the Senegal river valley, and the effects of the extension of farming based on irrigation into areas traditionally used for pasture. The study is well illustrated with numerous maps, tables and photographs. A summary of this work is contained in the author's paper 'Peul et aménagements hydro-agricoles dans la vallée du fleuve Sénégal' (The Peul and irrigation development in the Senegal river valley), in *Pastoralists of the West African Savanna*. Edited by M. Adamu, A. H. M Kirk-Greene (Manchester, England: Manchester University Press for the International African Institute, 1986, p. 191-213).

640 **The Senegal River valley: what kind of change?**
Adrian Adams. *Review of African Political Economy*, vol. 10 (1977), p. 325-53.

A critical account, written during the mid-1970s, of rural development in the Fleuve area, and the relations between the farmers and the organizations responsible for the implementation of development projects. The paper focuses on the different perceptions held by farmers and by technicians of the development process, and the problems of imposing 'development' from above. The paper was also reprinted in *Rural development in tropical Africa*, edited by J. Heyer (London: Macmillan, 1981).

641 **The state and rural development 1960-85.**
Sidi Kane, Baba Ba, Pap Sow. In: *African agriculture: the critical choices*. Edited by Hamid Ait Amara, Bernard Founou-Tchuigoua. London: Zed Books, 1990, p. 170-91.

A useful survey from an underdevelopment perspective of the failure of agricultural policy since independence, and the reasons for the comparative decline of the Senegalese economy compared with other former French colonies in West Africa. The authors place the blame on policies favouring export crops at the expense of those for local consumption, and the extraction of a surplus from the rural sector by the state.

642 **Structural change and managerial inefficiency in the development of rice cultivation in the Senegal River region.**
Kathleen M. Baker. *African Affairs*, vol. 81, no. 325 (1982), p. 499-510.

A critical account of SAED, the Société pour l'Aménagement et l'Exploitation du Delta, which was set up to develop agriculture in the delta of the Senegal River, and later further up-river. The article concludes that none of the structural changes in the organization of rice cultivation introduced by SAED resulted in significant increases in production, due to poor management and disillusionment among the farmers, and that much could be learned from the relationship between farmers and officials in China.

Les villages-centres du Sénégal. (Village centres of Senegal.)
See item no. 43.

Seeds of famine: ecological destruction and the development dilemma in the West African Sahel.
See item no. 71.

Cartes pour servir à l'aménagement du territoire. (Maps for use in territorial development.)
See item no. 78.

Le long voyage des gens du Fleuve. (The long journey of the people of the River region.)
See item no. 137.

Agricultural sector study: main report.
See item no. 334.

Organisation coopérative et modification des rapports de production et des formes de propriété en milieu rural africain. (Cooperative organization and modification of relations of production and of forms of ownership in a rural African setting.)
See item no. 344.

Quelques observations sur les blocages de la croissance dans l'agriculture sénégalaise. (Some observations on the obstacles to growth in Senegalese agriculture.)
See item no. 348.

Urban planning and development

643 **Une banlieue ouvrière: l'agglomération suburbaine de Grand Yoff.**
(A workers' suburb: the suburban region of Grand Yoff.)
Olivier Laurent. *Bulletin de l'IFAN*, vol. 32(B), no. 2 (1970),
p. 518-57.

A study of the growth of an unofficial suburb on the outskirts of Dakar, which began in 1953, and which had a population of 25,000 in 1968. The paper discusses the variable quality of the housing, the often inadequate service provision, and the household composition, ethnic origins and occupations of the residents.

644 **Une communauté en ville africaine: les castors de Dakar.** (A community in an African city: the 'beavers' of Dakar.)
Annick Osmont. Grenoble, France: Presses Universitaires de Grenoble, 1978. 192p.

This self-help housing cooperative, which built ninety houses in Dakar for its members between 1955 and 1958, has been intensively studied both as a model for low-cost housing provision, and as an example of the development of new social institutions in the city. The group started in an effort to provide better housing for its members, but it soon developed an internal solidarity based on kinship and ritual which enabled its members also to collaborate in building a school, a mosque, a stadium and a market. The author deals with similar issues in earlier papers 'Un cas réussi d'intégration urbaine: la cité des castors de Dékaheulé à Dakar' (A successful example of urban integration: the 'beaver city' of Dekaheule at Dakar), A. Osmont-Dottelonde, *Revue Française d'Etudes Politiques Africaines*, vol. 29 (1968), p. 51-60, and 'La formation d'une communauté locale à Dakar' (Formation of a local community in Dakar), *Cahiers d'Etudes Africaines*, vol. 13 (1973), p. 496-510.

645 **Crise urbaine et contrôle social à Pikine: bornes-fontaines et clientélisme.** (Urban crisis and social control at Pikine: drinking fountains and clientelism.)
Gérard Salem. *Politique Africaine*, vol. 45 (March 1992), p. 21-38.

An account of the structure of patronage and resource distribution in Pikine, an unplanned satellite town outside Dakar. A wide range of variables are discussed in the study, from ethnicity to the distribution of water taps.

646 **Dakar: ses origines – son avenir.** (Dakar: its origins, its future.)
Georges Ribot, Robert Lafon. Bordeaux, France: G. Delmas, 1908. 197p.

A study of Dakar at the turn of the century centred on the issue of public health. After chapters on the history and climate, there follow sections on housing, the population, the major diseases, and efforts to improve health in the city by cleaning it up, and improvements in housing, the water supply and medical services. In an appendix there is a list of health regulations in force in Dakar (subjects range from stray dogs to prostitution) and the text of important decrees in the public health campaign. There are some excellent black-and-white photographs of the town, coloured maps of Dakar and its harbour, and some memorable plans for the construction of public lavatories.

647 **The establishment of the Medina in Dakar, Senegal, 1914.**
Raymond F. Betts. *Africa*, vol. 41, no. 1 (1971), p. 143-52.
In the wake of an outbreak of plague in 1914, the French decided on a solution: a policy of residential segregation. This was achieved by rehousing the local people in the area known as the Medina. With the arrival on the political scene of Blaise Daigne, however, this policy was bitterly opposed by the local Lebu peoples and was finally abandoned. The Medina had been established by this time, but remained incomplete and badly planned, a blot on the urban landscape.

648 **The impact of policy conflict on the implementation of a government-assisted housing project in Senegal.**
Rodney R. White. *Canadian Journal of African Studies*, vol. 19, no. 3 (1985), p. 505-28.
An account of conflict between the Senegalese state and the World Bank over a housing project for the poor. As a result of the weakness of the Senegalese economy and the differing priorities of the organizations involved in the scheme, the actual benefits for the poor were minimal.

649 **Imperial designs: French colonial architecture and urban planning in sub-Saharan Africa.**
Raymond F. Betts. In: *Double impact: France and Africa in the age of imperialism.* Edited by G. Wesley Johnson. Westport, Connecticut; London: Greenwood Press, 1985, p. 191-207.
This short chapter examines French colonial planning and architecture with special reference to Dakar, the capital city of Senegal. Well illustrated with plates of buildings of architectural note in Dakar, it also includes further references to works on the city.

650 **Irrégularité urbaine et invention de la ville africaine au Cap-Vert (Sénégal).** (Urban irregularity and invention in the African town in Cap-Vert [Senegal].)
Roger Navarro. *Tiers-Monde*, vol. 29, no. 116 (1988), p. 1101-19.
A description of two settlements: Genaw-Rails, with a population of 30,000, which has sprung up on the southern coast of the Cap-Vert isthmus; and Dagoudane-Pikine, fifteen kilometres to the east of Dakar. The paper considers the legal aspects of the squatters' occupation of the land, the social structure of the settlements, whether they are characterized by community or chaos, and the threat of demolition of the sites, which can be to some extent reduced by the squatters developing links with the state.

La croissance urbaine dans les pays tropicaux: Ziguinchor en Casamance. Une ville moyenne du Sénégal. (Urban growth in tropical countries: Ziguinchor in the Casamance. A medium-sized town in Senegal.)
See item no. 32.

Dakar en devenir. (The development of Dakar.)
See item no. 33.

Dakar: métropole ouest-africaine. (Dakar: a West African metropolis.)
See item no. 34.

Espace Dakar-Rufisque en devenir. De l'héritage urbain à la croissance industrielle. (The spatial development of Dakar-Rufisque. From urban heritage to industrial growth.)
See item no. 36.

Language and Languages

General

651 **Enquête sur les langues parlées au Sénégal par les élèves de l'enseignement primaire.** (Investigation of the languages spoken in Senegal by primary school pupils.)
T. Wioland. Dakar: CLAD (Centre de Linguistique Appliquée de Dakar), 1965. 252p. (L'enseignement du français en Afrique, 11).
Based on a questionnaire sent out to all state primary schools, this report deals not only with the spoken languages, but also trends such as 'Wolofization' in the Senegalese population. The bulk of the report consists of a department-by-department survey of language use, and there is a useful country-wide summary at the end. The conclusion is that of all the Senegalese languages, only Wolof is expanding, and is widely spoken as a second language by Peul, Bambara, Serer and Diola children.

652 **Le français au Sénégal: interférences du wolof dans le français des élèves sénégalais.** (The French language in Senegal: Wolof influence in the French of Senegalese pupils.)
Maurice Calvet, Pierre Dumont. *Bulletin de l'IFAN*, vol. 31(B), no. 1 (1969), p. 239-63.
Studies the influence of the Wolof and French languages on each other. As eighty per cent of young school-age Senegalese are Wolof speakers, and the medium of instruction is French, the two languages have inevitably merged to form a patois. Not surprisingly, the prevailing view of French linguists is that the purity and separate identity of both languages should be maintained and protected.

653 **Le français et les langues africaines au Sénégal.** (French and the
African languages in Senegal.)
Pierre Dumont.   Paris: Karthala, 1983. 380p.

This is the standard account of the relationship between French and Wolof. After a
detailed comparison of the two languages, the main subjects discussed are the words in
the Wolof language borrowed from French, the characteristics of French spoken in
Senegal, and the political and educational issues of language in Senegal. With over
eighty per cent of the population speaking and understanding Wolof, French will never
become a means of national communication, but it does allow access to power. The
appendices include tables on language use in Senegal and the phonetics of the main
languages, an example of French teaching materials used in primary school, and the
text of official decrees on the orthography of Wolof and Serer. There is also a useful
bibliography.

Senegalese vernaculars

654 **Etudes dialectologique des parlers 'Mandingues' du Sénégal.**
(Dialectological studies of 'Manding' speech of Senegal.)
Abdoulaye Baldé.   Niamey: Centre d'Etudes Linguistiques et
Historiques par Tradition Orale, 1982. 2 vols. (CELTHO/Langues
Africaines/5).

The Niamey language centre, set up by the Organization of African Unity, has issued
many valuable publications on West African languages despite limited facilities: many
of them have been typed and duplicated on evidently antique equipment. These
volumes provide both a description of some of the major Manding dialects, and an
attempt to develop a 'standard' dialect which can be used throughout the region. Baldé
was also the author of a short collection of texts with French translations, published as
Textes Mandinka-Malinké (dialecte mandingue du Sénégal) (Mandinka-Malinké texts:
the Manding dialect of Senegal) (Niamey: Centre d'Etudes Linguistiques et
Historiques par Tradition Orale, 1982. 38p.), and a second comparative study of
Senegalese Manding dialects, *Etude comparative des parlers mandingues du Sénégal:
dialectologie et phonologie* (Comparative study of Manding speakers of Senegal:
dialectology and phonology) (Niamey: CELHTO, 1985. 102p.).

655 **Niger-Congo, Mande.**
Wm. E. Welmers.   In: *Current trends in linguistics*. Edited by
T. Sebeok.   Mouton: The Hague, 1971, vol. 7, p. 113-40.

A survey of the Mande languages, which are spoken by groups of people widely spread
over West Africa from Senegal in the west to northern Benin and Nigeria in the east.
For Senegal, the important grouping is the northern division which includes both
Soninke and Maninka-Bambara-Dyula. The paper also considers the origins of the
group, and ends with a three-page bibliography.

656   **La situation linguistique en Casamance et Guinée-Bissau.**
Alain Khim.   *Cahiers d'Etudes Africaines*, vol. 20, no. 3 (1980),
p. 369-86.

A brief sketch of the linguistic situation in the two areas, followed by a comparison of
the position of Portuguese Creole in the Casamance, Senegal, where it is the language
of a single group, and in Guinea where it is a lingua franca.

657   **West Atlantic: an inventory of the languages, their noun class systems**
and consonant alterations.
J. David Sapir.   In: *Current trends in linguistics*, Edited by
T. Sebeok.   The Hague: Mouton, 1971, vol. 7, p. 45-112.

The standard account of a large and diverse group of languages spoken in an area
extending from Mauritania to Liberia, which includes major Senegalese languages such
as Fula (the Pulaar of the Peul and Tukulor), Wolof and Serer, as well as minority
group languages such as Tenda, Basari and Bedik. On the basis of lexical similarity,
Sapir groups the languages into three groups. The first of these, the northern branch,
he subdivides into five subgroups, the most important of which contain the Senegalese
languages (Fula, Serer, Wolof). The others are the Cangin languages; the Bak
languages of the Lower Casamance (including the various Diola dialects); and the
eastern Guinea-Bissau languages (including Tanda, Basari, Bedik, and Konyagi); and
Nalu. The rest of the paper consists of a detailed technical comparison of the noun
class systems and consonant alternation systems of these languages.

French in Senegal

658   **Inventaire des particularités lexicales du français en Afrique noire.**
(Inventory of French usage specific to sub-Saharan Africa.)
Equipe IFA.   Paris: EDICEF, 1988. 2nd ed. 442p.

The standard work in its field, compiled by a team of distinguished French and African
scholars, this book has at its centre a 354-page lexicon of distinctive idioms which have
entered the French spoken in Africa, including both distinctive idiomatic uses of
French words, English loan-words, and words from African languages which have
become widespread. There is an important references index and bibliography at the
end.

659   **Lexique du français du Sénégal.** (Lexicon of Senegalese French.)
Jacques Blonde, Pierre Dumont, D. Gontier.   Dakar: Nouvelles
Editions Africaines; Paris: EDICEF, 1979. 159p.

A glossary of French usages in Senegal which diverge from standard French: these
include both French words used in non-standard ways or words borrowed from African
languages. Examples of usage are given for each item, many of them drawn from
Senegalese authors. At the end there is a section of illustrations of items of clothing,
types of musical instrument, etc., and, for the purpose of comparison, a short glossary
of the standard French usages of words contained in the main body of the text.

Grammars and dictionaries

Diola

660 **Dictionnaire français-dyola et dyola-français précédé d'un essai de grammaire.** (French-Diola and Diola-French dictionary, preceded by an essay on grammar.)
E. Wintz. Elinkiné, Senegal: Mission Catholique, 1909; Farnborough, England: Gregg Press, 1968. 185p.

According to Sapir, this study, by a Catholic priest, is based on the Kasa dialect of Diola spoken to the south of Ziguinchor, very similar to the Fogny dialect described by Sapir himself. In the grammatical section, Sapir argues, Wintz attempts to impose Latin categories on the language, and this fails to give a clear impression of its structure. However, the dictionary section is substantial and accurate.

661 **A grammar of Diola-Fogny: a language spoken in the Basse-Casamance region of Senegal.**
J. David Sapir. Cambridge, England: Cambridge University Press, 1965. 129p.

This book, by an American anthropologist and linguist, is the standard work on a Diola dialect in English. Fogny is the most important Diola dialect, and is spoken in an area extending north from Ziguinchor and Bignona to the Gambian border. With its modern transformational approach this is a book for the specialist rather than an introductory text. The main part is divided into two sections, dealing with the phonology of the language and with its morphology and syntax. At the end is a recorded text, transcribed with a commentary, and an index of morphemes.

Manding

662 **La langue mandingue et ses dialectes (Malinké, Bambara, Dioula). Tome II: Dictionnaire mandingue-français.** (The Manding language and its dialects [Malinke, Bambara, Diola]. Vol. 2: Manding-French dictionary.)
M. Delafosse. Paris: Imprimerie Nationale/Librairie Paul Geuthner, 1955. 857p.

Apart from his three-volume study of the peoples of the region, this dictionary was probably the most important work by Delafosse, the French administrator who acquired an unrivalled knowledge of West African languages. Perhaps not surprisingly, in view of its length, the work remained unpublished until nearly thirty years after his death in 1926.

Palor

663 **Le Palor: esquisse phonologique et grammaticale d'une langue cangin du Sénégal, suivi d'un lexique et de textes transcrits et traduits.** (Palor: a phonological and grammatical outline of a Cangin language in Senegal, followed by a lexicon and transcribed and translated texts.)
Paula D'Alton. Paris: Centre National de la Recherche Scientifique, 1987. 254p.

This is a detailed linguistic study of one of the rather neglected Cangin group of languages that belong to the northern branch of the West Atlantic family, and are thus related to both Wolof and Serer. Indeed, the Palor themselves, who number about 10,000 in an area between Dakar and Thiès, are often called 'Serer' by outsiders. Because of the proximity of the area to the economic centre of the country, a rapid process of 'Wolofization' is taking place, and there is a real danger of minority languages like Palor being lost completely. The bulk of the book is divided between sections on phonology and grammar, and it ends with a lexicon, including many examples of usage, and a series of texts, short Palor stories with word-by-word translations into French.

Pulaar (Peul, Tukulor)

664 **Grammaire moderne du pulaar.** (A modern grammar of Pulaar.)
Yero Sylla. Dakar: Les Nouvelles Editions Africaines, 1982. 233p.

A modern grammar in French, written by a linguist and native Pulaar speaker. After an introduction on phonemes and their pronunciation, the bulk of the book deals with the main features of the language in twenty-four sections. The appendices include a description of the standard system of word division, a list of grammatical terms in Pulaar for use in education, and a collection of texts.

665 **La langue des Peuls ou Foulbé.** (The language of the Peuls or Fulbe.)
H. Labouret. Dakar: IFAN, 1952. 268p. (Mémoires no. 16).

Apart from Gaden's work, the most important studies of Pulaar are those of Labouret. This thorough and expansive text is divided into four parts. The first deals with the morphology of the language, its elements and grammatical structures. The second part focuses on folktales in various dialects, such as that of the Fuuta Toro in northern Senegal, and further afield. The third and fourth parts consist of Peul-French, and French-Peul lexicons, and the book also contains a useful Pulaar bibliography. Labouret was also the author of *La langue des Peuls ou Foulbé. Lexique français-peul* (The language of the Peuls or Fulbe. French-Peul lexicon) (Dakar: IFAN, 1955. 160p. [Mémoires no. 41]), which complements and extends the coverage in this work.

666 **Le poular, dialecte peul du Fouta sénégalais. Tome II: lexique poular-français.** (Pulaar, the Peul dialect of the Senegalese Fuuta. Volume 2: Pulaar-French lexicon).
Henri Gaden. Paris: Ernest Leroux, 1914; Farnborough, England: Gregg Press, 1967, 263p. 1969.

As well as having a distinguished administrative career (rising to the rank of governor-general), Gaden was also the author of several magisterial books on the Pulaar language which have yet to be superseded. This lexicon, which is based on the dialect spoken in the Fuuta Toro, in the extreme north of the country, contains listings of words both by initial vowel sound and initial consonant. A revised version of the dictionary, using illustrations from Gaden's other studies, was issued as *Dictionnaire peul-français* (Peul-French dictionary) (Dakar: IFAN, 1969. 119p. [Catalogues et Documents, no. 22]).

Wolof

667 **Dakar Wolof: a basic course.**
Loren V. Nussbaum, William W. Gage, Daniel Varre. Washington, DC: Centre for Applied Linguistics, 1970. 455p.

Based on a teaching-aid by W. A. Stewart entitled *Introductory course in Dakar Wolof* and originally issued in 1966, this is the standard basic course available in English on the Wolof language spoken in contemporary Senegal.

668 **Grammaire de wolof moderne.** (Grammar of modern Wolof.)
Pathé Diagne. Paris: Présence Africaine, 1971. 229p.

A systematic linguistic analysis of modern Wolof, which covers the system of phonology, syntactical structures and the internal structure of Wolof discourse. It includes a comprehensive general bibliography for the specialist reader.

669 **Initiation à la grammaire wolof.** (An introduction to Wolof grammar.)
Amar Samb. Dakar: IFAN, 1983. 128p.

A concise and systematic treatment of Senegal's most widely-spoken language, organized around the division between the main parts of speech, and copiously illustrated with examples.

670 **Lexique wolof-francais.** (Wolof-French dictionary.)
Dakar: Centre de Linguistique Appliquée de Dakar, 1977-81. 4 vols.

The standard modern dictionary of the language.

Literature

Oral literature

671 **Contes et légendes soninké (Mali, Sénégal, Mauritanie).** (Soninke tales
and legends from Mali, Senegal and Mauritania.)
Collected by Oudiary Makan Dantioko.   Paris: EDICEF, for the
Conseil International de la Langue Française, 1978. 130p.
Twenty-two short tales about animals and people recited by *griots*, collected partly
for use in functional literacy campaigns.

672 **Les dits de la nuit: contes tenda (Sénégal oriental).** (Sayings of the night:
Tenda stories from Eastern Senegal.)
Texts transcribed and translated by M-P. Ferry.   Paris: Karthala, 1983.
303p.
This is a major collection of forty-nine stories gathered from local story tellers in the
Bedik and Beliyan areas of eastern Senegal by a leading writer on the region. The two
sections of the book are preceded by short ethnographic sketches of the peoples among
whom they were collected, and at the end there is a list of the story tellers and a list of
the plants and animals around which many of the tales revolve, together with their
scientific names.

673 **Un exemple d'oralité négro-africaine: les fables djugut (Basse
Casamance).** (An example of black African oral literature: Djugut
fables from the Lower Casamance.)
Louis-Vincent Thomas.   *Bulletin de l'IFAN*, vol. 31(B), no. 1 (1969),
p. 167-214.
A study of some of the main genres and characteristics of African oral literature, and
the religious aspects of words, based on the analysis of thirty folk tales collected among
a subgoup of the Diola of the Lower Casamance. They are typical of folk tales from

the region, both in their use of magical elements, and of animals symbolizing particular types of personality.

674 **Nouvel exemple d'oralité négro-africaine: récits Narang-Djiragon, Diola-Karaban et Dyiwat (Basse-Casamance.)** (A new example of black African oral literature: recitations from Narang-Djiragon, Diola-Karaban and Dyiwat, Lower Casamance.)
Louis-Vincent Thomas. *Bulletin de l'IFAN*, vol. 32(B), no. 1 (1970), p. 230-301.

A collection of Diola folk tales from three areas of the Casamance, where Islam, Catholicism and African traditional religion predominate, respectively. Many of the stories deal with animal characters, and each is preceded by a short introduction to the main themes.

675 **La parole à travers quelques proverbes peuls du Fouladou (Sénégal).** (The concept of speech, based on Peul proverbs from Fouladou, Senegal.)
Roger Labatut. *Journal des Africanistes*, vol. 57, no. 1/2, (1987), p. 67-76.

Approximately forty proverbs are used to highlight the major tendencies of the Fulbe conception of speech, which stands in contrast to, but cannot replace, actions. Speech is considered to be a cultural activity that underlies personal dignity and helps maintain group cohesion. Dangerous by nature, it follows strict rules and must be held under command.

676 **Proverbes et maximes peuls et toucouleurs, traduits, expliqués et annotés.** (Peul and Tukulor proverbs and maxims, translated, explained and annotated.)
Henri Gaden. Paris: Institut d'Ethnologie, 1931. 368p. (Travaux et Mémoires de l'Institut d'Ethnologie, 16).

A study of over 1,200 proverbs and maxims, covering all aspects of life from family and domestic arrangements to morality and indigenous wisdom. The book contains extensive information on Peul and Tukulor customs and beliefs, as well as grammatical notes on the Pulaar language.

677 **Proverbes malinké: à l'ombre des grands fromagers.** (Malinke proverbs: in the shade of the great kapok trees.)
Collected and translated by Gérard Meyer. Paris: EDICEF for the Conseil International de la Langue Française, 1985. 172p.

A collection of 309 Malinke proverbs collected in Niokholo in south-eastern Senegal, each transcribed in the original language with a French translation and short notes on origin and meaning. The proverbs are preceded by two short notes by the translator on the cultural background and the presentation of the main themes.

678 **Quelques proverbes sérères recueillis à Fadiout (Sénégal).** (Some Serer proverbs collected at Fadiout, Senegal.)
F. J. Ezanno. *Anthropos*, vol. 48, no. 3/4 (1953), p. 593-6.
A collection of over fifty proverbs with French translations collected in the Fadiout coastal area of Senegal.

679 **Recueil des traditions orales des Mandingues de Gambie et de Casamance.** (A collection of Manding oral traditions from Gambia and the Casamance.)
S.-M. Cissoko, K. Sambou. Niamey: Centre Régional de Documentation pour la Tradition Orale, 1974. 269p.
This work contains historical traditions, relating to the period before the mid-19th century and the rapid spread of Islam, which were collected in the main Mandinka kingdoms during 1969, and transcribed with an interlined word-for-word parallel translation in French. The volume contains important material, despite its understandably crude production.

680 **When talk isn't cheap: language and political economy.**
Judith T. Irvine. *American Ethnologist*, vol. 16, no. 2 (1989), p. 248-67.
A study of the economic functions of language with reference to the *griots* among the Wolof, who make a living out of praise-singing.

When is genealogy history? Wolof genealogies in comparative perspective.
See item no. 173.

Contemporary literature

General

681 **Anthologie de la nouvelle poésie nègre et malagache de langue française.** (Anthology of the new black and Malagasy poetry in French.)
Edited by Léopold Sédar Senghor. Paris: Presses Universitaires de France, 1969. 2nd ed. 227p.
The seminal anthology which established black writers as a force to be reckoned with in French literature and which helped launch Senghor's literary career. It contains the famous essay *Orphée noir* by Sartre and a short introduction by Senghor, together with selections from the work of poets from Guyana (including Damas and Césaire), Senegal (including Senghor, Birago Diop and David Diop) and Madagascar. Senghor's poems include early versions which were later reworked.

682 **Anthologie de la nouvelle sénégalaise (1970-1977).** (An anthology of the
Senegalese short story, 1970-1977.)
Dakar: Les Nouvelles Editions Africaines, 1978. 188p.

A collection of twenty-three stories, ranging from four to sixteen pages in length,
mainly by the generation of Senegalese writers born after 1940. The general tone of the
stories is critical of modern Senegalese society, though moderated with a sense of
humour.

683 **Essai sur la contribution du Sénégal à la littérature d'expression arabe.**
(Senegal's contribution to literature in Arabic.)
Amar Samb.   Dakar: Institut Fondamental d'Afrique Noire, 1972.
534p. (Mémoires no. 87).

The major study of a neglected area of Senegalese literature, this book focuses on the
work of fourteen 'schools', Arabic literary traditions transmitted from teacher to pupil.
The book contains many useful extracts and translations of this work, in which
religious texts predominate.

684 **French African verse.**
Edited and translated by John Reed, Clive Wake.   London:
Heinemann, 1972. 213p. (African Writers Series 106).

An important collection of French-language poetry drawn from all over Africa,
published with parallel translations in English. Senegal is well represented, with
selections from Senghor, David and Birago Diop, Malick Fall, Pauline Joachim, and
Lamine Diakhaté. The book also contains a brief but informative introduction, a
bibliography with biographical notes, and a glossary.

685 **Lectures africaines: a prose anthology of African writing in French.**
Edited by Abiola Irele.   London: Heinemann Educational Books,
1969, 118p.

This anthology, written for university students, contains a useful editorial introduction
discussing the major authors, followed by ten lengthy excerpts from their work. They
include Birago Diop, Sembène Ousmane, and Cheikh Hamidou Kane. The selections
are reproduced in French with marginal annotations in English.

686 **Negritude: black poetry from Africa and the Caribbean.**
Edited and translated by Norman R. Shapiro.   London: October
House, 1970. 247p.

A major anthology which brings together work by black francophone poets from both
the begetters of 'negritude' – Césaire, Damas and Senghor – and their successors, with
parallel translations in both English and French. There is a twenty-seven-page section
on Senegal in which Senghor, Malick Fall, David Diop, Lamine Diakhaté and Annette
M'Baye are represented, and at the end there are useful biographical notes on the
individual poets.

687 **Le Sénégal écrit: anthologie de la littérature sénégalaise d'expression française.** (Senegal writes: anthology of Senegalese literature in French.)
Edited by Gisela Bonn. Tübingen, Germany: Horst Erdmann Verlag; Dakar: Les Nouvelles Editions Africaines, [1975]. 508p.

An important anthology of Senegalese writing in French, complete with the *imprimatur* of a preface by Senghor. The collection contains essays, poetry, tales, recitations and excerpts from stage works. All of the important figures in Senegalese literature are represented, and there is a thirty-seven-page section of biographical notes on the authors. For readers of French, this is perhaps one of the best available one-volume overviews of the field from the period up to the 1970s.

Major authors

Mariama Bâ

688 **Une si longue lettre.** (Such a long letter.)
Mariama Bâ. Dakar: London: Heinemann, 1981; Virago, 1988. 131p.
(Originally published by Nouvelles Editions Africaine. 1979, 131p.).

Mariama Bâ completed two novels before her early death in 1981. This, the first, written with great sensitivity and generally considered to be a landmark in women's writing in Africa, takes up a familiar theme in African literature, that of the woman whose husband takes a second wife. The letter which she writes to a female friend, Aissatou, provides a commentary on Senegalese society and culture.

Birago Diop

689 **Birago Diop.**
Edited by Roger Mercier, Monique Battestini, Simon Battestini.
Paris: Fernand Nathan, 1964. 63p. (Littérature africaine, 6).

One of a series of concise introductions to the work of major African writers, this pocket-sized book contains a biographical sketch, a selection of poems from *Leurres et lueurs* (Snares and flashes) which Diop published in 1960, a selection of seven of his tales, some critical reactions and a glossary.

690 **Tales of Amadou Koumba.**
Birago Diop, translated by Dorothy S. Blair. London: Oxford University Press, 1966. 134p. (First published as *Contes d'Amadou Koumba*. Paris: Présence Africaine, 1947).

This collection of folk tales is, according to the author, based on traditional Wolof stories told to him in his childhood by Amadou Koumba, the household griot. Most of the stories have an obvious moral, and many of them revolve around animal characters such as Golo the monkey and Leuk the hare. The critical success of the volume was such that Diop followed it with two further collections, *Les nouveaux contes d'Amadou Koumba* (New tales of Amadou Koumba) in 1958, and *Contes et lavanes* (Tales and riddles) in 1963. This 1966 Blair translation includes five stories from the second collection, as well as a foreword which sketches in the background of Diop's career and the distinctive elements of his literary style.

Cheikh Anta Diop

691 **Nations nègres et culture: de l'antiquité nègre égyptienne aux problèmes culturels de l'Afrique noire d'aujourd'hui.** (Black nations and culture: from negro antiquity in Egypt to the cultural problems of Black Africa today.)
Cheikh Anta Diop. Paris: Présence Africaine, 1979. 2 vols.
This large-scale study was first published in 1954. In the first part, Diop argues the case for the African/Negro origins of Egyptian (and, by implication, much of European) civilization, as well as the Egyptian origins of many contemporary African peoples. In the second part, he discusses the development of language, philosophy, art and social structure. The appendices contain a comparative word-list of Wolof (which Diop idiosyncratically calls 'Valaf') and Serer, a glossary of archaeological terms, and a six-page bibliography. Diop covered similar territory in a number of other major works, including *L'Afrique noire pre-coloniale: étude comparée des systèmes politiques et sociaux de l'Europe et de l'Afrique Noire, de l'antiquité à la formation des états modernes* (Precolonial Black Africa: a comparative study of the political and social systems of Europe and Black Africa, from antiquity to the formation of the modern states) (Paris: Présence Africaine, 1960. 213p.).

692 **Black Africa: the economic and cultural basis for a federated state.**
Cheikh Anta Diop, translated from French by Harold J. Salemson.
Westport, Connecticut: Lawrence Hill, 1984. 2nd ed. 92p.
One of a series of works by Diop showing his concern for rediscovering Black Africa's history and cultural heritage. The book deals with the possibility of creating a political, economic and cultural unity among African nations. True independence, it argues, is based on an African identity that recognizes the underlying unity which still exists in spite of Africa's history of fragmentation through slavery and colonialism. A bold case is made for a pan-African federated state whose economy would be based on various energy sources, the natural wealth and abundant resources of the continent, and a programme of industrialization.

693 **Hommage à Cheikh Anta Diop.** (Tribute to Cheikh Anta Diop.)
Présence Africaine, no. 149/50 (1989). 420p. (special issue).
A memorial volume to the Senegalese scientist and historian, by the journal with which he had long been associated. The twenty-seven contributions (five of them in English) include reminiscences and appreciations of his work, and the texts of an interview and a conversation. An uncritical but important source of information on Diop's life and work.

694 **Origine et évolution de l'homme dans la pensée de Cheikh Anta Diop: une analyse critique.** (The origin and evolution of mankind according to Cheikh Anta Diop: a critical analysis.)
Alain Froment. *Cahiers d'Etudes Africaines*, vol. 31, no. 1/2 (1991), p. 29-64.

A sympathetic, but ultimately devastating, critique of Diop's ideas on the history of mankind, which are shown to be extremely simplistic, even in the light of the evidence available during his lifetime. The author concludes that Diop's importance lies in the history of African political consciousness rather than in the study of human evolution.

David Diop

695 **Hammer blows.**
David Mandessi Diop, translated and edited by Simon Mpondo, Frank Jones. London: Heinemann 1975. 53p. (African Writers Series 174), (First published as *Coups de pilon* in 1956).

David Diop established a reputation as 'the most interesting and talented new African poet in the fifties'. When he died at an early age in a plane crash in 1960, he was on his way to Paris with a second book of poems which was thus lost. Diop was born in Bordeaux of a Senegalese father and Cameroonian mother, but spent much of his short career teaching in revolutionary Guinea. The original French title of this volume, *Coups de pilon*, literally means pestle blows, or the pounding of the pestle, and alludes to the way in which grain is ground in Senegalese households. The majority of the seventeen poems in the collection are protests against colonialism, warfare and repression. In this edition they are reprinted, together with five other early poems which survive, in French with a parallel English translation. The book ends with a brief biographical note and a glossary.

696 **David Diop (1927-1960): témoignages – Etudes.** (David Diop, 1927-1960: testimonies and studies.)
Paris: Présence Africaine, 1983. 412p.

A memorial volume published to mark the twentieth anniversary of Diop's death. The contributions in the *témoignage* section are for the most part brief appreciations in both poetry and prose, including a short contribution from Senghor. The second half of the book contains fifteen more substantial critical essays, two of them in English, focusing on Diop's political views as reflected in *Coups de pilon* (q.v.).

Ousmane Socé Diop

697 **Karim: roman sénégalais** *suivi de* **Contes et légendes d'Afrique noire.**
(Karim: a Senegalese novel followed by black African tales and legends.)
Ousmane Socé Diop.   Dakar: Nouvelles Editions Latines, 1948. 238p.

Originally published in 1935, this novel was written while the author was training as a vet in France (his fellow student Birago Diop helped correct the proofs). *Karim* is one of the first major African works of fiction, and the prototype in a long series of novels in which the hero, living in a city, attempts to reconcile the differences between African and Western values. The 1948 edition also contained a collection of folk tales written by Socé in 1938. It was this pioneering work which helped pave the way for Birago Diop's own work in this genre.

698 **Mirages de Paris: roman.** (Visions of Paris: a novel.)
Ousmane Socé Diop.   Paris: Nouvelles Editions Latines: 1964. 4th ed. 187p.

Often regarded as less successful than its predecessor, Socé's second novel nevertheless established another genre, the story of the African in France subjected to racial prejudice and emotionally involved with a European girl. The 1948 edition also contained a group of poems by Socé, *Rythmes du Khalam* (Rhythms of Khalam), which was later published separately, also by Nouvelles Editions Latines, in 1962.

Aminata Sow Fall

699 **The beggars' strike** *or* **The dregs of society.**
Aminata Sow Fall, translated by Dorothy S. Blair.   London: Longman African Classics, 1981. (First published as *La grève les bàttu* [The strike of the oppressed], Dakar: Nouvelles Editions Africaines, 1979.

Mour Ndiaye, Director of the Department of Public Health and Hygiene, dreams of becoming Vice-President. His marabout advises him to sacrifice a bull and distribute its meat to the local beggars, in order to further his chances. Unfortunately, the beggars have vanished as a result of a clean-up campaign organized by Ndiaye's department. This hilarious social satire by Senegal's leading woman writer deals with the familiar themes of politics, class and religion in contemporary Africa.

700 **An interview with Aminata Sow Fall.**
Peter Hawkins.   *African Affairs*, vol. 87, no. 348 (1988), p. 419-30.

An introduction to the work and the novels of Senegal's leading woman writer, together with an interview in which she talks about her education and career, including her four novels (*Le revenant, La grève des bàttu, L'appel des arènes, L'ex-père de la nation*), and her views on feminism and religion.

Chiekh Hamidou Kane

701 **Ambiguous adventure.**
Chiekh Hamidou Kane. London: Heinemann, 1963. 178p. (African Writers Series 119).
Chiekh Hamidou Kane, born into an important Tukulor family living along the Senegal river, was initially taught in a Koranic school before eventually reading philosophy and law at the University of Paris. He later served for many years as a government minister, and has also worked for UNICEF. *Ambiguous Adventure* (first published as *L'aventure ambiguë*) is an autobiographical novel. The central character, Samba Diallo, is initially destined to be a local spiritual leader after a strict Islamic education, but instead is sent into the French schooling system and gains a university place to study in Paris. His adventure is ambiguous because he is torn between the Islamic faith of his youth and a European culture which at first sight seemed so appealing. The book is widely regarded as one of the most important philosophical novels to come out of Africa.

Sembène Ousmane

702 **Black docker.**
Sembène Ousmane, translated by Ros Schwarz. London: Heinemann, 1986. 223p.
Sembène's first major novel draws on the author's experiences in the early 1950s, when he worked as a docker and later as a trade union leader in Marseilles. Although stylistically less assured than his later novels, it remains a powerful indictment of French racism. The plot centres around the trial and imprisonment of a young Senegalese writer forced to work as a docker, and accused of the murder of a French woman who, it appears, has published his manuscript under her own name. This work was first published as *Le docker noir* (Paris: Nouvelles Editions Debresse, 1956).

703 **God's bits of wood.**
Ousmane Sembène, translated by Francis Price. London: Heinemann, 1960. 288p. (African Writers Series 63). (First published as *Les bouts de bois de dieu*, Paris: Le Livre Contemporain, Amiot Dumont, 1960. 381p.).
Sembène's third novel is his best known and probably his finest, forming a major landmark in the development of African fiction. As with *Black docker*, the inspiration for this work came from the author's involvement in workers' struggles, but this time the setting is Africa, the construction of the Dakar-Bamako railway line, and the events surrounding the strike of October 1947–March 1948. 'God's bits of wood' is the term which the Senegalese railway workers use to refer to themselves, and the book recounts their hardships during the strike in three towns through which the railway passes – Dakar, Thiès and Bamako. The book reflects the clash between traditional culture and the forces of progress, and between the differing aspirations of the workers and the Europeans.

704 **Tribal scars (Voltaïque).**
Ousmane Sembène, translated by Len Ortzen.   London: Heinemann,
1970. 210p. (African Writers Series 142).
A collection of twelve short stories dealing with themes similar to those which
Sembène explored at greater length in his novels: Islam; the relations between men
and women in a polygamous society; the struggles of workers; and exile in France. This
collection was first published in French as *Voltaïque: nouvelles* (Paris: Présence
Africaine, 1962).

705 **The money-order** with **White genesis.**
Sembène Ousmane, translated by Clive Wake.   London: Heinemann,
1972. 190p. (African Writers Series 92).
This book contains two novellas, a form in which Sembène excels, both set in present-
day Senegal. First published in French as *Vehi ciosane ou blanche genèse,* followed by
Le mandat, it was awarded the prize for literature at the first Festival of Negro Arts in
Dakar, 1966. *White genesis* deals with the theme of incest in a rural village. *The money-
order* describes the tragi-comic events which befall Ibrahima Dieng when he receives a
money order from a relative working in France through the post and tries to cash it.
Sembène turned the story into one of his finest films, first screened at the Venice Film
Festival in 1968.

706 **Xala.**
Sembène Ousmane, translated from the French by Clive Wake.
London: Heinemann, 1976. 114p. (African Writers Series 175).
This novel, an acerbic commentary on contemporary African society, which Sembène
also made into a film, tells the story of a rich and powerful Senegalese businessman
who takes a third wife and sets up a separate household for her. Sembène portrays the
man's opulent European lifestyle, and the jealousies and tensions between the
households of his different wives. Not only does his business fail and his wives quarrel,
but he finds himself impotent and humiliated on his wedding night.

707 **The last of the empire: novel.**
Sembène Ousmane, translated by Adrian Adams.   London:
Heinemann, 1983. 238p. (First published as *Le dernier de l'empire.*
2 vols, Paris: L'Harmattan, 1981).
Despite the author's disclaimer at the start, this novel is a thinly veiled satire of
Senegalese politics and political figures during the late 1970s. It is a story of corruption,
manipulation and double-dealing among the second-generation politicians of an
African country during the six days of a political crisis, precipitated when the eighty-
year-old president disappears in mysterious circumstances. This leaves the Prime
Minister in a dilemma as to whether or not he should take over as the constitutional
successor.

708 **Didactic realism in Ousmane Sembène's *Les bouts de bois de Dieu*.**
V. O. Aire.   *Canadian Journal of African Studies,* vol. 11, no. 2
(1977), p. 283-94.
A study of the political themes in Sembène's novel about striking railway workers, this
paper provides a useful introduction to the major issues with which he has been

preoccupied over the years, such as the plight of the masses, race relations, religion and the position of women, and to the techniques through which the author conveys his political message.

709 **Sembène Ousmane et l'esthétique du roman négro-africain.** (Sembène Ousmane and the aesthetic of the black African novel.)
Martin T. Bestman. Sherbrooke, Quebec, Canada: Editions Naaman, 1981. 349p.
A major study which deals with the social background to Sembène's work, his critique of both African and Western society, his political philisophy, and his narrative style, which draws on both European and griot models. An appendix contains a detailed analysis of the novel *Xala*, and there is a useful bibliography.

Art and ideology in the work of Sembène Ousmane and Hailé Gerima.
See item no. 757.

The cinema of Ousmane Sembène, a pioneer of African film.
See item no. 760.

The silent revolutionaries: Ousmane Sembène's *Emitai*, *Xala* and *Ceddo*.
See item no. 761.

'Xala': a cinema of wax and gold.
See item no. 763.

Abdoulaye Sadji

710 **Nini, mulâtresse du Sénégal.** (Nini, mulattress of Senegal.)
Abdoulaye Sadji. Paris: Présence Africaine, 1965. 2nd ed.
Sadji's first novel, actually written as early as 1935 but only published several years later, is a morality tale with an unlikely protagonist, a blonde, blue-eyed Creole girl, who longs to become fully assimilated into European society, even if it means turning her back on her African family and roots. She has an affair with an expatriate, turns down an honourable offer of marriage with an African, and eventually deserts her relatives in order to see the world.

711 **Tounka: nouvelle.** (Tounka: a novella.)
Abdoulaye Sadji. Paris: Présence Africaine, 1965. 90p.
Although it remained unpublished until four years after the author's death, *Tounka* was in fact completed in 1946, making it was one of the first, and also one of the most successful, treatments of a legendary theme in African literature. It describes the migration of a people to the coast from the drought-stricken interior, and the later career of a mythical hero, N'Galka, a favourite of the gods until his pride leads them to destroy him.

712 **Maimouna: roman.** (Maimouna: a novel.)
Abdoulaye Sadji. Paris: Présence Africaine, 1958. 252p.
Although this is Sadji's third novel, it was the first to be published. It is similar to *Nini* in that it is a morality tale, but this story is more tragic. The heroine is a beautiful country girl who abandons the safety of village life with her mother to visit her sister in Dakar where she becomes pregnant. After she returns to the village in disgrace, disaster strikes again. She survives a smallpox epidemic, though disfigured, but loses her child.

713 **Ce que dit la musique africaine.** (What the music of Africa says.)
Abdoulaye Sadji. Paris: Présence Africaine, 1985. 121p.
Sadji combined his writing with a career as an education official. This may be reflected in this short collection of ten tales aimed at children and published posthumously. Like Birago Diop, Sadji says that the tales were told to him by a griot. They deal with legendary figures from the past, including the famous conquerors Soundiata and Samory.

Léopold Sédar Senghor

714 **Poèmes.** (Poems.)
Léopold Sédar Senghor. Paris: Editions du Seuil, 1964. 254p.
This, the first edition of Senghor's collected verse includes the four major collections *Chants d'ombre* (1945), *Hosties noires* (1948), *Ethiopiques* (1956) and *Nocturnes* (1961), together with ten others poems and five prose translations of African texts. At the end is a brief glossary of African words used in the poems.

715 **Selected poems.**
Léopold Sédar Senghor, translated from the French by Clive Wake, John Reed. London: Oxford University Press, 1964. 120p.
A still useful selection of thirty-seven poems in translation, drawn from the first five collections of Senghor's verse: *Chants d'ombre; Hosties noires* (written during and about the years of the Second World War); *Chants pour Naëtt* (love poems, later revised as *Chants pour Signare* and included in *Nocturnes*); *Nocturnes*; and *Ethiopiques* (which includes the long dramatic poem 'Chaka'). The thirteen-page introduction traces the origins of Senghor's style in African and European literature, and there is also a useful glossary.

716 **La belle histoire de Leuk-le-Lièvre.** (The beautiful story of Leuk the Hare.)
Léopold Sédar Senghor, Abdoulaye Sadji, edited by J. M. Winch. London: Harrap, 1965. 154p.
A school text consisting of forty-two short folk tales selected from a larger collection originally published by Hachette in Paris in 1953. Here, Senghor and Sadji have produced a collection of folk stories for children in the manner of Birago Diop. Their tales describe the exploits of one of the favourite animal characters in Senegalese folk-

lore, Leuk the hare, who also features in Diop's tales. This edition contains a brief editorial introduction, notes on syntax and a vocabulary.

717 **Nocturnes: love poems.**
Léopold Sédar Senghor, translated from the French by Clive Wake, John Reed. London: Heinemann, 1970. 64p. (African Writers Series 71).

The standard translation in English of Senghor's fourth volume of poems, originally published in French in 1960. The poems fall into two groups: twenty-four intimate and sensual lyrics entitled 'Songs for Signare' which are revised versions of love poems originally published in 1949 as *Chants pour Naëtt*; and five longer elegies which deal with themes such as the nature of poetry and the role of the poet. This translation includes the twenty-nine poems, together with a six-page introduction which traces Senghor's stylistic development, and a glossary.

718 **Léopold Sédar Senghor – prose and poetry.**
Léopold Sédar Senghor, selected and translated by John Reed, Clive Wake. London: Heinemann, 1976. 182p. (African Writers Series 180).

This book consists of a selection of the prose and poetry of Léopold Senghor, and is still one of the best introductions available in English to the whole range of his work. The introduction traces the relationship between Senghor's political and literary careers. This is followed by thirty-two passages drawn from his speeches and prose writings, arranged so as to present his ideas on issues relating to culture, politics, art, and negritude, and translations of twenty-four of the poems. The volume ends with a glossary and select bibliography.

719 **Léopold Sédar Senghor: selected poems/poésies choisies. A bilingual text.**
Léopold Sédar Senghor, translated with an introduction by Craig Williamson. London: Rex Collings, 1976. 135p.

An invaluable introduction to Senghor's poetry, this book contains parallel texts in French and English of over forty of the poems from Senghor's first four collections, *Chants d'ombre*, *Hosties noires*, *Ethiopiques* and *Nocturnes*. There is also a brief but useful introduction which discusses the African roots of Senghor's poetry, and the background to negritude.

720 **Selected poems of Léopold Sédar Senghor.**
Edited by Abiola Irele. Cambridge, England: Cambridge University Press, 1977. 135p.

A selection of thirty-two of Senghor's best-known poems, reproduced in French with extensive notes in English, prepared apparently with Senghor's help. A useful thirty-seven-page introduction provides a sketch of Senghor's career, the philosophy of negritude, a survey of the first four major collections of poems, a discussion of Senghor's poetic technique, and a brief bibliography.

721 **Elégies majeures** *suivi de* **Dialogue sur la poésie francophone.** ('Major elegies', followed by 'A dialogue on poetry in French'.)
Léopold Sédar Senghor.   Paris: Editions du Seuil, 1979. 124p.
This, the last of Senghor's collections to be published, contains six large-scale elegies, including memorial pieces for Martin Luther King and the poet's old friend from student days, Georges Pompidou. The second half of the book consists of a dialogue on French-language poetry, which takes the form of essays by Alain Bosquet and Jean-Claude Renard, a poem by Pierre Emmanuel, and Senghor's lengthy response to them.

722 **Oeuvre poétique.** (Poetic works.)
Léopold Sédar Senghor.   Paris: Editions du Seuil, 1990. 430p.
This latest definitive edition of Senghor's poetry, one of the glories of African literature, includes the four collections previously published in *Poèmes*, together with *Lettres d'hivernage* (Letters from the rainy season) (1972), the *Elégies majeures* (1979), a handful of poems published separately, and the youthful 'lost poems', once rejected but rescued by Senghor's wife, and now reinstated for the sake of completeness. The *Dialogue sur la poésie francophone* is also included, as are the prose translations of African texts and the glossary from the earlier edition.

723 **Liberté.** (Liberty.)
Léopold Sédar Senghor.   Paris: Editions du Seuil, 1964- .
From the early 1960s onwards, Senghor began to collect together his scattered prose writings with a view to publishing them in volumes focused loosely around related themes. Five volumes, under the general title *Liberty* were published. *Négritude et humanisme* (Negritude and humanism); *Nation et voie africaine du socialisme* (The nation and the African way of socialism); *Négritude et civilisation de l'universel* (Negritude and civilization of the universal); *Pour un socialisme africain et démocratique* (For an African socialism and democracy); and *Négritude et dialogue des cultures* (Negritude and dialogue of cultures). Throughout the set, which alternates literary and political themes, the essays constantly return to the familiar Senghorian territory of the the nature of man, of negritude, and of the relations between the cultures of Europe and Africa.

724 **Ce que je crois.** (What I believe.)
Léopold Sédar Senghor.   Paris: Bernard Grasset, 1990. 254p.
Senghor's most recent volume of essays, obviously intended as a summary of the themes which have preoccupied him during his career, contains five pieces dealing with the significance of African prehistory, the distinctive characteristics of African philosophy, and the emergence of 'La civilisation de l'universel', in which the African elements will be finally subsumed.

725 **Léopold Sédar Senghor: l'homme et l'oeuvre.** (Léopold Sédar Senghor: the man and his work.)
Armand Guibert.   Paris: Présence Africaine, 1962. 188p.
A pocket-sized introduction to Senghor's work, this book consists of a biographical and critical introduction, the texts of ten of the major poems with commentaries, further selections from the four early collections of poems, two brief pieces of prose, the text of a conversation between Guibert and Senghor about the poetry, and a selection of critical reactions to Senghor's writing.

726 **Léopold Sédar Senghor and African socialism.**
Walter A. E. Skurnik. *Journal of Modern African Studies*, vol. 3,
no. 3 (1965), p. 349-69.

A study of Senghor's ideas on African socialism, both as a means of promoting African
development, and as a set of assumptions about Africa's place in the world.

727 **Négritude or black cultural nationalism.**
Abiola Irele. *Journal of Modern African Studies*, vol. 3, no. 3 (1965),
p. 321-448.

A useful summary of the development of the negritude movement which Irele
regards as the only significant African expression of cultural nationalism. It deals with
the antecedents of the movement, in the colonial situation and the black diaspora; the
precedents in cultural and literary movements in Cuba, the US and Haiti; and modern
influences, including the intellectual climate in Europe, particularly Marxism, the work
of anthropologists such as Frobenius and Lévy Bruhl, and the work of francophone
black writers such as René Maran, Alioune Diop (the founder of Présence Africaine),
and the three poets, Césaire, Damas and Senghor.

728 **Négritude – literature and ideology.**
Abiola Irele. *Journal of Modern African Studies*, vol. 3, no. 4 (1965),
p. 499-526.

A sequel to Irele's first paper on negritude, this is a useful summary of the movement's
main ideas and main literature up to the 1960s. The first part, illustrated with poems by
Senghor and David Diop, deals with creative writing, and with the themes of
alienation, revolt, and the rediscovery of Africa as a source of pride. The second part
deals with ideology, and includes a summary of Senghor's ideas on the distinctiveness
of African culture and thought: emotionality, sensibility to rhythm, and a sense of the
divine. The paper ends with a useful select bibliography.

729 **Léopold Sédar Senghor et la naissance de l'Afrique moderne.** (Léopold
Sédar Senghor and the birth of modern Africa.)
Ernest Milcent, Monique Sordet. Paris: Editions Seghers, 1969. 271p.

An important French biography of Senghor dealing with his entire career, from
childhood and student days to the presidency. It contains an interesting selection of
plates, a chronology and a preface by his old friend, who became a fellow president,
Georges Pompidou.

730 **Léopold Sédar Senghor and the politics of negritude.**
Irving Leonard Markovitz. New York: Atheneum, 1969. 300p.

This important study, by an American political scientist, gives a critical account of
negritude and Senegalese politics during the first decade of independence, presenting
Senghor as a good man whose personal and intellectual style were out of tune with
those of most Senegalese. Markovitz gives an account of Senghor's thought as a basis
for a developing nation – negritude, Senegalese socialism, and humanism – based on
lengthy quotations from Senghor's own writings. At the end is an important and very
extensive forty-nine-page bibliography.

Literature. Major authors. Léopold Sédar Senghor

731 **Léopold Sédar Senghor: an intellectual biography.**
Jacques Louis Hymans.   Edinburgh: Edinburgh University Press,
1971. 312p.

One of the major works on Senghor in English, this biography is based on research carried out in the 1960s. Hymans traces the early influences on Senghor as he grew up in Africa at the end of the 1920s, through his period of higher education and teaching in France, when he developed his concept of negritude, to the period marking the transition from poetry to politics, when he became President of Senegal in 1960. During his career, Senghor is seen as wandering intellectually between the two civilizations of France and Africa, in an attempt to restore the equilibrium destroyed by the colonial period. The book ends with a lengthy bibliographical note which is an excellent survey of the Senghor literature up to the late 1960s.

732 **The concept of negritude in the poetry of Léopold Sédar Senghor.**
Sylvia Washington Bâ.   Princeton, New Jersey: Princeton University
Press, 1973. 305p.

A major study of Senghor's poetry in English, with a preface by the poet himself. After a biographical introduction there are sections on the basis of negritude, expressions of negritude, the fundamental traits of negritude in rhythm and imagery, and the future of negritude. The book also includes a generous selection of translations, a glossary and a seven-page bibliography.

733 **A dance of masks: Senghor, Achebe, Soyinka.**
Jonathan Peters.   Washington, DC: Three Continents Press, 1978.
270p.

A major comparative, critical study of three of the giants of African literature. Peters argues that although they draw on a common African culture and are agreed that art in Africa must serve more than a purely aesthetic purpose, they have used its symbols in different ways in order to express different philosophical standpoints. The chapters on Senghor discuss each of the four major early collections of poems with numerous quotations in English translation, and the book ends with a comparative assessment which is highly critical of Senghor's depiction of African reality.

734 **Léopold Sédar Senghor: critique littéraire.** (Léopold Sédar Senghor: a
literary critique.)
Daniel Garrot.   Dakar: Nouvelles Editions Africaines, 1978. 155p.

A study of Senghor's literary criticism, containing discussions of his views on engagement, realism and humour, the themes of love, exile and childhood, and on imagery and rhythm. Senghor's thinking is illustrated with numerous quotations from his work, and the book ends with the text of Senghor's responses to a series of questions from the author, and a short bibliography.

735 **La poésie de l'action: conversations avec Mohamed Aziza.** (The poetry
   of action: conversations with Mohamed Aziza.)
   Léopold Sédar Senghor.   Paris: Stock, 1980. 360p.

In this book, based on lengthy conversations with a Tunisian journalist, Senghor
reminisces about his life and career, and reveals his views on a wide variety of topics
relating to history and politics, literature and art.

736 **Léopold Sédar Senghor: négritude ou servitude?** (Léopold Sédar
   Senghor: negritude or servitude?)
   Marcien Towa.   Yaounde: Editions CLE, 1980. 115p.

Originally part of the author's doctoral thesis, this brief critical study unfavourably
compares Senghor's concept of negritude as expressed in his poetry with that of
Césaire. The author's conclusion is that the two concepts are similar in name only.
While Césaire's is genuinely liberating, Senghor's has more in common with European
racist stereotypes.

737 **Léopold Sédar Senghor.**
   Janice Spleth.   Boston, Massachusetts: Twayne Publishers, 1985.
   184p.

The standard recent study of Senghor's writing in English. After an introductory
outline of his career and an analysis of the concept of negritude, most of the book
concentrates on the major poetic works. The author's conclusion is that the more
intimate pieces will be remembered better than the circumstantial and rhetorical
works. The book ends with notes which contain some useful references, and a brief
bibliography of standard works.

738 **Black, French and African. A life of Léopold Sédar Senghor.**
   Janet G. Vaillant.   Cambridge, Massachusetts: Harvard University
   Press, 1990. 388p.

The fullest available biography of Senghor, perhaps the only one to date which
balances coverage of his political and literary careers. Based on interviews with
participants and on archival sources, the thirteen chapters survey every phase of
Senghor's career, from his childhood, through his years in France and his development
of the philosophy of negritude, to his long political career from 1945 to 1980 and the
main crises which he faced.

739 **Born again African.**
   Roger Shattuck, Samba Ka.   *New York Review of Books*, vol. 37,
   no. 20 (20 Dec. 1990), p. 11-21.

Starting with a review of Vaillant's biography of Senghor (see previous item), and
Senghor's *Oeuvre poétique* and *Ce que je crois*, this lengthy article provides a
sympathetic survey of the roots of Senghor's poetry and philosophy in the cultures of
Europe and Africa, and of his political and literary careers.

Other authors

740 **Les trois volontés de Malic: Force-Bonté: Kairée.** (Malik's three wishes: Force-Bonté: Kairée.)
Ahmadou M. Diagne, Bakary Diallo, Cheik A. Ndao. Nedeln, Germany: Kraus Reprint, 1973. various paginations.

This three-in-one volume of facsimile reprints includes two early classics of Senegalese literature. Diagne's novella, a morality tale for school children published in 1920, was perhaps the first piece of African fiction in French written in modern times. Malik's three wishes are to be allowed to work his way through the successive stages of the colonial education system in a search for success. Diallo's *Force-Bonté*, published in 1926, was the first full-length Senegalese novel, a heavily romanticized autobiographical account of a Fula (Peul) shepherd boy conscripted into the French army during the First World War. *Kairée* by Ndao, best known as perhaps Senegal's finest dramatic writer, date from 1962. Many of them deal with political themes, including a section entitled 'Larmes de flammes pour Lumumba' (Tears of flame for Lumumba). Unfortunately, the reprints in this edition appear to be from poor photocopies of the originals, and the detail of the illustrations in the Diagne tale is completely lost.

741 **A Dakar childhood.**
Nafissatou Diallo, translated by D. S. Blair. Harlow, England: Longmans, 1982. 134p.

Originally published as *De Tilène au Plateau: une enfance dakaroise* (From Tilène to the Plateau: a Dakar childhood) (Dakar: Nouvelles Editions Africaines, 1976), and one of a long series of fine autobiographies or autobiographical novels by Senegalese writers, this book presents a fascinating view of family life from the perspective of a child growing up in Dakar in the postwar years. The French title reflects the move from Tilène, a district in the Dakar Medina to the more élite residential area of the Plateau. The book describes the writer's education and training as a midwife, and ends with a moving account of the death of her father, and her marriage, after which she leaves for France.

General literary criticism

742 **African literature in French: a history of creative writing in French from West and Equatorial Africa.**
Dorothy S. Blair. Cambridge, England: Cambridge University Press, 1976. 348p.

One of the standard studies of the field in English, this book discusses the social, educational and political origins of African francophone literature, and the development of the major genres. There is a valuable discussion of the uses of African oral traditions, and lengthy analyses of drama, poetry and the novel. At the end there is a useful sixteen-page bibliographical section with annotated references arranged chapter by chapter. Senegalese writers are well represented, including Senghor, David Diop,

Birago Diop, Ousmane Socé Diop, Abdoulaye Sadji, Sembène Ousmane, Cheikh Hamidou Kane, and Malick Fall.

743 **Black writers in French: a literary history of negritude.**
Lilyan Kesteloot, translated by Ellen Conroy Kennedy. Philadelphia, Pennsylvania: Temple University Press, 1974. 401p.

This book, based on research carried out from 1958 and 1961, was originally published in French as *Les écrivains noirs de langue française: naissance d'une littérature* (Black writers in French: birth of a literature) (Brussels: Editions de l'Université de Bruxelles, 1963), was the first major study of African literature in French. It traces the roots of contemporary African literature back to European Surrealism and Communism, Black American writing and European anthropology. There is a section on negritude, a discussion of its inventors, Damas, Césaire and Senghor, and a history of the publishing house Présence Africaine. The English version includes an informative translator's introduction, the author's 1973 preface, a completely updated bibliography, and a useful index.

744 **Islam in Senegalese literature and film.**
Mbye B. Cham. *Africa*, vol. 55, no. 4 (1985), p. 447-64.

In this paper, the author examines the varying reactions of Senegalese artists and writers to Islam, ranging from acceptance (Kane and Sow Fall) through irreverence (Birago Diop) and iconoclasm (Mahama Traoré), to apostacy (Sembène Ousmane). However, even the work of Sembène is saturated with Arabic terms, idioms and religious symbols. All of these groups, however, reject Western culture.

745 **Journeys through the French African novel.**
Mildred Mortimore. London: James Currey; Portsmouth, New Hampshire: Heinemann, 1990. 230p.

A recent survey of the field by a leading authority on Algerian literature, which analyses selected novels dealing with related themes of political change and the position of women in society. The Senegalese novels analysed in detail are by Kane (*Aventure ambiguë*), Sembène (*Bouts de bois de Dieu*), and Mariama Bâ (*Une si longue lettre*).

746 **Littérature nègre.** (Black literature.)
Jacques Chevie, Armand Coli. Dakar: Nouvelles Editions Africaines, 1984. 272p.

Another standard account from the 1980s, with chapters on the origins of black writing, including the negritude movement, Senghor, Birago Diop, Kane's *Ambiguous adventure* and Sembène's *The money-order*. There is also a discussion of African theatre. The book finishes with sections on the social responsibility of the writer (a reflection of the involvement of writers such as Senghor in both literary and public life), the transition from oral to written literature, and the future of black writing.

747 **La littérature sénégalaise.** (Senegalese literature.)
Notre Librairie: revue du livre, no. 81 (Oct.-Dec. 1985). 219p.

A concise and extremely informative overview of the field, in a journal which specializes in single-issue surveys of individual African countries and their literatures.

The bulk of the book is made up of short essays on various important themes: types of discourse, language, oral and written literature, uses of history, poetry and negritude, the novel, the uses of literature, and the book industry. This last section is one of the few sources of information on publishing, libraries, local cultural activity, and the work of literary foundations and associations. The writers include many of the best-known writers and critics in the field, and at the end is an important list of the main works in the main genres, and some very useful notes on a wide variety of important works by major authors. For readers of French, this is one of the best introductions to the field available.

748 **Roman africain et tradition.** (The African novel and tradition.)
Mohamadou K. Kane. Dakar: Les Nouvelles Editions Africaines, 1982. 519p.

This major study deals with the ways in which African novelists writing in French have dealt with problems and issues relating to tradition. These include problems of identity in the face of colonialism; the relationship between tradition and progress, in the face of urbanization; and conflicts involving divisions of generation, gender, religion and race. In the conclusion the author discusses the changing themes in the African novel, and the declining importance of tradition as an issue in the post-colonial era.

749 **Senegalese literature: a critical history.**
Dorothy S. Blair. Boston, Massachusetts: Twayne Publishers, 1984. 176p. (Twayne's World Authors Series, 696.)

The best introduction to the subject currently available in English, by a distinguished critic and translator, which explains the wealth of Senegalese literary talent in terms of French education policy in West Africa. After the preface, a chronology of Senegalese history, and an invaluable chronological list of Senegalese literary publications from 1850 to 1983, the body of the book consists of four chapters. The first describes the country, its peoples and its history, and the literature which this has inspired, particularly the historical dramas of Cheik Aliou Ndao such as *L'exil d'Alboury, le fils d'Almamy* (The exile of Alboury, son of the Almamy). The second is an account of the beginnings of Senegalese writing in the work of Panet, Boileau, Ahmadou Mpaté Diagne, and Bakary Diallo. The third chapter is a long discussion of the 'Negritude generation', and its roots in black nationalism and cultural currents in Europe. The fourth chapter deals with the period after independence and includes discussion of the work of the three women writers, Nafissatou Diallo, Aminata Sow Fall and Mariama Bâ. There is an invaluable bibliography.

750 **Theories of Africans: francophone literature and anthropology in Africa.**
Christopher L. Miller. Chicago, London: University of Chicago Press, 1990. 328p.

A complex and ambitious study, by one of the leading younger American writers on French African literature, on the question of whether Western critics can avoid the distorting effects of Western academic language and accurately describe African literature. Senegalese authors are well represented in the writers covered, and the sixth chapter is an important discussion of women's fiction, particularly Mariama Bâ's *Such a long letter*.

Arts and Crafts

General

751 **Aminata Sow Fall and the Centre Africain d'Animation et d'Echanges Culturels in Senegal.**
Rosa Bobia. *Journal of Modern African Studies*, vol. 29, no. 3 (1991), p. 529-32.
A note on this leading Senegalese woman writer, which includes both brief summaries of her four novels to date, and of her other activities, including the establishment of the 'Centre Africain d'Animation et d'Echanges Culturels' which runs a book store in Dakar and attempts to promote the interests of Senegalese arts, literature and writers.

752 **L'art africain et la société sénégalaise.** (African art and Senegalese society.)
Louis-Vincent Thomas, Pierre Fougeyrollas. Dakar: Faculté des Lettres et Sciences Humaines, 1967. 109p.
A discussion, based on questionnaire data, of the the problems of defining and understanding African art. The authors examine ideas of beauty, the classification of objects as art, the social, aesthetic and religious functions of material culture, and the role of museums and the artisan in the production and conservation of art objects.

753 **Art sénégalais d'aujourd'hui.** (Senegalese art today.)
Paris: Galeries Nationales du Grand Palais, 1974. 87p.
The catalogue of an exhibition held in Paris of Senegalese painting, this handsome volume introduces the reader to some of the major established Senegalese artists, graduates of l'Ecole des Arts, established in Dakar as one of President Senghor's cultural initiatives.

754 **Cultural policy in Senegal.**
Mamadou Seyni M'Bengue. Paris: UNESCO, 1973. 61p. (Studies and Documents on Cultural Policies).

An uncritical survey of the main cultural activities in Senegal, including a brief sketch of the history of IFAN, unfortunately without any references or supporting documentation.

755 **Les Diola et les objets d'art.** (The Diola and art objects.)
Louis Vincent Thomas. *Bulletin de l'IFAN*, vol. 31(B), no. 2 (1969), p. 452-530.

A second excursion by Thomas into the sociology of art, based on a survey of 388 people in the Casamance. Although he established that art is appreciated for its function rather than its aesthetic qualities in this area, in other ways the results of the survey must have been disappointing: questions dealing with the status of craftsmen, black arts festivals and the museum system, perhaps not surprisingly, produced rather vague responses, suggesting a low level of awareness, or possibly interest, in these matters.

756 **The lantern festival in Senegambia.**
Judith Bettelheim. *African Arts*, vol. 18, no. 2 (1985), p. 50-3, 95-7, 101-2.

A description of the festival known also as 'Lanterns' or 'Fanal', which is held on Christmas Eve during the Christmas-New Year holiday or during Ramadan in urban Senegal and The Gambia. A feature of the festival is the construction of lanterns, some of them very large, out of wood and finely cut paper in a variety of shapes, ships being among the most popular. The lanterns are then paraded in the streets, and formal competitions have developed around them. The paper traces the development of these festivals in the historical records and compares them with similar events in the Caribbean.

Cinema

757 **Art and ideology in the work of Sembène Ousmane and Hailé Gerima.**
Mbye Baboucar Cham. *Présence Africaine*, no. 129 (1984), p. 79-91.

A short survey of the aesthetics and ideology of the films of two politically committed directors, Sembène from Senegal and Gerima from Ethiopia, who between them account for a significant number of feature films made by Africans between 1960 and 1980. The main Sembène films discussed are *Ceddo* and *Emitai*.

758 **Caught in a cultural crossfire.**
West Africa, no. 3723 (19-25 Dec. 1988), p. 2,372-24.

A feature on the state of West African cinema which includes a review of Sembène's *Camp Thiaroye* and an interview with the director himself.

759 **Le cinéma au Sénégal.** (Cinema in Senegal.)
Paulin Soumanou Vieyra. Brussels: OCIC (Organisation Catholique
Internationale du Cinéma); L'Harmattan. 1983. 170p. bibliog.

Paulin Vieyra, an authority on African cinema in general and the producer of a
number of films about Senegal, has published two works on Senegalese cinema. This
study covers the last fifty years of the history and structure of Senegalese film-making,
one of the richest and most important cinema traditions in Africa, from which has
emerged some of the most highly regarded African films and film-makers. The
development of cinema and the systems of film distribution in the country are
described, and the contributions made by its leading figures are also discussed. This
work is an important text on Senegalese cinema, and includes a valuable twelve-page
chronological bibliography on the subject. See also Vieyra's book entitled *Sembène
Ousmane, cinéaste: première periode 1962-1971* (Sembène Ousmane, film-maker: the
first period, 1962-1971) (Paris: Présence Africaine, 1972. 244p.); the first full-length
study of Sembène's work in the cinema up to the release of *Emitai* in 1971, the bulk
of which contains credits, scenarios and critical discussion of each of his films in
chronological order.

760 **The cinema of Ousmane Sembène, a pioneer of African film.**
Françoise Pfaff. Westport, Connecticut; London: Greenwood Press,
1984. 209p.

The standard work in English on Sembène's films, dealing with his work up to and
including *Ceddo* (1976). The first part contains chapters on the background to
Sembène's work, and discusses the African background to the films, drawing parallels
with the narrative technique of the *griot*. The second part is a survey of the films
themselves, *Bombom Sarret* (1963), *Black Girl* (1966), *Mandabi* (1968), *Emitai* (1971),
Xala (1974), and *Ceddo* (1976). There are eighteen pages of black-and-white stills from
the films, a biographical sketch of the director, a list of his film credits, and a selection
of critical reaction to his work.

761 **The silent revolutionaries: Ousmane Sembène's *Emitai*, *Xala* and *Ceddo*.**
David Uru Iyam. *African Studies Review*, vol. 29, no. 4 (1986),
p. 79-87.

This paper presents a complex analysis of three of Sembène's films from the 1970s
(*Emitai*, *Xala* and *Ceddo*) and the relationship between film technique and political
message. He argues that by leaving important groups of characters silent, these
apparently powerless groups (in these films, beggars and women) appear to be
endowed with the strength to be able to effect a transformation in power relations
within their societies.

762 **Sub-Saharan African films and filmmakers: an annotated bibliography.**
Nancy Schmidt. London: Hans Zell, 1988. 410p.

An attempt to pull together the rather scattered literature on African film, the bulk of
this book consists of two bibliographies: the first includes books, monographs and
theses, and the second (nearly 4,000 references) includes mainly articles and reviews.
There are indexes for actors, film festivals, film titles, filmmakers, countries and
general subjects.

763   'Xala': a cinema of wax and gold.
Teshome H. Gabriel.   *Présence Africaine*, no. 116 (1980), p. 202-14.
A study in English of one of Sembène's greatest films, as both a moral tale of a man
who loses everything through living beyond his means, and a satire on the neocolonial
leaders of Africa. 'Wax and gold' is a reference to the distinction between surface
appearance and a deeper meaning.

Theatre

764   Actes du colloque sur le théâtre négro-africain. (Proceedings of a
colloquium on the black African theatre.)
Paris: Présence Africaine, 1971. 249p.
These papers from a conference held at the Ecole des Letters et Sciences Humaines,
University of Abidjan in 1970, deal with major issues in African theatre, including its
origins and development, sources of inspiration, theatrical techniques, its impact on
the public, and the relationship between African theatre and theatre elsewhere in the
world. Most of the papers are short. Two (by Bernard Mouralis and Bakary Traoré)
are concerned with the development of African theatre at the Ecole William Ponty and
one (by R. Hermantier) considers the relationship between drama and cultural
development in Senegal.

765   Black theatre in French: a guide.
Harold A. Waters.   Sherbrooke, Canada: Editions Naaman, 1987.
96p.
A brief survey of this genre, tracing its origins to the Ecole Normale William Ponty at
Gorée in the 1930s, and providing information on over 130 plays, including publication
details and plots. The plays are also listed by title, order of publication, country and
theme. The author has also published a more extensive study of the same field in
French under the title *Théâtre noir: encyclopédie des pièces écrites en français par des
auteurs noirs.* (Black théâtre: encyclopaedia of plays written in French by black
authors) (Washington, DC: Three Continents Press, 1988. 214p.).

Painting

766   Peinture sous verre du Sénégal. (Senegalese glass painting.)
Michel Renaudeau, Michèle Strobel.   Paris: Editions Fernand Nathan;
Dakar: Nouvelles Editions Africaines. 1984. 111p.
A beautifully produced coffee-table book examining one of Senegal's most attractive
popular arts, glass painting. The book traces the origins of the technique and the main
themes and motifs of contemporary glass painting, in particular the influence of Islam.
The bulk of the book consists of sumptuous photographs by Renaudeau.

767 **Peintures populaires du Sénégal 'souweres'.** (Popular paintings of Senegal, 'souweres'.)
Paris: Musée National des Arts africains et océaniens (Editions ADEIAO), 1987. 47p.

The catalogue of an exhibition held in Paris from May to September 1987, this little book consists of short essays on the origins, techniques and main themes of Senegalese glass painting. It is beautifully illustrated with photographs by the ubiquitous Michel Renaudeau. 'Souweres' is a Wolof word derived from the French 'sous-verre' meaning 'under glass'.

768 **Senegalese art [graphics] today.**
B. Pataux. *African Arts*, vol. 8, no.1 (1974), p. 26-31, 56-9, 87.

A beautifully illustrated article reviewing an exhibition of contemporary Senegalese art, 'Art sénégalais d'aujourd'hui' held at the Grand Palais in Paris, from 26 April to 24 June 1974 (see item no. 753). Generally Senegal had a less rich artistic heritage than some other parts of the region, due to the country's early conversion to Islam, and therefore contemporary Senegalese art is seen as a product of acculturation. The bulk of the paper discusses the main themes and characteristics of the tapestries and paintings, and it ends with a brief note on sculpture.

769 **Senegalese glass painting: through a glass colourfully.**
Howard Schissel. *West Africa*, no. 3547 (19 Aug. 1985), p. 1699.

A short report on the work of Gora-Mbengue, one of Senegal's leading glass painters.

Music

770 **The construction and tuning of the *kora*.**
Anthony King. *African Language Studies*, vol. 13 (1972), p. 113-36.

A detailed study of the construction, decoration, pitch levels and tuning systems of the *kora*, the West African 'harp-lute', a type of instrument popular among Mandinka professional musicians in Senegambia, including the Casamance, but rarely encountered elsewhere.

771 **Diola-Fogny funeral songs and the native critic.**
David J. Sapir. *African Language Review*, vol. 8 (1969), p. 176-91.

An interesting discussion of the ways in which the local listeners judge excellence in the songs, which any man attending a funeral is entitled to perform. A man's extemporized performance tends to be judged by his ability to take up the song, finish a section of it correctly, and direct the chorus. Sapir uses three songs to illustrate his argument.

772 **Mandinka drumming.**
Roderic Knight. *African Arts*, vol. 7, no. 4 (1974), p. 24-35.
This detailed study is based on research in The Gambia, but describes a style of music common in Senegal as well. It deals with the organization of drumming, the types of instruments in use, rhythm, dancing and singing, and is illustrated with numerous photographs, diagrams and musical examples.

773 **Music in Africa: the Manding contexts.**
Roderic Knight. In: *Peformance practice: ethnomusicological perspectives*. Edited by Gerard Behague. Westport, Connecticut: Greenwood Press, 1984. p. 53-90.
A study of Manding music in Senegambia, which deals with performance practice, the social setting of performances, the role of musicians, aesthetic judgements, music teaching, and the content of song texts, together with a discussion of the relationship between the performer and the audience. In particular it focuses on the distinction between the 'art music' of the *jali*, the professional singer, and the more popular music of the drummer.

774 **Musical style and social change among the Kujamaat Diola.**
Judith T. Irvine, J. David Sapir. *Ethnomusicology*, vol. 20. no. 1 (1976), p. 67-86.
This is a study of musical style among the Kujamaat (Fogny) Diola of the Casamance region of Senegal, and in particular a study of what they mean when they call certain songs 'old fashioned' and others 'new'. The paper outlines the main features of the local musical style, and the changes that are taking place.

775 **Performance and ambiguity: a study of Tukulor weavers' songs.**
R. M. Dilley. In: *Discourse and its disguises: the interpretation of African oral texts*. Edited by Karin Barber, Paul de Farias. Birmingham, England: Centre of West African Studies, 1989, p. 138-51. (Birmingham University African Studies Series no. 1).
This chapter focuses on the songs of Tukulor weavers, many of whom also perform as praise singers. A description of the functions and social position of this category of craftsmen is given, followed by details of the context in which songs are performed. The contents of songs are analysed, and the author suggests that although they are ostensibly sung to eulogise particular hosts or patrons, the weavers also sing of their own deeds, abilities and powers. Indeed, they reveal through such songs their own conceptions of their social and cultural identity that they consider to mark them off from non-weavers.

776 **Senegal.**
Tolia Nikiprowetzky. *The New Grove Dictionary of Music and Musicians*. Edited by Stanley Sadie. London: Macmillan, 1980. vol. 17, p. 127-9.
An entry in the standard musical dictionary, which gives background information on the country, details of the main musical instruments, including the harp-lute (*kora*),

plucked lute (*khalam*), drums, xylophone (*balafon*), musical styles and the role of the griots or professional musicians, together with a short bibliography.

777 **Sweet mother: modern African music.**
Wolfgang Bender, translated by Wolfgang Freis. Chicago, Illinois: Chicago University Press, 1991. 235p. bibliog.

The best available account to date of the development of contemporary popular music throughout Africa, from its traditional roots to the clubs and dance halls of the urban centres. The first chapter, 'The griot style', deals with Senegambia, and includes short sections on Youssou N'Dour and his band Super Etoile, and of the groups Le Xalam and Touré Kunda. At the end of the book is a bibliography and a discography which lists thirty-one items for Senegal and The Gambia.

778 **West African music village. Kew Gardens June 15th-25th 1989.**
London: Cultural Co-operation in association with Royal Botanic Gardens, Kew and City Limits World Music Series, 1989. 30p.

This illustrated publication was written as an accompayning text to the 1989 West African Music Village at which West African musicians and artists performed in Kew Gardens, London. A section is included on Senegambian music and performers, giving details of the position of the 'griots' or singers in Senegambian societies and the type of instruments they play. A separate section on music and musical instruments of West Africa is also included.

779 **Xylophones-sur-jambes chez les Bédik et les Bassari de Kédougou.** ('Leg xylophones' among the Bedik and Bassari of Kédougou.)
Marie-Paule Ferry. *Objets et Mondes*, vol. 9, no. 3 (1969), p. 307-12.

These 'xylophones' of the title consist of three or four pieces of wood resting across the thighs of a player who sits down with his legs outstretched. The wood is then beaten with sticks. In both cultures they are associated with initiation rituals, but both the context and the instruments differ. Among the Bedik, young initiates play them in the bush schools which follow initiation, and among the Bassari they are used on the occasion of great festivals by skilled musicians.

Crafts

780 **L'artisanat féminin dans la région du Fleuve Sénégal.** (Female craft production in the Fleuve region of Senegal.)
Christine Lagoutte. *Canadian Journal of African Studies*, vol. 22, no. 3 (1988), p. 448-71.

A useful addition to the literature on women's craft production in Senegal, which discusses the position of potters and dyers in Tukulor and Sarakole society, their organization, the transmission of knowledge, techniques of production, and the possibilities of development.

781 **Le coton chez les noirs.** (Cotton among the blacks.)
Charles Monteil. *Bulletin du Comité des Etudes Historiques et Scientifiques de l'Afrique Occcidentale Française*, vol. 9, no. 4 (1926), p. 585-684.

This is an old, but still a very useful, source of historical information on the indigenous textile industry and the traditional uses of cotton in French West Africa, written by a colonial administrator. It deals with the development of the industry, the influence of Islam, and the impact of European influence, particularly the import of cheap manufactured goods. Many of the techniques of cloth production in the region which he describes are still in use.

782 **Le déclin social du forgeron diallonké au Sénégal oriental.** (The social decline of the Diallonke smith in Eastern Senegal.)
Daniele Fouchier. *Journal des Africanistes*, vol. 53 (1983), p. 185-95.

A discussion of the changing role of the blacksmiths among a small ethnic group situated along the border with Guinea, and in the town of Kédougou. The paper discusses: the traditional role of the blacksmiths who formed an endogamous group, both in the economy and in ritual; their declining importance due to the changing economy, the end of warfare, and the influence of Islam on the community; and their contemporary migration to Kédougou.

783 **Dreams, inspiration and craftwork among Tukulor weavers.**
R. M. Dilley. In: *Dreaming, religion and society in Africa.* Edited by M. C. Jedrej, R. Shaw. Leiden, The Netherlands: E. J. Brill, 1992, p. 71-85.

This chapter discusses the role of dreams and dream divination among the Tukulor in general, and more specifically, dreams as a source of inspiration for Tukulor weavers. Not only do cloth patterns and weave designs appear as dream-inspired, but aspects of the secret corpus of weaving lore, such as incantations and spells, are thought to derive from spirits who use the medium of dreams to transmit this knowledge to man.

784 **Enquête sur les structures et l'exploitation de l'artisanat en milieu urbain, 1973-1975.** (Survey of the structures and working of urban arts and crafts, 1973-1975.)
Dakar: Direction de la Statistique, Ministère des Finances et des Affaires Economiques, 1977. [n.p.].

Based on a survey carried out by the Statistical Office of the Ministry of Finance and Economic Affairs, this study, in typescript form, presents a quantitative analysis of the state of the art and craft industry in the seven major urban centres of the country: Dakar, Ziguinchor, Diourbel, Saint-Louis, Tambacounda, Kaolack and Thiès.

785 **Les forgerons de Kaolack: travail non-salarié et déploiement d'une caste au Sénégal.** (The blacksmiths of Kaolack: non-salaried work and the deployment of a caste in Senegal.)
Alan Morice. Paris: Ecole des Hautes Etudes en Science Sociales, 1982. 350p.

A doctoral thesis which also forms a major study of the organization of a Senegalese craft industry. After introductory sections on the Senegalese economy and the blacksmith caste, the main body of the book presents the author's detailed findings on the means of production, markets, labour (organized around kinship), and on career and marriage strategies, illustrated through the detailed histories of seven 'families'. The book is well illustrated with the texts of interviews, genealogies and photographs.

786 **The iconography of the Diola *ebanken* shield.**
Peter Mark. *Paideuma*, vol. 32 (1986), p. 277-83.

A study of a non-written 'text', an anti-witchcraft amulet made in the form of a small shield, eight to ten inches in diameter, and made of raffia, decorated with fragments of broken mirror, cowries, buttons and red seeds, which could be used either in dances or hung from the ceiling as a form of protection. The paper discusses the meaning of these elements, the role they play in creating a power-charged object which could protect the owner against witchcraft, and the relationship of the *ebanken* with the *bukut* initiation ceremony, the central ritual of Diola society.

787 **Memorandum au gouvernement du Sénégal sur le développement de l'artisanat du tissage.** (Memorandum to the Senegalese government on the development of small-scale weaving.)
Roger Deschamps. Geneva: International Labour Organisation, 1962. 34p.

Based on one month's research commissioned by the Senegalese government, this study investigates the possibilities for development within the traditional hand-weaving industry, as well as the idea of promoting weaving in the Casamance and Senegal river regions as a measure to combat rural migration to urban areas. The author recommends that the traditional handloom, being described as archaic, unusable and unadaptable, should be totally abandoned in favour of semi-industrial production.

788 **Le 'mystère' et ses masques chez les Bédik.** (The 'mystery' and its masques among the Bedik.)
Pierre Smith. *L'Homme*, vol. 24, no. 3/4 (1984), p. 5-33.

An account of the masks which 'materialize' during male initiation ceremonies among the Bedik in the extreme south east of Senegal and the extent to which they constitute a 'mystery'. Ritual action can be considered separately from beliefs. In fact, the men know that they are only acting a role imposed on them by tradition, and the women know that they only have to appear to believe in the spirits the masks represent. The mystery is not, therefore, really a mystery, but nevertheless the tradition continues.

789 **Myth and meaning and the Tukulor loom.**
R. M. Dilley. *Man*, vol. 22, no. 2 (1987), p. 256-66.

This is a study of the Tukulor weavers' loom, and the cultural and religious meanings attached to it. The structure is seen to embody a set of ideas and conceptions about the loom and the weavers' craft. These ideas are retold among the weavers in their myths of origin about the craft, and are acted out each time a loom is built or used to produce cloth. The author suggests that because of such cultural associations, attempts at modernizing the loom are frequently unfruitful and discounted by weavers.

790 **Notes sur quelques bijoux sénégalaise.** (Notes on some Senegalese jewels).
Béatrice Appia-Dabit. *Bulletin de l'IFAN*, vol. 5(B) (1943), p. 27-33.
This short article describes the work and methods of Senegalese jewellers.

791 **La place et le rôle du secteur artisanal dans l'économie sénégalaise.** (The place and role of the arts and crafts in the Senegalese economy.)
Dakar: Ministère du Développement Industriel et de l'Artisanat, 1980. [n.p.].
An official review of government plans for the arts and crafts sector, the role of official agencies, and financial schemes to aid its development.

792 **Politique générale de l'artisanat: plan directeur 1981-1985. Stratégie et programme d'action au seuil du vie plan.** (General policy towards arts and crafts management plan 1981-1985. Strategy and programme of action at the inception of the sixth plan.)
Dakar: Ministère du Développement Industriel et de l'Artisanat, 1981.
Published by the Ministry of Industrial Development and Arts and Crafts, this document outlines the government policy towards the sector, and its role in developing it. Schemes for the organization of craft fairs and exhibitions, and for the setting up of experimental workshops are described.

793 **Quelques artisans noirs.** (Some black craftsmen.)
Béatrice Appia-Dabit. *Bulletin de l'IFAN*, vol. 3(B), no. 14 (1941), p. 1-44.
Describing the work and methods of the specialist 'caste' groups of Tukulor weavers, potters and woodcarvers, this article also includes fascinating detail on the spiritual aspects of these crafts, and in particular the incantations these artisans use during various stages in production.

794 **Secrets and skills: apprenticeship among Tukulor weavers.**
R. M. Dilley. In: *Apprenticeship: from theory to method and back again.* Edited by Michael Coy. Albany, New York: State University of New York Press, p. 181-98.
The system of apprenticeship among Tukulor weavers is examined, describing not only the techniques and methods of the craft that are passed from master to apprentice, but also the types of initial instruction in the secret lore and knowledge of the craft that are given to youths. The author argues that apprenticeship is not simply a mechanism for restricting and controlling access to this particular trade, but it is a means by which ideas about the cultural self-definitions of weavers are passed from one generation to the next.

795 **Sénégal: l'artisanat créateur.** (Senegal: creative craftsmanship.)
Jacques Anquetil. Paris: Agence de Coopération Culturelle et
Technique, 1977. 107p.

This well-illustrated volume describes the arts and crafts of each of the main ethnic
groups in or bordering on Senegal. After a general introduction to the craft industries
and main centres of production, the book describes the social, economic and artistic
life of the Wolof, Serer, Diola, Bassari and 'nomadic groups' including (surprisingly)
the Tukulor.

796 **Le textile au Sénégal: le marché intérieur et l'industrie locale. Tomes I
& II.** (The textile industry in Senegal: the internal market and local
industry. Volumes one and two).
Dakar: Ministère du Développement Industriel et de l'Artisanat [n.d.].
2 vols.

A study of the organization of the Senegalese textile industry, this work outlines the
operations of the country's cotton producers as well as of its spinning and weaving
mills. It gives a breakdown of levels of production in all sectors of the industry between
the years 1974 and 1978, together with the proportions of cotton products that find
their way on to the internal market.

797 **Les tissus de l'Afrique Occidentale: méthode de classification et
catalogue raisonné des étoffes tissées de l'Afrique de l'Ouest établis à
partir de données techniques et historiques.** (Textiles of West Africa:
method of classification and systematic catalogue of West African
woven materials based on technical and historical data.)
Renée Boser-Sarivaxévanis. Basel, Switzerland: Pharos-Verlag, 1972.

A study by a leading authority on West African textiles, the second part of which
contains illustrations and descriptions of thirty-eight textiles from the Senegambian
region, together with notes on the history, the use of traditional cloth and the
craftsmen.

798 **Tukulor weavers and the organisation of their craft in village and town.**
R. M. Dilley. *Africa*, vol. 56, no. 2 (1986), p. 123-47.

This article describes the socio-economic organization of weaving among Tukulor
craftsmen of the villages of Fuuta Toro, and compares it with that found among those
craftsmen who have migrated from the area to towns further south in the central
regions of the country. Moving from a system of village patronage, Tukulor weavers
have now established new forms for the organization of the production of cloth,
centring on distribution through the market places and market traders operating in
urban areas such as Dakar and Diourbel.

799 **Tukulor weaving origin myths: Islam and reinterpretation.**
R. M. Dilley. In: *The diversity of the Islamic community:
anthropological essays in memory of P. A. Lienhardt.* Edited by
A. al-Shahi. London: Ithaca Press, 1987, p. 70-9.

A study of weaving origin myths among Tukulor weavers, this chapter examines the
extent to which the ideology of Islam has been used by narrators to reinterpret

particular aspects of the mythical origins of weaving. Such versions, however, have not gained an especially wide currency since, it is argued, they undermine some of the crucial features at the heart of the social and cultural identity of this closed, somewhat secret category of craftsmen.

800 **The wild bull and the sacred forest: form, meaning and change in Senegambian initiation masks.**
Peter Mark.   Cambridge, England: Cambridge University Press, 1992. 170p.

A detailed discussion of the horned masks associated with the *bukut* male initiation ceremony, held once in a generation. The masks are unusual in that specimens have survived from the 18th century, making it possible to study the changes in style over time. This book discusses Diola society, initiation, and the masks themselves, and places them in the context of the cultural history of the region and Islam. It is well illustrated with both contemporary and recent black-and-white photographs. See also related discussion in Mark's earlier paper 'Diola masking traditions and the history of the Casamance (Senegal)', *Paideuma*, vol. 29 (1983), p. 3-22.

Un village de la vallée du Sénégal: Amadi Ounaré. (A village in the Senegal valley: Amadi Ounare.)
See item no. 42.

Migration artisanale et solidarité villageoise: le cas de Kanèn Njob, au Sénégal. (Migration of craftsmen and village solidarity: the case of Kanen Njob, Senegal.)
See item no. 128.

Media

801 **The African book world and press: a directory.**
Edited by Hans Zell, Carol Bundy.   Munich, Germany: Hans Zell,
1983. 3rd ed. 285p.
A country-by-country survey, which gives details of booksellers, publishers, institutional publishers, periodicals and magazines, newspapers, book industry associations and literary societies, and both private and government printers.

802 **African books in print: an index by author, subject and title: volume I,
author index; volume II, subject index, title index.**
Edited by Hans Zell.   London: Mansell, 895p. 2nd ed. 1978. 2 vols.
A standard bibliographical resource, first published in 1973. The first volume of the edition consulted contains a directory of publishers, six of which are from Senegal, and an alphabetical list of authors and titles. The second volume contains a useful subject index including entries by country.

803 **Attitudes et comportments de la population rurale sénégalaise vis-à-vis
des moyens audio-visuels de formation.** (The attitudes and behaviour of
the Senegalese rural population towards audio-visual education.)
Michel Bourgeois.   *Tiers-Monde*, vol. 19, no. 70 (1977), p. 381-96.
An account by a UNESCO consultant of the impact of broadcasting, and particularly radio, on the rural areas of Senegal. The paper surveys the reactions of the peasantry to radio, its role in allowing a dialogue to develop between the peasantry and their leaders, and the importance of this dialogue in the development process, particularly in allowing problems to be identified at an early stage.

804 **Les débuts de la presse au Sénégal.** (The beginnings of the press in
Senegal.)
Roger Pasquier. *Cahiers d'Etudes Africaines*, vol. 2, no. 3 (1962),
p. 477-90.

A brief historical sketch of the origins of the Senegalese press, which includes a list of
holdings at the Bibliothèque Nationale.

805 **La presse au Sénégal avant 1939. Bibliographie.** (The press in Senegal
before 1939. A bibliography.)
Marguerite Boulègue. *Bulletin de l'IFAN*, 27 (B), no. 3-4, 1965,
715-54.

The standard survey of the early Senegalese press, listing eighty-two titles dating from
before 1939, with full information on titles, editor, format and availability. There is a
seven-page introduction, as well as a chronological and alphabetical index.

Parks, Recreation and Sport

Parks

806 **Le Haute Gambie et le Parc National du Niokolo Koba.** (Upper Gambia
and the National Park of Niokolo Koba.)
G. Rouré (et al.).   Dakar: Editions GIA, 1956. 192p.

An early guide which contains sections on the history and geography of the area, the
park itself, a note by Monique de Lestrange on the local Koniagui and Bassari peoples,
and a guide to local tourist sites. There are a number of maps and numerous
photographs and drawings of variable quality. Rouré was in charge of water and
forestry in the region, and was the author of several books on wildlife and hunting.

807 **Le Parc National du Niokolo-Koba. Fascicules I-III.** (The National Park
of Niokolo-Koba. Parts I-III).
Dakar: IFAN, 1956- . 3 vols. (Mémoires no. 48, 62, 84.)

Le Parc National du Niokolo-Koba was the first national park to be established in
French West Africa. It was created in the south-east corner of Senegal, first as a
hunting reserve and then as a park in 1954. These three volumes are the major
scientific study of its wildlife. The first volume contains a general introduction and
specialist chapters on its larger fauna: mammals, birds, reptiles and amphibians. Parts
II and III deal with insects, and Part III also contains a general bibliography of over
200 items.

808 **Recherches scientifiques dans les parcs nationaux de Sénégal.** (Scientific
research in the national parks of Senegal.)
Dakar: IFAN, 1982. 364p.

This volume contains twenty-six chapters written by various authors on a range of
geological, zoological and botanical subjects. The studies centre on the animal and
plant life of the six areas of the country which were designated as national parks in
1982. This volume is a further addition to the earlier scientific studies initiated by

IFAN in Dakar on the flora and fauna of the national park at Niokolo-Koba (see previous item). All four volumes tend to be aimed at the specialist scientific audience rather than the general reader.

809   **Sénégal: ses parcs, ses animaux.** (Senegal: its parks and animals.)
      J. Larivière, A. R. Dupuy.   Paris: Fernand Nathan, 1978. 142p.

A lavish introduction to the national parks, co-authored by a director of the Service des Parcs Nationaux and with an officially sanctioned preface by Senghor. Senegal's national parks are substantial, covering 1.3 million hectares or 1.5 per cent of the land area of the country. The first part of the book is a coloured photographic survey of scenery and wildlife. The second part, entitled 'Carnet de voyage' is a more systematic survey with maps and information on the main attractions to be seen in terms of ecosystem and animal species.

Diet of wild chimpanzees *(Pan troglodytes verus)* **at Mt. Assirik, Senegal.**
See item no. 59.

The forest dwellers.
See item no. 61.

Recreation

810   **Jeux et jouets de l'ouest africain. Tomes I et II.** (Games and toys of
      West Africa. 2 vols).
      Ch. Béart.   Dakar: IFAN, 1955. 888p. (Mémoires no. 42).

A monumental descriptive inventory of games and toys throughout West Africa, full of illustrations, figures and photographs. The two volumes are organized not according to region or culture, but, rather idiosyncratically, according to the type of activity or amusement. However, they offer a wealth of information. The first volume includes dolls, designs, graffiti, athletics, wrestling, and games of chance. The second volume deals with ritual and festivals, dance and music, word games, and the theatre.

811   **Sports.**
      In: *The Gambia and Senegal.* Edited by Philip Sweeny.   Hong Kong:
      Insight Guides, APA Publications (HK), 1990, p. 115-22.

A description of Senegal's sporting facilities for tourists, including golf, watersports, fishing and hunting, and the notorious Dakar Rally.

Tourism

812 **La Casamance ouvre ses cases: tourisme au Sénégal.** (The Casamance opens its huts: tourism in Senegal.)
Muriel Scibilia.   Paris: L'Harmattan. 1986. 172p.

A lively and enthusiastic account by a French teacher and journalist of 'integrated rural tourism', the *campement* movement developed by the French anthropologist Christian Saglio in the early 1970s. His aim was to integrate tourism into local rural life, while at the same time encouraging dialogue between peoples of different cultures. The first chapter of the book deals with the early attempts to get the system running, and the resistance which it met at first from the local people. The second chapter provides a whistle-stop tour of several sites in the Casamance area, while the third deals with the organization of the movement. The fourth chapter deals with the tourists themselves. The conclusions assess the role of tourism in economic development and the ways in which this new form of tourism alters the traditional relationship between the tourist and the local people. At the end there are facts and figures on the main sites and plans of *campement* buildings.

813 **Destination Senegal.**
Laurent Marcaillou.   *Jeune Afrique*, no. 1610. (6-12 Nov. 1991) p. 52-4.

A report on attempts to stimulate tourism, aimed at increasing the annual number of tourists from 300,000 to 1 million. Receipts from tourism declined from 1988 to 1990, having grown between 1984 and 1988. The article contains a report on an interview with Jacques Baudin, the Senegalese minister responsible for tourism, who blamed some of the problems of the industry on the high cost of air travel due to quotas imposed by Air Afrique.

814 **Diola traditions and the village hotel.**
Prudence Lambert. *West Africa*, no. 3517 (21 Jan. 1985), p. 103-05.

Discusses the administration of local *campements* and Diola tradition.

815 **Tourisme balnéaire ou tourisme rural intégré? Deux modèles de développement sénégalais.** (Seaside tourism or integrated rural tourism? Two models of development in Senegal.)
Marguerite Schlechten. Fribourg, Switzerland: Editions Universitaires, 1988. 442p.

This book, which was the author's PhD thesis, is perhaps the most important academic study of tourism in Senegal yet written. It consists of a detailed comparison of the economic and social effects of seaside tourism on the Petite Côte with those of integrated rural tourism in the Casamance. The second chapter provides an important overview of the development of tourism in Senegal, while the fourth and fifth deal with tourism in the two regions. The conclusion is that as a model of development, integrated rural tourism is preferable, despite its shortcomings. The kind of seaside tourism found on the Petite Côte only exacerbates the country's economic and social problems by creating an economic enclave into which consumer goods from the industrial countries flow, and to which the local people are denied access. The study also contains a number of black-and-white photographs and a food bibliography.

The Gambia and Senegal.
See item no. 7.

Guide de Dakar et du Sénégal. (Guide to Dakar and Senegal.)
See item no. 84.

Traveller's guide to West Africa.
See item no. 87.

West Africa: a travel survival kit.
See item no. 88.

West Africa: the rough guide.
See item no. 89.

Research Resources

Museums

816 **A propos du plan de réorganisation des réserves du Musée d'art africain de l'IFAN, Dakar.** (A plan for store-room reorganization at the Museum of African Art in Dakar.)
Coumba Ndoffène Diouf. *WAMP Bulletin*, vol. 3 (1992), p. 26-31.

The article reports on major renovation work carried out to the store-room in the African Art Museum in Dakar, during which objects were documented, restored and placed in new receptacles to prevent further deterioration.

817 **Bulletin de WAMP/WAMP (West African Museums Project, Dakar) Bulletin.**
London: International African Institute, 1990- . annual.

A new journal, first published in 1990, which aims to provide articles and news on developments in museums in West African countries. Organized and edited in Dakar, the journal is published in English and French, and often includes information on museums in Senegal.

818 **Collections Bassari du Musée de l'Homme, de Département d'Anthropologie de l'Université de Montréal, Canada, du Musée de l'IFAN à Dakar et du CRDS à Saint-Louis, Sénégal.** (The Bassari collection of the Museum of Man, Department of Anthropology, University of Montreal, Canada, the IFAN Museum, Dakar, and the CRDS, Saint-Louis, Senegal.)
Marie-Thérèse de Lestrange, Monique Gessain.   Paris: Musée de l'Homme, 1976. 342p. (Catalogues du Musée de l'Homme, Série C, Afrique Noire II).

An important reference work on the material culture of the Bassari people, now divided between southern Senegal and neighbouring Guinea. The first part of the book is a lengthy general survey of Bassari material culture, including basketry, pottery, housebuilding, clothing, ornaments, and musical instruments. The rest of the book is a catalogue of Bassari materials in four major museum collections. The whole book is illustrated with numerous excellent black-and-white photographs, and at the end there are details of the origins of the collections, indexes of plants and animals, a bibliography, a list of films, and a detailed table of contents.

819 **Gorée.**
Shelley Moore.   *Crisis*, vol. 93, no. 6 (1986), p. 18-21, 56.

A description of La Maison des Esclaves, the slavery museum on the island of Gorée, once a centre of the slave trade for the Dutch, Portuguese, British and French.

820 **Le Musée historique du Sénégal à Gorée.** (The Historical Museum of Senegal at Gorée.)
Abdoulaye Camara.   *WAMP Bulletin*, no. 2 (1991), p. 15.

A short account written by the Museum's *conservateur*. Opened in March 1989, the museum exhibitions retrace the history of Senegal, particularly of the Atlantic slave trade based on the island of Gorée, just off the Dakar coast.

821 **Les musées du Sénégal. The museums of Senegal.**
Jean Girard.   *Museum*, vol. 18, no. 3 (1965), p. 134-7.

A brief summary, in both French and English, of the aims and main collections of the four Senegalese museums of the period: those of the University of Dakar, Saint-Louis, and the history and oceanography museums on the island of Gorée.

822 **Naissance d'un éco-musée en Basse-Casamance (Sénégal).** (The birth of an eco-museum in Senegal's Lower Casamance.)
Maria Donata Rinaldi.   *WAMP Bulletin*, no 2 (1991), p. 5-9.

A report on the establishment of a museum village in which the environment and the lifestyles of the local populations (their cultural, economic and other activities) are part of the exhibition. The article, written by one of the founders of the museum, describes the aims of the project, including rural development, the provision of tourist facilities and the creation of local employment, as well as some of the problems which have hindered its completion.

Libraries and archives

823 **The A.O.F. archives and the study of African history.**
Mary Niles Maack. *Bulletin de l'IFAN*, vol. 42(B), no. 2 (1980),
p. 277-98.
An account of the history of the French West African archives in Dakar, which date
back to 1816, though they had varied fortunes during the 19th century. In 1911, a
comprehensive West African archives system was created, and the existence of this,
probably one of the best collections in the former colonial world, helps account for the
enormous amount of research which has been done on Senegal over the years, as well
as for the high quality of much of it.

824 **The archival system of former French West Africa.**
G. Wesley Johnson. *African Studies Bulletin*, vol. 8, no. 1 (1965),
p 48-58.
One of a group of short articles on research resources for Senegal and the rest of the
former French West Africa, written following a visit in 1964. See also the author's
'Archival materials of Senegal', *Africana Newsletter*, vol. 2, no. 1 (1964), p. 74-6.

825 **Bulletin bibliographique des Archives du Sénégal.** (Bibliographical
Bulletin of the Archives of Senegal.)
Dakar: Centre de Documentation, Archives Nationales. 1963- .
quarterly.
Published since 1963, this bulletin is the main source of regular information on these
important archives.

826 **Guide des archives de l'Afrique Occidentale Française.** (Guide to
archives of French West Africa.)
Saliou Mbaye. Dakar: Archives de Sénégal, 1990. 204p.
The most recent guide to Dakar archives, written by the current director. It contains a
brief history of the collection, a list of complementary archives, a list of the main
collections, and details on utilization and access. There are valuable bibliographical
references throughout, and a lengthy index of names and subjects at the end.

827 **Libraries in Senegal: continuity and change in an emerging nation.**
Mary Niles Maack. Chicago, Illinois: American Library Association,
1981. 250p.
Based on the author's PhD thesis, this work traces the historical development of
library institutions in Senegal from the early colonial period at the start of the 19th
century to the mid-1970s. The library as an institution is a foreign import, and as such,
it has tended to follow the European model. The author examines this French political
and cultural legacy in the establishment of libraries in the country, as well as the
significant departures from these colonial precedents started post-independence by
multinational or by local agencies. The book covers institutions with holdings of 2,000
or more volumes, and includes not just academic and special libraries but also national
archives, documentation centres and information services that are offered by various
agencies. Maack also considers the cultural goals motivating the organization of

libraries as well as the emergence of librarianship as a profession in Senegal after independence. A select bibliography of unpublished materials, of library archive and documentation sources, and of general works is appended.

Bibliographies

828 **Africa bibliography.**
Edited by Hector Blackhurst. Manchester, England: Manchester University Press, 1984- . annual.

Published annually in one volume since 1984, this authoritative bibliography is based mainly on the holdings of the Manchester University Library and material received by the International African Institute. After a preliminary section on the continent as a whole, the bulk of the references are grouped by region and country. It includes mainly periodical articles, books and essays in edited volumes, and there are separate author and subject indexes.

829 **Africa south of the Sahara: index to periodical literature, 1900-1970.**
African Section, General Reference and Bibliography Division, Reference Department, Library of Congress. Boston, Massachusetts: G. K. Hall, 1971.

This valuable bibliography is based on photocopies of the card index of the State Library of Congress, so the quality of reproduction is variable. The list is divided by country and by subject, and there are in total around 1,500 references to Senegal (p. 558-65), most of them annotated.

830 **The African book publishing record.**
Edited by Hans M. Zell. Borough Green, England: Hans Zell, 1974- . quarterly.

This is the major source of information on new publications on Africa. In addition to specialist articles, the periodical contains a section on reference sources for each country, and a lengthy general bibliography with subject, country and author indexes.

831 **Bibliographie des régions du Sénégal.** (Bibliography of the regions of Senegal.)
Laurence Porgès. Dakar: République du Sénégal, Ministère du Plan et du Développement, 1967. 705p.

This monumental reference work is the fullest bibliographical source on Senegal up to the late 1960s. The introduction contains a list of previous bibliographies on the country, lists of periodicals and archival sources. The bulk of the work consists of sections on the different regions of Senegal: Cap-Vert, Casamance, Diourbel, Fleuve, Sénégal Oriental, Sine-Saloum, and Thiès. Each chapter includes lists of relevant files from the Archives de l'AOF, official periodicals and reports series, and a long list of references arranged by author in alphabetical order, over 2,800 in total. At the end there are comprehensive author and subject indexes, and administrative maps covering the period from 1909 to 1965.

832 **Bibliographie des régions du Sénégal. Complément pour la période des origines et mise à jour 1966-1973.** (Bibliography of the regions of Senegal. Supplement for the early period and updated to 1966-73.) Laurence Porgès. Paris: Mouton, for the Agence de Coopération Culturelle et Technique, 1977. 637p.

This supplement to Porgès' original volume contains mainly references for the period 1966-73, in a similar format. Together the two volumes contain over 7,200 references.

833 **Bibliographie générale des colonies françaises.** (General bibliography of French colonies.) G. Grandidier, E. Joucla. Paris: Société d'Editions Géographiques, Maritimes et Coloniales, 1937. 704p.

A vast compendium of over 9,500 references arranged in alphabetical order by both subject and author. The coverage of early Senegalese sources is excellent, and the lengthy index, which is broken down both by subject and territory, makes it possible to trace a large number of relevant sources very quickly.

834 **Bibliographie générale du Mali (anciens Soudan français et Haut-Sénégal-Niger).** (General bibliography of Mali, formerly French Sudan and Upper-Senegal-Niger.) Paule Brasseur. Dakar: IFAN, 1964. 461p. (Catalogues et documents xvi).

Together with a companion volume, *Bibliographie générale du Mali (1961-1970)* (General bibliography of Mali, 1961-1970) (Dakar: IFAN/Les Nouvelles Editions Africaines, 1976. 284p. [Catalogues et documents xvi-2]), this volume provides in total nearly 8,000 annotated references under the headings of physical environment, human environment, institutions and development. Given the arbitrariness of African state boundaries, many of the entries are relevant to the region as a whole or to the peoples of Senegal. Both volumes have excellent indexes.

835 **Cumulative bibliography of African studies: International African Institute, London, England. Author Catalogue, 2 vols. Classified Catalogue, 2 vols.** Boston, Massachusetts: G. K. Hall, 1973. 4 vols.

A bibliography compiled from the card index of the IAI dating up to about 1970. The most important section on Senegal is in volume 2 of the Classified Catalogue, p. 309-18.

836 **Current contents Africa.**
Munich, Germany; New York; London; Paris: K. G. Saur. 1976-
quarterly.
This publication consists of facsimiles of the contents pages of over 120 Africanist
serials, including the standard academic journals, together with *West Africa* and *Jeune
Afrique*.

837 **The Gambia.**
Compiled by David P. Gamble. Oxford: Clio Press, 1988. 137p.
(World Bibliographical Series, vol. 91).
Given the nature of the boundaries between Senegal and The Gambia, Gamble's
bibliography is also a useful source of information on the peoples and cultures of the
region as a whole. This work contains 334 items, most of them with excellent, long
annotations. Of particular relevance to Senegal are the sections on ethnography,
language and foreign relations. The author, together with Louise Sperling, has also
compiled a much longer bibliography on The Gambia, *A general bibliography of The
Gambia (up to 31 December 1977)* (Boston, Massachusetts: G. K. Hall, 1979. 266p.),
and two volumes of updates which, taken together, include over 8,000 references.

838 **Guide to research and reference works on sub-Saharan Africa.**
Edited by Peter Duignan. Stanford, California: Hoover Institution
Press, [n.d.]. 1102p. (Hoover Institution Bibliographical Series, 46).
Probably one of the most useful one-volume bibliographies on Africa available for its
period, this book contains sections on centres, institutions and records of research;
libraries and archives in Europe, America and Africa; bibliographies for Africa in
general; a subject guide; and an area guide by former colonial power, region and
country. In all there are 3,127 entries, most of them with excellent annotations, and a
useful fifty-eight-page index at the end. Similar ground is covered in another
bibliography which the author compiled with L. H. Gann, *Colonialism in Africa 1870-
1960. Volume 5. A bibliographical guide to colonialism in Sub-Saharan Africa.*
(Cambridge, England: Cambridge University Press, 1973. 552p.).

839 **International African bibliography: current books, articles and papers in
African studies.**
Compiled and edited by David Hall. London: Hans Zell Publishers.
quarterly.
This standard bibliography, issued quarterly since 1970, and compiled at the Library of
the School of Oriental and African Studies in London, includes, in addition to general
and regional sections, references divided by country. Each issue ends with a subject
index, and the last issue of each year contains an annual index of subjects, names,
ethnic groups and languages.

840 **Les manuscrits historiques arabo-africains (II).** (Arab and African
historical manuscripts.)
Vincent Monteil. *Bulletin de l'IFAN*, vol. 28(B), no. 3-4 (1966),
p. 668-75.
A survey of the Arabic literature of the region, dealing with Nigeria, Cameroon, Chad,
Senegal, Mali and Niger.

Historical dictionary of Senegal.
See item no. 198.

Santé et population en Sénégambie des origines à 1960. (Health and population in Senegambia from its origins to 1960.)
See item no. 622.

Vingt ans de travaux à la clinique psychiatrique de Fann-Dakar. (Twenty years of work at the Fann-Dakar psychiatric clinic.)
See item no. 624.

Agricultural development and policy in Senegal: annotated bibliography of recent studies, 1983-89.
See item no. 626.

The African book world and press: a directory.
See item no. 801.

African books in print: an index by author, subject and title.
See item no. 802.

La presse au Sénégal avant 1939. Bibliographie. (The press in Senegal before 1939. A bibliography.)
See item no. 805.

General periodicals and newspapers

841 **Jeune Afrique.** (Young Africa.)
Paris: Groupe JA, 1955- . weekly.
For readers of French, this is the most easily available source of regular news on the country, with particularly good coverage of politics and the economy. The periodical was published monthly between 1955 and 1960.

842 **Le Politicien.** (The Politician.)
Dakar: 1977- . fortnightly.
A weekly satirical independent publication which has spawned a similar, separate newspaper named *Le Cafard Libéré*, published in Dakar (1987- . weekly).

843 **Le Soleil.** (The Sun.)
Dakar: 1970- . daily.
This is the largest-circulation national daily newspaper and is broadly sympathetic to the government.

844 **Sopi.**
Dakar: 1988- . weekly.

Sopi is the official organ of the PDS, the Parti Démocratique Socialiste, the main opposition to the ruling Parti Socialiste of President Diouf and ex-president Senghor. It is published weekly.

845 **Sud Hebdo.** (South Weekly.)
Edited by Sudcom. Dakar: Groupe Multimedia Sud Communications (18 rue Raffenel), 1990- . weekly.

This newspaper is published weekly and takes an independent editorial stance. It was established in the late 1980s.

846 **Le Témoin.** (The Witness.)
Dakar: 1990- . weekly.

Launched in April 1990 by an ex-editor of *Sopi*, this publication was originally issued fortnighly, but now appears every Tuesday. It was one of a number of new papers launched during the period after the 1988 elections.

847 **Wal fadiri. L'Aurore.** (The Dawn.)
Dakar. 1985- . weekly.

Now in its 9th year of publication, this weekly paper gives a broadly Muslim perspective on current affairs.

848 **West Africa.**
London: West Africa Publishing Company. 1917- . weekly.

Published weekly since 1917, this is the main source of regular information about West Africa and its constitutent countries available in English. It also carries regular articles on regional organizations such as ECOWAS and the Organisation of African Unity (OAU). There is an annual index.

849 **Xabaar.**
New York: West African Business Association Inc. Jan. 1993- . monthly.

Published monthly for the Senegalese immigrant community in the United States, this new newspaper deals with trade, entertainment and other news.

Professional periodicals

850 **Bulletin de l'Institut Fondamental d'Afrique Noire (IFAN).**
Dakar: IFAN. 1954- . quarterly.

IFAN, which has probably produced more scholarly publications on Senegal than any other institution, started as the Institut Français d'Afrique Noire, with 'français' changing to 'fondamental' at independence. Series B of the journal is devoted mainly to articles on Senegal, concentrating mainly on history, culture and ethnography, but with wide coverage across the other social sciences and literature; series A concentrates on the natural sciences. In 1939 the present Bulletin replaced the *Bulletin du Comité d'Etudes historiques et scientifiques de l'AOF*, which itself succeeded in 1918 *Annuaires et Mémoires du Comité d'Etudes historiques et scientifiques de l'AOF*, first published in 1916. In 1954 the Bulletin was divided into series A and B, both of which are now published quarterly.

851 **Cahiers d'Etudes Africaines.** (African Studies Notebooks.)
Paris: Editions de l'Ecole des Hautes Etudes en Sciences Sociales.
1961- .

The best of the French-based general academic journals on the region, covering history, the social sciences, and literature. About a third of the articles are in English, and the French articles are usually printed with English summaries.

852 **Journal (de la Société) des Africainists.** (Journal of [the Society of] Africanistes.)
Paris: Musée de l'Homme, Société des Africainistes. 1911- .

With its museum base, this journal tends to be ethnographic in emphasis and is almost entirely in French, with abstracts in French and English.

853 **Présence Africaine.** (African Presence.)
Paris: Présence Africaine. 1947- .

The journal of the publishing house founded by Alioune Diop in 1947, this is probably one of the most important journals focusing on literature, history and the social sciences in francophone Africa. The PA imprint has also been responsible for introducing the work of many of Senegal's most famous authors over the years, and there have also been a number of important special issues and memorial volumes devoted to their work.

854 **Psychopathologie Africaine.** (African Psychopathology.)
Dakar: Société de Psychopathologie et d'Hygiène mentale de Dakar.
1965- . [3 per year].

This journal which has appeared usually three times a year since 1965, arose out of the work carried out by Henri Collomb and his psychiatric research group in Dakar, and is one of the main sources of information on their research. The journal is in fact more inter-disciplinary than its name would suggest, and much of the work in it is of direct interest to anthropologists and sociologists, in addition to doctors and psychiatrists. It includes numerous articles on Senegal.

Directories and encyclopaedias

855   **Africa contemporary record.**
Edited by Colin Legum.   New York: Africana Publishing (Holmes and Meier). 1969- . annual.

Issued annually since 1969, this is one of the best sources of information available on the recent history, politics, and economy of each African country. As well as the country sections, it also carries special articles, and sections on relations with France and regional organizations such as ECOWAS and the Senegambian Federation.

856   **Africa South of the Sahara.**
London: Europa Publication, 1991. 20th ed. p. 847-67.

A standard African yearbook issued annually, which carries brief articles on the geography, recent history and economy of each country, together with a lengthy statistical survey, and a directory of government departments, embassies and major organizations. The general sections of the volume include directories for the United Nations and other international and regional organizations.

857   **Cities of the world, volume 1: Africa.**
Edited by Margaret Walsh Young, Susan L. Stetler.   Detroit, Michigan: Gale Research Company.

Pages 564-83 of this city directory, which also contains general background information on each country, deal with Senegal, including Dakar and Saint-Louis. The Dakar section is obviously aimed at the long-term foreign resident, with information on schools for foreigners, recreation and entertainment. It is followed by a twelve-page country profile.

858   **Encyclopedia Britannica.**
Wallington, England: Encyclopedia Britannica International. annual.

The current Britannica article on Senegal written by H. J. Deschamps, a former colonial official and leading authority, is subsumed within a much longer section on Western Africa. It gives brief details of the physical and human geography, peoples, the economy, administrative and social conditions, and history, and rather limited bibliographical information. The annual update to the *Encyclopedia Britannica*, *Encyclopedia Britannica World data (book of the year)*, is also a useful source of information, particularly 'The year in review' which includes brief summaries of the main events for each country, and the final statistical section on world data.

859   **Encyclopedia of the Third World.**
George Thomas Kuriam.   New York: Facts on File Inc., 1987. 3rd ed. 3 vols.

A useful source of concise and well-presented information. The Senegal entry (volume 3, p. 1713-31) starts with a table of basic facts, and continues with a general survey of geography, social and ethnic composition, politics, and the economy. There is a companion volume, *Atlas of the Third World* (George Kuriam. New York: Facts on File, 1983. 381p.) which is a useful, if poorly designed, source of sketch maps and pie charts on each country, relating to geography, demography and economics.

860   **Europa World Year Book.**
London: Europa Publications. Vol. 16, 1993. 2 vols.

Perhaps the best and most informative of all the yearbooks. The 1993 edition consulted has a sixteen-page section on Senegal, consisting of an introductory survey of the country and its recent history, a statistical survey and a political, social and diplomatic directory.

Indexes

There follow three separate indexes: authors (personal and corporate); titles; and subjects. Title entries are italicized and refer either to the main titles, or to many other works cited in the annotations. The numbers refer to bibliographic entry rather than page numbers. Individual index entries are arranged in alphabetical sequence.

Index of Authors

Index of Titles

A

272

Index of Subjects

A

Administration 32, 34, 37, 43, 75, 78, 79, 126, 459-467, 625
African languages 651-670
African socialism 443, 628-629, 632, 723-724, 726, 730-731, 738
Age 119, 121, 145, 158, 162, 170
Agriculture 5, 21-22, 27-28, 37-38, 40, 43, 49-50, 65, 70-72, 174, 326, 332, 334-354, 358, 416, 419, 422, 481, 497, 530, 571, 604-607, 609, 625-642
Ahmadu Bamba 149, 303, 571, 582 see also Mouride Brotherhood
Aid 421, 424
Al-Bouri Ndiaye 149, 290
Animation rurale 627-628, 630, 632-633, 635
Anthologies 681-682, 684-687, 718
Arab sources 12, 90, 93-94, 201, 210, 212, 216, 221, 240
Arabic literature 228, 683, 840
Archeology 201, 203-208, 226
Architecture 249, 649
Archives 823-827, 831
Army 302, 304, 311
Arts 1, 86, 249, 751-769
Assassinations 430
Assimilation 258, 261, 277, 293, 316, 440, 590
Atlas 75-76, 81, 83, 105

B

Badyaranke 544, 551, 556, 570

Bakel 64, 114, 117, 129, 185, 388
Bakel livestock project 71
Bambara 10, 54, 114, 651, 655
Banjal 473
Banks 427
Baol 168
Baptisms 142
Bassari 121, 125, 176-177, 180, 335, 535, 548, 657, 779, 806, 818
Bedik 179-180, 548, 657, 672, 779
Beggars 523
Belief systems 536-589
Beliyan 176, 180, 548, 672
Bibliography 1, 5, 27, 34, 155, 198, 622, 626, 747, 762, 805, 816, 828-840
Birds 58, 60, 62
Blacksmiths 128, 547, 782, 785
Boghé 388
Bordeaux, 126, 259, 286
Bud Senegal 341
Bundu 212, 225, 235, 243, 253-254

C

Caillié, R. 92
Campements 812, 814-815
Cangin languages 657, 663
Cannabis 616
Cap-Vert 106-107, 147, 263, 341, 831
Carving 136
Casamance 7, 10, 16, 27, 32, 49, 88, 101, 109, 116, 130, 147, 210, 246, 254, 346, 363, 373, 444, 454-455, 473, 540, 545, 654, 656, 674, 679, 770, 774, 812, 815, 831

Caste 128, 162, 172, 601, 782, 785, 793
Catholic Church 143, 166, 258, 586-587, 589
CEAO, 494, 496
Censuses 144-145, 147-148
Centres d'Expansion Rurale 632, 636
Child socialization 170
Children 170-171, 527, 543, 549, 551, 554
Chimpanzees 59, 61
Christianity 142-143, 151, 536-537, 586-589
Cinema 89, 744, 757-763
Cities 6, 12, 27, 31, 33-34, 49, 50, 52, 66
Civil servants 461, 465
Class 32-33, 291, 475, 482, 520-521, 524, 594
Climate 6, 11, 30, 34, 37, 48, 67, 78, 88, 199, 222, 326, 419
Clothing 531
Club de Sahel 69, 631
Coastline 48, 109
Collin, Jean 458
Colonial period 3-6, 11, 15, 18-19, 21, 23, 34, 39, 275-318, 439-442, 463, 467, 748 see also History, colonial
Commodities 422, 427
Communes: see Dakar, Gorée, Rufisque, Saint-Louis
Communications 12, 22, 32, 75, 416, 418
Compagnie des Indes 99
Companies 99, 196, 257, 260, 262, 264, 315
Constitution 19, 435, 486, 487
Consumption patterns 38, 142, 345, 519, 526, 532
Conversion 134, 570, 578, 588

279

Map of Senegal

This map shows the more important towns and other features.

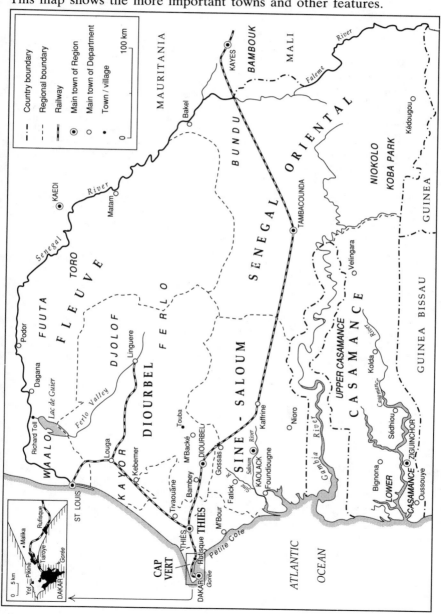